*Remember your leaders, who spoke the word of God to you. Consider the outcome of their way of life and imitate their faith. Obey your leaders and submit to their authority. They keep watch over you as men who must give an account. Obey them so that their work will be a joy, not a burden, for that would be of no advantage to you (Hebrews 13:7,17).*

*With practical and proven principles, the authors have teamed to provide a rich resource that elders, and those who oversee them, may return to many times for specific guidance.*

—Keith E. Yoder
Teaching The Word Ministries, Leola, PA

*Nothing causes more confusion in the body of Christ than putting the wrong people in the wrong whirlhole at the wrong time. Team based leadership in the local church is essential for unity, vision, and building a healthy, life-giving church. This book serves this need like no other book available right now. I highly commend it!*

—Floyd McClung, Senior Pastor
Metro Christian Fellowship, Kansas City, MO

*Larry Kreider and the DOVE Christian Fellowship International team are a priceless gift to the body of Christ. These pages are filled with wise and inspiring counsel. Regardless of your church culture, these practical insights will help you to keep a clear head in the middle of the seasons of leadership.*

—Dave Hess, Pastor
Christ Community Church, Camp Hill, PA.

# The Biblical Role of ELDERS for Today's Church

Larry Kreider

Ron Myer

Steve Prokopchak

Brian Sauder

House to House Publications
www.dcfi.org

# The Biblical Role of Elders for Today's Church

Updated edition © 2004
© 2003  by House to House Publications
Ephrata, Pennsylvania  USA
Tele:  717.738.3751
www.dcfi.org/house2house

ISBN: 1-886973-62-8

Printed in the United States of America

# Dedication

This book is dedicated to our Lord Jesus Christ who is our supreme model for servant-leadership. It is also dedicated to all those in the body of Christ who have faithfully served in local church leadership and to many who will obey the call to serve as local church elders, helping His church to be salt and light and filled with His glory.

# Acknowledgments

A very special thanks goes to Karen Ruiz, editor, and Sarah Mohler for cover design and layout. Another big "thank you" to those who gave valuable insight to the book, Greg Baird, Peter Bunton, Pamela Druhen, Karen Hugo, Diane Omondi, Keith Yoder, Glen Yoder, proof-reader Carolyn Sprague, and many others who contributed to this book. We love and appreciate all of you.

# Contents

# Introduction

## Building a Strong Team

Local churches usually rise and fall on leadership. In the New Testament, Peter admonishes the leadership of the early church,

> To the elders among you, I appeal as a fellow elder, a witness of Christ's sufferings and one who also will share in the glory to be revealed. Be shepherds of God's flock that is under your care, serving as overseers—not because you must, but because you are willing, as God wants you to be; not greedy for money, but eager to serve; not lording it over those entrusted to you, but being examples to the flock. And when Christ the Chief Shepherd appears, you will receive the crown of glory that will never fade away (1 Peter 5:1-4).

What is an elder? The term has many different meanings from congregation to congregation, denomination to denomination and ministry movement to ministry movement. Biblically, elders are those who have a God-given calling to give oversight to the local church. Many churches call their governing leaders "pastors, vicars, overseers or bishops." We call them "elders." The terminology is not as important as is the clear biblical model of teamwork needed to govern the local church.

Of course, just because a church uses the term *elder,* it does not always mean those in positions of leadership function in a biblical pattern. Even church government by elders can be ineffective when key biblical leadership ingredients are missing.

We wrote this book for those who want to understand how an authentic New Testament model of church government can help every member of the body of Christ become mature and properly equipped. Every member is a priest who is called by God to do the work of ministry while the elders promote this priesthood as they give governmental oversight to the church. This model communicates the family character of the local church. Believers are brothers and sisters in Christ who are in loving relationship with one another. Elders function as spiritual parents to the family.

Are you a present or future church leader who desires to learn how to lead as a shepherd and make wise decisions? Do you wish to know what qualifies a person to be an elder and what are the responsibilities? How can your leadership team deal with discipline issues in the church or conflict on the team? How do you raise up and train elders?

This book answers these questions and much more. We write from personal experience. As co-authors of this book, we each have more than two decades of experience in local church leadership. We have had the privilege of consulting and training leadership teams of many churches and denominations during the past years and have come to love the church and love her leaders. It is our desire to share that experience with you in this book. We will tell on ourselves—the mistakes we made. We would like to help you avoid making these same mistakes. Our examples and our stories are real even though some of the names have been changed.

The biblical principles taught in this book apply to the leadership of the community churches that dot the landscape of your community, along with the mega churches and the small house churches. The key is not the size of the church or the denomination you represent, but the key is following a biblical pattern for healthy leadership and healthy churches.

It is our prayer that this book answers your questions, provokes some questions, challenges your beliefs, and ministers to you and your spiritual family all at the same time. We love the body of Christ and pray daily for healthy elders and eldership teams.

You will find our value of healthy churches having healthy eldership teams threaded throughout this book because we believe it to be true. We pray that the pages to follow will be a blessing to you and your spiritual family.

Larry Kreider, Ron Myer, Steve Prokopchak, Brian Sauder
DOVE Christian Fellowship International
1924 West Main St.
Ephrata, PA 17522

*Throughout this book we have utilized the pronoun "he" when referring to a church elder. We do this to make the text easier to read. We recognize that different denominations have various understandings of the role of women in church leadership. This will be discussed later in the book.*

# Elders For Today's Church

It was our first attempt at an elders' retreat for our "new" church. Our fifteen-year-old church that had grown from 25 people to over 2,300 had just decentralized into eight separate churches, each led by its own team of elders. None of us really knew exactly what we were doing. We only knew that God directed our particular leadership team to take a few days away—away from our families, our jobs and our routines to listen to God and to one another.

By the time the weekend ended, we knew that we had met God. We felt closer to one another and to the One who had brought us together. God met us in that place as we laid aside our personal agendas and came together to hear what God was saying about providing oversight, nurture and guidance for our church. It's hard to describe, but we even felt closer to our surroundings: the bed we slept in, the table where we gathered to eat, even the floor where we fell prostrate. It became a familiar place, a place that we would miss and a place to which we would look forward to returning.

Over the next several years, we did return, many times. Committed to working together and taking responsibility to guide our church through its trials and blessings, our team of elders learned to serve in unity and Christ-like humility. We were discovering and experiencing *eldership* as an effective biblical model for leading a local church.

## Building leadership in our churches

Through the course of history there has been much debate over the roles and responsibilities of elders in the church. For the past two thousand years, the church has used various leadership structures with varying degrees of effectiveness. Differing models have their strengths and weaknesses, benefits and dangers.

Although the early church started out with the biblical model of elders, this leadership style was lost for centuries, during which a widening chasm developed between the clergy and the laity. Attempts were made to restore biblical eldership going back to the Brethren movement in England and the Restoration movement in America, but many today are confused about what the role of biblical eldership really is because it is rarely practiced in our churches today.

It is the intention of this book to clarify what true biblical eldership is and how these leaders function and give oversight to the church. We recognize that today a majority of churches call the one who gives primary oversight to the local church a "pastor." Although the language may be different, the same individual is being referred to. We call the primary leader a "senior elder." The terms we use should not alienate us. We simply prefer to use this terminology because we feel it more accurately portrays biblical church leadership.

Godly stewardship requires continual evaluation of principles of leadership to determine if they are consistent with the New Testament. In looking for more effective models, biblical *elders* have been rediscovered.

## A New Testament model

Biblical eldership tends to focus on the entire body of believers becoming equipped to minister, thus discouraging spectator Christianity.

Christ gave leaders to the church "to prepare God's people for works of service, so that the body of Christ may be built up" (Ephesians 4:12). Biblical church elders are to provide direction, protection and correction to the local church. Elders have the role of giving oversight to the affairs of the church as they empower believers for ministry and direct them to areas of service. As equipped believers grow, the church grows.

This was Jesus' approach to leadership. "Nevertheless I tell you the truth. It is to your advantage that I go away; for if I do not go away, the Helper will not come to you; but if I depart, I will send Him to you" (John 16:7). Jesus knew that it was important for Him to go so that the Holy Spirit might come and fill each of us. Jesus desired that the number of people who were filled with the Spirit of God would multiply greatly. He said we would do all the things that He did and even greater things! Every believer has that potential.

Just as each believer has a vital role to play in God's plan, each local church also has an essential role to play. Churches can move ahead with clear direction when they understand how leadership functions and how biblical elders can govern the church so that every believer has the opportunity to become involved in the Lord's service.

## The 2-2-2 blueprint

The blueprint we have discovered in the New Testament for organizing the church begins simply and remains easy to replicate. You do not have to be a master builder to understand it. Anyone can examine the design and follow its instructions to build solid leadership in the church.

The first foundational truths for building successfully are found in 2 Timothy 2:2. Paul, the apostle, exhorts Timothy, his protege, to pass on what he had learned to mature believers who would in turn pass on what they had learned to others. "And the things you have heard me say in the presence of many witnesses entrust to reliable men who will also be qualified to teach others."

The unlimited potential of this kind of in-house training is obvious. It is the potential that starts at ground level and continues to develop ordinary people into world-changers! It is the potential that says, "We believe in you, so we trust you to God. The Lord is going to use you in big ways if you allow Him to! We are here to equip you, and God will do the rest." This is how church leaders of all kinds, from small group leaders to church elders, can eventually be formed!

Brian was fresh out of college with a degree in industrial engineering when leaders in our church, DOVE Christian Fellowship International (DCFI), saw potential in him and encouraged him in church leadership roles, first as a youth pastor and eventually as an elder in the church. Over the years, the leadership believed in Brian and helped set in motion the calling in his life to understand the development and design of the local church. Rather than engineering ways to make a product or provide a service, these days Brian determines effective ways to plant churches as he oversees our Church Planting and Leadership School.

An ideal blueprint for governmental leadership in the local church is to raise up leaders in-house who are trusted, faithful examples of Christian living. According to our understanding of New Testament leadership, these church leaders are called *elders*, and they are in place to lead the local church. That is why God gave them to the church.

Every Christian is a minister; however, elders are appointed to give governmental oversight to the church. As they provide direction, protection and correction to the local church, elders help equip the believers and bring them to maturity.

## What is so important about church government?

For many, the topic of local church government is one that seems unimportant. In *Biblical Eldership,* author Alexander Strauch challenges this kind of thinking.

> For many people, the issue of church government...is as irrelevant an issue as the color of the church pews. Indeed, for many people the color of the church pews inspires greater interest! To these people, the organizational structure of the church really doesn't matter. The average church member's disinterest in how the church is governed needs to be challenged, how-

ever. Church government is an extremely practical and theologically significant issue.[1]

The New Testament church was governed in a way that personally affected every member. Every member is a priest who is to do the work of ministry, while the elders promote this priesthood by equipping them to do so. This model communicates the family character of the local church.

Believers are brothers and sisters in Christ in loving relationship with each other. Elders are considered spiritual fathers and mothers called to model, equip and govern other family members. They are to be servant-leaders working for the benefit of the family.

This is a clear, simple pattern for healthy local church leadership: healthy elders, secure in the Lord's love and call, serve as spiritual parents to the local church body.

Effective eldership like this requires a certain leadership style that decreases the distance between leaders and followers. It paves the way for leaders to lead with servants' hearts, leading as humble examples of Christian living. At its best, a senior elder and his team aims to provide loving oversight for a congregation and encourage everyone to become active ministers.

## Churches of all kinds need elders

The Lord is using multiple types of churches today—from conventional church structures to those that operate outside traditional patterns. Many options need to be made available to us for the immense task of equipping the saints for ministry and bringing the gospel of Jesus Christ to a lost and dying world.

Whether you serve in a community church, a larger mega-church or in a house church (sometimes called a "micro church"),[2] godly elders will help the church to function as a healthy church family. Although different in size, shape and vision, all churches need an effective model of church government, and many are finding that biblical eldership is the way to lead the local church.

It is our goal in this book to challenge and encourage church leaders to practice authentic biblical eldership as they shepherd the flock of God. We write as a labor of love to help equip both present and future servant-leaders in the local church.

## Questions to discuss

1. What should the main focus of biblical eldership be?
2. Explain how in-house training of elders could result in unlimited potential in your church (2 Timothy 2:2).
3. What is the importance of church government?
4. How is an elder similar to a spiritual parent?

---

[1] Alexander Strauch, *Biblical Eldership,* (Littleton, CO: Lewis and Roth Publishers, 1995), p. 101.
[2] For more on micro churches, read Larry Kreider's *House Church Networks, A Church for a New Generation,* (Ephrata, PA: House to House Publications, 2001).

# Elders Serve as Overseers and Shepherds

In the New Testament, the term *elders* normally refers to those in positions of spiritual authority, governing and guiding the local church. Paul speaks to the *elders* of the church many places throughout scripture. He calls on *elders* to shepherd the church.[1] He instructs his spiritual son Titus to install *elders* in every church.[2]

In the early church, the apostles birthed a church (or churches) in a city and returned later to entrust it to mature believers they called *elders*.[3] C. Peter Wagner gives us insights into how the apostles and elders worked together to fulfill these crucial roles in the church:

> Paul told Titus to "appoint elders." In the New Testament terms, elders is another word for the pastors of the churches. At that time, all churches were house churches, and each one was governed by an elder. Pastors did not appoint elders back then; apostles appointed elders.[4]

The fruit of the apostles' work was handed over to the care of local elders who stayed and gave spiritual care and oversight to the local church. This gave the apostles freedom to continue in their apostolic ministry.

In Acts 15 and 16, both the apostles and elders had distinct roles in church government. Simply stated, the role of the elders was to oversee the local church, and the role of the apostles was to oversee the local church elders.

## Elders oversee and shepherd God's people

The Greek words used to describe local church leaders in the New Testament include the word for "elder" (*presbuteros*); the word for "overseer" (*episkopos*); and the word for "shepherd" (*poimen*). Scripture uses the terms "elders, overseers and shepherds" interchangeably. These terms are all used to describe one and the same office or person.

In Acts 20:28, Paul is addressing the elders of the church in Ephesus when he refers to them as overseers and shepherds:

> Keep watch over yourselves and all the flock of which the Holy Spirit has made you overseers. Be shepherds of the church of God....

An analogy can be made between an elder and a carpenter to help think through this concept. An elder oversees in much the same way that a carpenter builds. *Elder* is what the person is called; *overseeing* is what he does. A *carpenter* is the person; *building* is what he does.

Just as a carpenter is also called a builder, elders are also called overseers and shepherds because it is what they do. They oversee and shepherd the local church.

In a nutshell, the different titles given to the spiritual leaders of the early church reveal the various aspects of their work. These words describe the elders and help us gain a picture of *the person* involved (a spiritually mature individual), *the function* of the ministry he is given (overseer), and *the manner* in which he accomplishes his ministry (as a shepherd) as indicated by the following chart:

| Title | Greek | Meaning | Describes |
|-------|-------|---------|-----------|
| elder | presbuteros | mature elder | the person |
| overseer | episkopos | giving oversight | the function |
| shepherd | poimen | as a shepherd | the manner |

## Elder: the person

*Elder* is a term referring to the person—a mature person of wisdom and experience. The term *elder* is used several different ways in the scriptures. In the Old Testament, the term *elder* referred to a person of age, experience and authority.[5] These were people respected by their families and communities simply due to their age and experience.

In the nation of Israel, elders led and ruled society corporately. These community leaders were responsible to protect, govern and administer justice. Moses appointed elders to help him judge the nation of Israel. These elders, being mature men, set the example for others, and gave leadership to cities, regions and later to the local synagogues.

In the New Testament, the Greek word for elder is *presbuteros*. This term also means "elder, older person or a senior." The application of this word, however, was applied several ways. Like the Old Testament, it referred to "an older person, advanced in years."[6] It also referred to the "official leaders of the Jewish people."[7] Apparently, the early church borrowed the term "elder" from the Jewish synagogue to designate leaders to whom the responsibility of teaching and ruling was given, because *presbuteros* also referred to "the leaders of the New Testament local churches."[8] These elders were those who were called upon to rule, govern or give oversight to the church. Government in the early church was first through Christ, then the apostles, and then through elders, who led the churches.

Acts 14:23 indicates that Paul and Barnabas returned to Antioch with its growing number of believers and "appointed elders for them in each church...." It was standard practice for apostles to appoint elders to the churches they founded, giving them oversight responsibility.

## An elder is an overseer

*Overseer* refers to the elder's function. As an elder, he oversees. That is what he does. An overseer watches over the matters pertaining to the church. *Overseer* is a designation for a New Testament church leader who gave oversight to the church (1 Timothy 3:1; Philippians 1:1).

The Greek word *episkopos* described the church leader's *leadership function*. As overseers, they were like the watchman of Israel who stood in a tower above the flocks to view the sheep. God commanded Ezekiel as a "watchman for the house of Israel..." (Ezekiel 33:7). This was a position of leadership where the overseer was in place to watch over and protect the flock. The term *overseer* describes the function of the elder who leads the local church.

## An elder leads as a shepherd

The manner in which an elder oversees is the same as that of a *shepherd.* "Be shepherds of God's flock that is under your care, serving as overseers—not because you must, but because you are willing, as God wants you to be" (1 Peter 5:2). An elder gives oversight to the church with the love of a shepherd caring for his sheep. As a leader, he is patient, attentive and leads the church with a gentle touch.

The word *shepherd* is a translation of the Greek work *poimen*, one who cares for the flock. This term is only used twice in the New Testament, in both cases when describing the duties and responsibilities of the leaders to *shepherd* and feed the church (Acts 20:28; 1 Peter 5:2).

We already mentioned Acts 20:28, where Paul is addressing the elders of the church and he refers to them as shepherds, "Keep watch over yourselves and all the flock of which the Holy Spirit has made you overseers. Be shepherds of the church of God...."

In 1 Peter 5:2-3, the author mentions that overseers who lead the church should lead as shepherds, "Be shepherds of God's flock that is under your care, serving as overseers...not lording it over those entrusted to you, but being examples to the flock."

An elder is a mature leader, and his work involves giving oversight to the local church. The manner in which he gives oversight is that of a shepherd who is compassionate and concerned for his sheep. He cares for, protects, guides and leads his sheep to good nourishment.

If an elder functions more strongly in the leadership or oversight role and is weak when it comes to shepherding the sheep, he should ask the Lord to give him a greater love and compassion for the sheep. If he is weaker on the leadership end, he should ask the Lord to give him greater wisdom to oversee the church so the sheep do not wander aimlessly! That is why having a team of elders is so important. Those on the team will have different gifts that complement those of the other elders and fill in the gaps.

## Plurality of elders

In the Old Testament, leadership was largely singular, but in the New Testament, eldership functioned on the principle of plurality. Jesus introduced the pattern when He chose twelve disciples. He did not send them out alone but two by two.

The appointment of elders in the early church was plural. Paul told Titus to appoint elders in every town in Crete (Titus 1:5). These churches were young and were probably quite small. Nevertheless, it appears that more than one elder was appointed to each church.

In 1 Thessalonians 5:12-13, we see that the congregation is to respect its leaders (plural). "Now we ask you, brothers, to respect those who work hard among you, who are over you in the Lord and who admonish you. Hold them in the highest regard in love because of their work..." Also in Hebrews 13:7, we are admonished, "remember your leaders" (plural), "for they watch out for your souls..." (v. 17, NKJ).

Working together as a team of elders seems to have been normal procedure for the New Testament church. Elders working together as a team learn to submit to each other and love each other. A plurality of leadership offers an example to the church of working together in love despite differences of opinions and personalities.

## Co-equal elders, with one who leads

Along with the plurality of leadership, the New Testament teaches a co-equality within that plurality.[9] Since every believer is on equal footing before God, and God does not show favoritism (Romans 2:11), no one elder should be exalted over another. A team of elders must maintain a spirit of humility as they work together in unity.

However, although all elders are equal as persons, they are not co-equal in responsibility. In his informative book, *The Church in the New Testament*, Kevin Conner maintains that on a team of elders, one elder will stand out and lead the way as a "first among equals."

Christ will place a mantle of leadership upon one elder to direct the people of God. This is done in conjunction with the multiple eldership. The thought of "first among equals" is illustrated in the very persons in the Godhead. The Father is the first person, the Son is second, and the Holy Spirit is third. However, Father, Son and Holy Spirit are equal as persons. For the purposes of creation and redemption, however, there is this order in the Godhead. The Father is indeed "first among equals." There is no competition, but recognition. Each person has distinctive function and ministry, yet are one in mind, will and judgment.

[Leaders of elder teams] are not set there as leaders of the rest because they are better than the others, but because God set them there, equipping, anointing and enabling them to be "first among equals." [10]

## Senior elder—head of the team

There is no such thing as a leaderless group. On a team, there must be one who leads; otherwise chaos occurs. Within a team of elders, final decisions must rest upon someone, or frustration and a lack of direction ensues. Every sports team has a captain; every school has a principal; every store has a manager; every town has a mayor; and every team of elders needs a senior elder.

In a plurality of elders there is a leader. The leader can be designated or allowed to emerge. The terminology as mentioned earlier for the one who leads the church leadership team is the "senior elder," and this term will be used throughout this book. Most churches today give different names for the head of a leadership team: pastor, senior pastor, minister, lead elder, overseer, vicar, etc. The name is not nearly as important as the practice of having a clear leader for the team.

Biblically, the senior elder shares the power and authority with the other elders. A healthy team, functioning together in unity with the biblical headship of a senior elder, is vital for effective church government.

## Two extremes

Without a clear understanding of the plurality of eldership with a senior elder as the head of the team, two extremes may develop in the local church. Since some churches have been burned by an authoritarian "pastor," they intentionally do not choose to recognize a leader of a team of elders. They instead say they will be led by the Holy Spirit alone. This pronouncement may sound very spiritual, but this lack of healthy church leadership will eventually cause frustration and pain equal to that of being burned by authoritarian leadership. When no one leads, the church flounders.

Others allow their church leadership to lead in autocratic, abusive ways. In the early church, Paul had to address this issue. In 1 Peter 5:3, he encourages the elders to be "eager to serve" and additionally cautions them against any kind of abusive practices as leaders by telling them they should not be "lording it over those entrusted to [them]...."

Power-hungry elders, who dominate their congregation by excessive use of their power, think they are "above the law" and cannot be questioned about their decisions. One local church had to go to court to force the "elders" to make financial reports available to the church. The elders believed that they had the authority to keep that information from church members. Healthy New Testament leadership is not secretive!

Hebrews 13:17 tells us that elders must give an account to the Lord for how they serve as shepherds and overseers. Elders must be loving leaders who provide an example of humility and submission for the congregation to follow. They lead as shepherds, laying down their lives for the sheep because they want the sheep to flourish and prosper.

## Questions to discuss

1.  Describe the function of an elder. Describe the function of an apostle.
2.  What is the difference between the role of an elder and the role of an apostle?
3.  How is working together as a team of elders beneficial? What is the importance of a team leader?

1  Acts 20
2  Titus 1:5
3  Acts 14:23
4  C. P. Wagner, *Apostles and Prophets*, (Ventura, California: Regal Books, 2000), p. 45.
5  Elders in Old Testament (older person who was a person of age) - Genesis 10:21; 25:23; Deuteronomy 5:23; 1 Samuel 4:3; 1 Chronicles 11:3
6  Elders in New Testament (older person, advanced in years) - John 8:9; Luke 15:25; Acts 2:17; 1 Timothy 5:2; Philemon 9; Luke 1:18; Titus 2:2-3
7  Official leaders of the Jewish people - Luke 7:3; Matthew 5:22; 10:17; 16:21; Luke 22:66; Acts 4:5-8; 6:12; Mark 13:9; 14:55
8  Leaders of the New Testament local churches
    Acts 11:30 - Elders at the church of Antioch
    Acts 14:23 - Paul and Barnabas appoint "elders in every church."
    Acts 15:2,4,6,22-23; 16:4 - Elders at the church in Jerusalem
    Acts 20:17, 28 - Elders/bishops at the church of Ephesus (v. 17 "elders of the church")
    Acts 21:18 - Elders at the church in Jerusalem
    Philippians 1:1 - The church at Philippi has bishops (elders) and deacons
    1 Timothy 5:17-19 - Elders at the church of Ephesus
    Titus 1:5 - Titus is to appoint elders in every town.
    James 5:14 - "The elders of the church"
    1 Peter 5:1 - "The elders among you"
9  Co-equality of elders:
    Acts 2:14 - Peter stands with the eleven as a co-equal apostle
    Galatians 2:9 - Peter, James and John are fellow-apostles, fellow-elders
    Revelation 4:4; 5:8-10 - The 24 elders in Revelation are co-equal
10 Kevin J. Conner, *The Church in the New Testament*, (Portland, OR: Bible Temple Publishing, 1989), p. 93-94.

# Biblical Qualifications for Elders

3

"Career training in as little as six months!" reads an appealing job opportunity in the local newspaper. Some jobs require intense short-term training and others require an individual to dig in for the long haul. What qualifies a person to become an elder of a local church? Does he have to study seven long years to become qualified? Can he take a crash course?

Our modern method of training church leaders often runs contrary to what we see modeled in the early church. In today's church world, an individual prepares for church leadership much like any other vocation. He feels called to go into "full-time ministry" so he goes to seminary to train and prepare for his desired point of entry into ministry. Upon graduation, he presents himself as a pastoral candidate and sends out a resume to churches needing pastors. A church that is looking for a pastor interviews him, and if he is acceptable to the church board, he is hired to serve. He becomes the leader of the church because he is the one with biblical training. He is the one who prepares the sermons every Sunday morning, visits the sick, and performs baptisms, weddings and funerals.

All too often, after a few years of ministry, the church board decides that this pastor is no longer "called to ministry" in this local church because he is not performing to their expectations. So the pastor is forced to seek a "call" elsewhere and the whole process starts all over again.

The early church did not recruit elders from a distant seminary. Seminary experience was not a prerequisite to leadership in the New Testament church, although some leaders, like Paul, were trained theologians, having studied the law under the strict religious sect of the Pharisees.

Make no mistake: studying for church leadership is very helpful for eldership and is not to be discouraged. However, a person who has studied in an academic setting to become a full-time minister should progress through the same requirements of anyone else in the local body. He must prove himself faithful with the little responsibilities he is given before he is handed the greater. Character requires more than functional knowledge. It is advantageous for individuals who are trained outside the local church to have a period of training within the context of the local church before they are released to serve.

If the New Testament church was not overly concerned with formal education for its elders, what then did they look for? Elders were found from within the local church and developed into leaders over time on the basis of their willingness to serve and their moral and spiritual maturity. They were spiritually growing individuals who were chosen because of their maturity and character.

Paul expressed concern over an elder's character; since for an individual to oversee others, he needed to watch over himself. His life was to be an example for others to follow, and he needed to display integrity, self-control and spiritual progress.

The qualifications for elders listed in 1 Timothy 3:1-7 and Titus 1:5-9 give spiritual leaders a checkpoint for their own spiritual lives. When the apostles chose a new elder to lead the church, they looked for a person with the attributes spoken of within these verses. These qualifications emphasized the person's character and maturity as a Christian as well as his leadership ability. Leadership ability cannot compensate for a lack of character.

Admittedly, the qualifications listed in these chapters require a high standard. Absolute perfection, however, is not demanded. If it were, no one would qualify! For example, in order to meet the qualification of being "above reproach," does that mean the elder is required to have no faults whatsoever? Does the qualification "have the ability to teach" mean that the elder must have eloquent oratorical skills? Does "not quick tempered" mean that the elder has total control of himself at all times and never gets angry? No, of course not! Rather than requiring sinless perfection, the qualifications require that an elder be consistent as a life-style in all areas of the Christian life. He is a spiritual father who is an example deserving imitation.

An elder sets the example of godly behavior, according to Coy Wylie, and he describes it this way:

> An elder's character and conduct are not called into question. He is free from any accusation. You can throw mud at him all day long and because of the quality of his life, none will stick to him. He is a man of impeccable integrity, unwavering honesty and consistent morality. He is a man that you would trust with your family and your money. If you loaned him your car, he would return it with a full tank of gas and a fresh wash job! [1]

How does God's Word describe the qualifications for elders? The description is found in both 1 Timothy 3 and Titus 1.

> Here is a trustworthy saying: If anyone sets his heart on being an overseer, he desires a noble task. Now the overseer must be above reproach, the husband of but one wife, temperate, self-controlled, respectable, hospitable, able to teach, not given to drunkenness, not violent but gentle, not quarrelsome, not a lover of money. He must manage his own family well and see that his children obey him with proper respect. (If anyone does not know how to manage his own family, how can he take care of God's church?) He must not be a recent convert, or he may become conceited and fall under the same judgment as the devil. He must also have a good reputation with outsiders, so

that he will not fall into disgrace and into the devil's trap (1 Timothy 3:1-7).

The reason I left you in Crete was that you might straighten out what was left unfinished and appoint elders in every town, as I directed you. An elder must be blameless, the husband of but one wife, a man whose children believe and are not open to the charge of being wild and disobedient. Since an overseer is entrusted with God's work, he must be blameless-not overbearing, not quick-tempered, not given to drunkenness, not violent, not pursuing dishonest gain. Rather he must be hospitable, one who loves what is good, who is self-controlled, upright, holy and disciplined. He must hold firmly to the trustworthy message as it has been taught, so that he can encourage others by sound doctrine and refute those who oppose it (Titus 1:5-9).

It can be seen in the above verses that there are both positive and negative qualifications for elders. These qualifications serve to protect both the leaders and the people from unnecessary pain and sorrow. Installing an elder lacking in these qualifications could result in a crisis of leadership. "We cannot ignore these qualifications," says Duane Britton, senior elder of one of DOVE Christian Fellowship International's churches in Ephrata, Pennsylvania:

An unqualified individual in the position of elder will inevitably be a detriment to the church and the gospel's testimony. God, in His grace, gives clear and ample instruction in His Word regarding the moral and spiritual requirements for those seeking church oversight.

People often take one of two extreme positions regarding the qualifications of elders. The first is to ignore the full range of scriptural qualifications, thus permitting unqualified individuals to fill a crucial position of leadership. The other extreme is to add qualifications or restrictions that God doesn't demand, thus excluding needed and qualified individuals from church leadership. Such practices only serve to hold a congregation back from reaching its full potential.

What God prizes among the leaders of His people is not education, wealth, social status, success, or even spiritual gifts. Rather, He values personal moral and spiritual character, requiring that those who lead His people be just, devout, self-controlled, peaceable, and forbearing with others. They must also be loyal spouses, good parents, and loyal students of God's Word.

As we take a closer look at 1 Timothy 3:1-7 and Titus 1:5-9, we can glean the character and the qualifications of a godly elder.

## To serve the church, an elder...
### ...is willing

According to 1 Timothy 3:1, an evidence of God's calling a person to serve as an elder is a desire for it. "If anyone sets his heart on being an overseer, he desires a noble task." It is a good thing to desire to serve Christ by being a leader in the church. This is not a human ambition; it is a calling from God—a deep desire and compulsion to love and shepherd the Lord's people.

God creates a burden within a person, a Spirit-generated concern for the flock. An elder knows he will devote much time and energy caring for the sheep in sacrificial, loving service. "Be shepherds of God's flock that is under your care, serving as overseers—not because you must, but because you are willing, as God wants you to be; not greedy for money, but eager to serve" (1 Peter 5:2). The elder is humbly willing to serve and has the heart of a shepherd for the sheep he oversees as he surrenders himself in sacrificial service to the congregation.

### ...is above reproach

"Being above reproach" is not referring to perfection. Paul was calling attention to a person's reputation. How do others view this individual? What is his character? An elder lives his life in such a way that no one can legitimately find fault with him. He is free from the taint of scandal and accusation (1 Peter 3:16) and has unquestionable integrity. If people look at his life and try to find something they can use against him they will find it difficult, because he is blameless and above reproach. His character sets an example for all to follow.

Why is it so important to be "above reproach"? Elders are often targets. Satan will assault elders because it is the best way to destroy the church. If an elder falls, it causes great, often devastating, harm to the church. An elder has a great responsibility to live a life of integrity before the people.

Integrity means having high moral standards combined with brutal honesty about where you are still falling short. Elders are willing to admit that they are still growing and that they need the Lord's help daily. This models a teachable heart.

## ...is the husband of one wife

The Greek translates this as a "one woman man." An elder has eyes only for his spouse. He maintains God's standard of morality. This passage in 1 Timothy 3:2 is sometimes used as proof text that a divorced person cannot serve as an elder. However, if we look at the time it was written, we see that some of the converted Jews still had several wives as permitted under Semitic Law. It was this practice of having multiple wives that was being discouraged at the time of Christ, hence the reference to "being the husband of one wife." When he came to Christ, the new convert was faced with a new standard of morality—God's standard. The same standard applied for any Christian woman. She too was to be faithful to one husband.

The real question today is, "Can divorced persons serve in any capacity of leadership?" We believe they can. We have chosen to address each person  who has divorced individually. There are far too many situations to make a blanket rule. While every divorce is the result of sin, not every divorce is sinful. There are those who have been abandoned and had no choice to divorce or not to divorce.[2] We choose to consider each situation separately by praying, fasting and doing whatever it takes to hear from God about His desire and desired use of a divorced potential leader.

Finally, "being the husband of one wife" does not mean that an elder must be married. Paul probably was not, yet he clearly called himself an elder and an apostle. Obviously, if an elder is married, he is to faithfully love one wife (1 Timothy 3:2; Titus 1:6).

## ...is temperate; self-controlled

Self-control consists of the right use of one's will under the controlling power and performance of the Holy Spirit. It must be an outgrowth of the Spirit's working in an elder "both to will and to do of His good pleasure" (Philippians 2:13).

Elders are disciplined people. They are able to control their desires and impulses. They are sober, cautious, vigilant and clearheaded, yet at the same time filled with the joy of the Lord. Elders are able to discern the many church matters that come before them and have a sound mind, enabling them to make good judgments. Elders are not double-minded or tossed to and fro by every wind of doctrine. As leaders, they are watchful regarding themselves and the flock they oversee (Hebrews 13:17).

They have a well-organized life and are disciplined in their stewardship of time. Elders are hard-working and thoughtful. They live a committed, Spirit-filled, godly life and model godly conduct.

## ...is respectable

The Greek word translated "respectable" is *kosmios*. The English word "cosmetics" comes from the same root word. In Titus 2:10, the verb *kosmeo* is translated "to adorn." In the book, *Leaders on Leadership*, Gene Getz writes:

> In essence, Paul is teaching that a mature leader's life will be like "cosmetics to the gospel." When non-Christians observe

their attitudes and actions, they should be attracted to the gospel message and to the One who incarnates that message.[3]

Getz goes on to tell a personal story of purchasing a house in a new neighborhood whose previous owner was a Christian minister. In this particular community, everyone kept their lawns well-manicured, except for the previous owner—the minister who allowed his expansive lawn to become a weedy hay field. After Getz, a minister himself, moved into the neighborhood, it took months for him and his family to build bridges with their neighbors because everyone was convinced all ministers were a bad lot—unconcerned and irresponsible. But they won their neighbors respect by diligently and consistently keeping their property manicured and orderly. They could once again "adorn" the gospel of Christ by living a life-style that properly corresponded with the character of God.

## ...is hospitable

Quite simply, "being hospitable" means being "fond of guests." The Greek word for hospitable translates to "love of strangers." Elders welcome new people, even people who are different than they. The home of an elder is an open home where people of all kinds feel welcome. An elder maintains a gracious and generous attitude toward others.

Elders are willing to help, to come to others' aid; they enjoy fellowshipping and associating with others.

Several years ago, as a senior elder of a cell-based congregation, Ron realized that hospitality was lacking in his local church. How could he motivate people to be "fond of guests?" One Saturday at about four o'clock in the afternoon, he had a spontaneous idea, "Wouldn't it be really neat to have a bunch of people over for lunch tomorrow?" he asked his wife, Bonnie. "We could really hit this hospitality thing 'big time.' I am thinking that about 40 people would be a good number," Ron continued.

Bonnie sort of gasped, and caught her breath. "That's a great idea, honey, and *you* can do it!" Bonnie's less than enthusiastic response did not deter Ron's last-minute idea. He decided he was up for the challenge!

Ron rushed off to the soon-to-close grocery store and headed for the meat counter. He asked how much ham he needed for sandwiches to feed 40 people. Then he bought several large cans of soup, two large cans of fruit salad, celery, several large bags of chips and some ice-cream. He ended up spending $1.65 per person.

On Sunday, after the service, Ron asked 40 people to raise their hands if they wanted to come for lunch that day. He had no problem quickly recruiting people for a free lunch! Before they ate, Ron read Acts 2:46-47. Several times over the next few months, Ron asked people from the congregation to come for lunch. One Sunday they had as many as 63.

After a number of weeks, of this, the cashier at the grocery store became curious. When Ron told her he was having 40 people from his church over for lunch, she wanted to know where his church met! So you see, hospitality is not about putting out a four-course meal. Hospitality is simply inviting people into your life and home. Be warned, this can be habit-forming and highly contagious!

### ...has the ability to teach

This does not necessarily mean that all elders have the gift of teaching or are great orators and speakers. Rather it implies they have the ability to communicate God's Word so that they can help others. Some elders are gifted to teach large groups, while others are gifted to teach one-on-one in a mentoring type relationship.

Elders know the truth of God's Word well enough to be able to confront and admonish others when needed. They cannot teach what they do not know. "He must hold firmly to the trustworthy message as it has been taught, so that he can encourage others by sound doctrine and refute those who oppose it" (Titus 1:9).

Elders are capable of teaching in a language the flock understands, reaching and connecting with their target audience. They have a compulsion to pass on to others what they have learned. Elders have a genuine love for God's Word and a desire to impart it to others.

## ...is not given to drunkenness

"Not given to drunkenness" literally means "not tarrying at wine." Elders are not infatuated with alcoholic beverages and defiled by the life-style often associated with drinking. They have an exemplary life-style that is without the negative influence of alcohol or intemperance. "Do not get drunk on wine, which leads to debauchery. Instead, be filled with the Spirit" (Ephesians 5:18). It is always wrong to be addicted to anything. This includes wine, drugs, sex, and even food (Proverbs 23:20-21).

## ...is not overbearing, but humble

An elder must be selfless. He is not self-willed and arrogant (1 Peter 5:3). His desire is for the people to be all they can be in God. He gives of himself for those in his care.

One senior elder, Bob, learned the hard way that his overbearing behavior was getting in the way of leading the flock in his care. The church and the eldership team were in turmoil, and Bob was forced to take a hard look at himself. He learned that he behaved as he did in order to protect himself. He could not admit that he was scared, so he tried to win by intimidation. Bob finally realized that the people viewed him as smug, proud, self-righteous and driving, and those were labels he did not desire! When he stopped trying to control others in order to feel secure, his overbearing attitude diminished. Due to this experience, Bob began thinking more about helping his team and the congregation than about his own welfare.

Elders know that their dependence is totally on God. This keeps them walking in humility, rather than lording it over others. Elders are examples to the church they serve. "Not lording it over those entrusted to you, but being examples to the flock" (1 Peter 5:3). The flock will not rise above the example set by the elders. When the flock recognizes the elder's humility before God, they will follow his example of grace. "God opposes the proud but gives grace to the humble" (James 4:6).

Prestige and the desire to be admired and respected can overshadow an elder's ministry. Proverbs 8:13 tells us that God hates pride. Pride is at the center of "selfish ambition" according to James 3:16. Selfish ambition prompts us to promote our own interests, and we start to believe in our own merit, superiority and accomplishments. This verse goes on to say that selfish ambition leads to "every evil practice." Humility, as opposed to selfish ambition, causes us to consider others as better than ourselves (Philippians 2:3).

## ...is not quick tempered or quarrelsome

Elders are not cranky or irritable and are not quick to get in verbal disputes. They do not lose their tempers and react when they are challenged or irritated. If elders quickly become angry, they will make matters worse when dealing with conflicts. This makes reconciliation difficult. James gives this timely advice: "My dear brothers, take note of this: Everyone should be quick to listen, slow to speak and slow to become angry" (James 1:19). Elders are well-balanced in judgment, not impulsive or given to extremes.

An elder is a person of peace. He is not pushy or hard to get along with. He is not contentious or moody but peaceable, pleasant and positive. Elders are not given to strife, debate or argument for argument's sake. This is very important when there are struggles in the church. An elder is more concerned with understanding others than he is with being understood by others. An elder lays his life down for the sheep.

## ...is gentle, not violent

An elder maintains relational integrity. He does not use force of character to get his way. He is not a bully in his relationships with others. Even under provocation, he does not strike out at people who try his patience. Elders are courteous and considerate of others, in addition to being patient, kind, considerate, forbearing and not easily disturbed. They are individuals who are willing to yield or concede in a matter without compromising the truth.

Sheep must be led, not driven. Ron was leading a meeting with a senior elder and his team who were working through some difficult issues. At one point, the senior elder responded to one disgruntled member of his team by saying, "I think you need to respond better to the prodding of your senior elder. You really should learn to listen to my prodding."

Ron made a mental note of his statement and later confronted the senior elder alone, "You know, brother, I think that it is 'goats' that need to be prodded," Ron reminded him. "As a shepherd, remember that sheep must be led."

Being gentle means we are forbearing and patient. That's how Jesus deals with us. An elder's greatest weapon is love.

## ...is free from the love of money

An elder is free of greed. He is free of the love of money and the things that money can obtain. He believes money is a tool for God to use to bless others and is not to be hoarded.

An elder is not out for personal gain or profit as a result of serving as an elder. In the New Testament, it appears that certain elders were financially supported in their work (1 Timothy 5:17). The churches were probably generous in their support which could lead one to be tempted to serve as an elder for the money. When an elder has his heart focused on possessions, he becomes discontented with ministry. "...Godliness with contentment is great gain" (1 Timothy 6:6).

Elders are examples of how to honestly earn, spend and save money. They tithe to the local church and give generously in a way that honors the kingdom of God and values the flock.

## ...is able to manage his own house well

A church resembles a family because it is made up of a group of brothers and sisters in Christ with the elders as the spiritual parents. An elder presides over the family with the feelings of a father, loving all the members without prejudice, partiality or selfish aims. Elders conduct the affairs of the church family in a godly way, caring for all things pertaining to the family.

It is especially important for elders to set the example for the flock as they lovingly discipline and nurture their children into adulthood. A natural father has strong ties with his children and "manages" them so his children are not wild and unruly. He disciplines and trains them with dignity and respect. Children will want to do what is right because they respect and love their parents.

Elders preside over their church family, tenderly caring for the church so people are encouraged to move ahead with common purposes and goals. Parents make decisions that are best for the family. The same is true of elders. They make decisions that are not always based on their own preferences but that are best for the church as a whole.

## ...has a good reputation with those outside the body

An elder has a good testimony with the unsaved and stays away from compromising circumstances. "Live such good lives among the pagans that, though they accuse you of doing wrong, they may see your good deeds and glorify God on the day he visits us" (1 Peter 2:12).

Ron tells the story of a time he spoke quite directly to an unsaved individual who had taken advantage of him, lied to him, and furthermore would not acknowledge it. Ron was firm (perhaps "righteously indignant") and spoke his mind. However, when Ron walked away, he had to ask himself this question, "Could I have followed up that confrontation by witnessing to that individual, or was I too upset?" As a Christian and church elder, Ron says he learned a hard lesson that day. He realized he would have to make some attitude adjustments.

Elders have a "soundness of speech that cannot be condemned, so that those who oppose you may be ashamed because they have nothing bad to say about [you]" (Titus 2:8). We have probably all been frustrated with leaders who said one thing but did the opposite.

## ...loves what is good

God is good, therefore an elder's desires are focused on the good things of God and not defiled by questionable or evil things. An elder is a godly person, one not defiled by sin. He hates sin and has a compassion for those whose lives are entangled by sin.

Elders see the good in others and in situations that are less than desirable. Since they see some of the negative things within the church, they also have the ability to see the good that can come out of these situations. Elders have a strong desire to see others succeed. They know that as others in the church succeed, they in turn succeed!

## ...is upright; holy

Being upright and holy is doing what is right in God's sight regardless of the circumstances. It is doing right even when no one is looking or listening. It is having a heart that is pleasing to God. David said, "As the deer pants for streams of water, so my soul pants for you, O God" (Psalm 42:1). That is holiness.

Elders are upright in character and equal and fair in their judgment toward all. Godly elders do not simply react; they have the wisdom to judge rightly, making the proper choices and sound decisions. When dealing with others, they do not allow prejudice or passion to cloud their decisions.

As a father, Steve realizes that his children watch his every move. "Our children must see an example of holiness behind our closed doors. While we can often fool those in the church, we will not fool our families."

## ...is not a new convert

Elders are not newly saved but have a history with God. When spiritual babies are given adult roles, they may become conceited. Spiritual growth should always precede responsibility.

Elders need to be Christians for a long enough time to be properly tested. The congregation needs to observe an individual when the going gets tough. They are spiritually mature and experienced.

Healthy elders depend on God's grace and power to do the job assigned to them. Leading a cell group can be a great training ground for a future elder. If we are faithful in little, we will be faithful in much (Matthew 25:21) .

There is no chronological age requirement for an elder, but maturity can be developed through life experiences. While all of us experience different life events, our level of maturity determines how we will respond to those events.

## ...is willing to be tested

An elder realizes that there will be tests and "...many are called, but few are chosen" (Matthew 22:14 NKJ). Many leaders who are rightly called by God fail the test of leadership and are no longer in leadership today. We learn from James 1:2-4 that the trials of life will either draw us closer to Jesus or drive us away from Jesus.

God allows an elder to go through tests to see how he will respond under pressure. By his response, he either qualifies or disqualifies himself.

Ron used to be in a farm partnership that did testing of new prototype farm equipment. The engineers who lived in the production room first put the equipment through their tests, and then they gave it to farmers like Ron who subjected it to a genuine field test. If the engineers said the machine would work in dry conditions, Ron also tested it in wet conditions. What good is a machine that only works in the best of conditions? Ron wanted to know what it would do in the worst conditions. Similarly, God allows us to be tested so that we have the opportunity to respond in a godly manner, passing the test.

In the church, elders are sometimes harshly tested. When the pressure is on, what will they do? The true test of a leader is the way he responds and reacts to adverse situations. How an elder reacts at the point of confrontation or pressure defines his character as a leader.

George was an elder who finally realized that when confronted with a weakness in his life, he often brought up others' mistakes so that he could look better. "I lived in a place of protectionism rather than freedom" he admitted. When he stopped selfishly looking after himself first so he would not get hurt, he experienced the freedom that comes from learning to take constructive criticism.

The Lord wants to make elders tough on the outside and soft on the inside. Tough on the outside does not mean "brash" but rather means "being able to take it." Elders are able to take the heat and withstand the weathering brought about from leading. Inside, an elder's heart is soft. He sincerely cares about others' problems and emotions. His heart is tender and soft to the prompting of the Holy Spirit.

When Ron's youngest son was born, he remained in the neonatal intensive care unit in the hospital for a harrowing nine days. Ron had one thought in mind—to get his son out of there with a clean bill of health. On the fourth day, as Ron entered the unit, the Holy Spirit spoke to him and said, "You know you are missing it. You are so concerned about your own needs that you are missing all of the hurting people around you." From that day on, Ron entered the hospital with a new focus—to notice and reach out to those around him who also had critical family health issues to face. Ron was not the only one with problems!

According to 2 Corinthians 10:7, elders focusing on their own needs alone are being quite shallow. "You are looking only on the surface of things. If anyone is confident that he belongs to Christ, he should consider again that we belong to Christ just as much as he."

## ...has the heart of a servant

Years ago, Larry observed a well-known church leader at a conference who provided a wonderful example of servanthood. This man took every opportunity to notice those around him and he was sensitive to their individual needs. On one particular occasion Larry watched this man lead a busboy to the Lord and he even went so far as to help him find a church to attend where he could receive fellowship. Larry observed this particular church leader serving wherever he had an opportunity. This man's example had a profound impact on Larry's life.

Jesus by nature is a servant and looks for those who have a servant's heart. "Jesus called them together and said, 'You know that the rulers of the Gentiles lord it over them, and their high officials exercise authority over them. Not so with you. Instead, whoever wants to become great among you must be your servant, and whoever wants to be first must be your slave—just as the Son of Man did not come to be served, but to serve, and to give his life as a ransom for many'" (Matthew 20:25-28).

Jesus is our ultimate role model for leadership. He led by being a servant to all those around Him. He knew who He was because of His intimate relationship with His Father, and out of that relationship, He ministered to the others' needs. From God's perspective, leaders and servants are synonymous in the body of Christ. In the world's system, leaders are expected to dominate those under them, but God has called elders to follow the example of His Son, and be servants.

Servanthood requires perseverance. Elders are shepherds who do not run away when the wolves attack, leaving the sheep defenseless. Elders have a personal love for the sheep, an investment of the heart. They keep their eyes on the final goal and serve without expecting applause.

### ...is full of the Holy Spirit

The qualifications for an elder are challenging, and in fact, daunting. Without the Holy Spirit on whom to depend an elder cannot succeed! It is only by being full of the Holy Spirit's power that anyone, including elders, can walk in victory and live the overcoming life. "So I say, live by the Spirit, and you will not gratify the desires of the sinful nature" (Galatians 5:16-18).

Without being baptized in the Holy Spirit, elders can find leading a local church to be a drudgery. Being baptized in the Holy Spirit is the

Lord's provision for releasing the power of the Spirit in each person's life. After the disciples' encounter with the Holy Spirit when Jesus breathed on them and told them to "receive the Holy Spirit," Jesus made it clear that their experience was still incomplete. In His final words to them before His ascension, He commanded them not to go out and preach immediately, but to go back to Jerusalem and wait there until they were baptized in the Holy Spirit and thus given the power they needed to be effective witnesses. "But you will receive power when the Holy Spirit comes on you..." (Acts 1:8).

So the disciples prayed and waited. During the festival of Pentecost, 120 of His disciples were gathered together in one place, and it happened! They were baptized in the Holy Spirit. Although they had received the life of the Holy Spirit only a few weeks before when Jesus breathed on them (John 20:22), this time they were baptized in the Holy Spirit. This baptism gave them the power they needed for ministry.[4]

When we try to lead in our own strength, we can easily fall flat on our faces, but being baptized in the Holy Spirit will empower us to do what we can't muster up on our own!

## ...knows he is called by God

Paul mentions that "to desire eldership is a good thing." It is a good work, not to be despised (1 Timothy 3:1). God sovereignly calls an elder into His service. If God calls, He equips an elder for the task because the Lord "...has saved us and called us to a holy life—not because of anything we have done but because of his own purpose and grace" (2 Timothy 1:9).

An elder knows that God has called him, not man. If he is appointed without God's affirmation in his spirit, he will not have the grace from God to face the hard times, and the good times will be meaningless to him. Paul was clear about his calling to spiritual leadership—he knew that God had called him (Galatians 1:1).

## ...is in love with Jesus

Remember what the Lord said to Peter? "...Do you truly love me?...take care of my sheep... (John 1:16-17). The foundation for shepherding is love—not love for the sheep, but love for the Lord Jesus. Jesus wanted Peter to focus on Him, not on the job description of shepherding the sheep. When elders major on loving Jesus, their job of shepherding the flock flows smoothly from that love.

Elders love Jesus and see others through the filter of His love. They know that Jesus loves them passionately and unconditionally and extend His lavish love to others. Elders, therefore, reflect a generosity of spirit, a love for mercy, and the ability to forgive.

People feel comfortable around godly elders because they are able to relate to people from all walks of life. One time, a young man with a head of teased high hair, dyed blue, came into a church service Ron was  leading. After the service, Ron talked to him at length showing genuine love and concern. Later, the young man told the friend who brought him how impressed he was that Ron, a church leader, treated him as a normal human being and looked beyond his rather unusual hair style to see the person inside.

## ...has endurance

An elder sees the big picture and does not give up easily when the going gets tough. "Therefore, since we are surrounded by such a great cloud of witnesses, let us throw off everything that hinders and the sin that so easily entangles, and let us run with perseverance the race marked out for us" (Hebrews 12:1-2).

The Christian life is to be run in such a way as to get the prize. "Do you not know that in a race all the runners run, but only one gets the prize? Run in such a way as to get the prize" (1 Corinthians 9:24). An elder stays in the race and does not get sidelined by problems life throws at him. One of the greatest acts of spiritual warfare is to not quit. Charles Spurgeon once said, "Through great perseverance, the snail finally reached the ark!"

## Conclusion

You might be thinking, "How can anybody meet all these criteria for eldership? It's impossible." You're right. They can't, but God can! Mature and wise elders know that they have no choice but to live out of a deep sense of God's grace, drawing on that grace daily. This is the key to meeting the qualifications for eldership and what gives an elder the motivation to help lead the church. Elders are qualified as elders because their character has been and is being molded and shaped by God's compassion and grace. They realize with humility that without the development of God's character in them, eldership and the qualifications for this leadership office are unattainable.

> And we pray this in order that you may live a life worthy of the Lord and may please him in every way: bearing fruit in every good work, growing in the knowledge of God, being strengthened with all power according to his glorious might so that you may have great endurance and patience... (Colossians 1:10-12).

## Questions to discuss

1. How did the New Testament church choose their elders?
2. Is it possible for an elder to meet all of the qualifications listed in 1 Timothy 3? Explain.
3. Which areas is the Lord calling you to focus on for growth?

---

[1] "Qualifications for Spiritual Leaders," from a sermon by Coy Wylie, pastor of Cornerstone Baptist Church in Amarillo, TX.

[2] For more on divorce read, "When Christians Remarry," in Steve Prokopchak's book, *Called Together,* (Camp Hill, PA: Horizon Books, 1999), pp.137-148.

[3] George Barna, editor, *Leaders on Leadership*, Gene Getz, "Becoming a Spiritually Mature Leader," (Ventura, California: Regal, 1997), p. 90.

[4] For more on being baptized in the Holy Spirit, see *Biblical Foundation Series, New Testament Baptisms* by Larry Kreider, (Ephrata, PA: House to House Publications, 2002), pp.25-43.

# The Responsibilities of Elders

**4**

Elders are called by God to provide three basic foundational responsibilities in the life of the church—protection, direction and correction. There are many different issues involved in these three basic responsibilities, but they are foundational for the health and well-being of the local church. Without them, the church will not reach its full potential.

In Acts 20:28-30, Paul notes some of the primary duties of elders. As overseers, they were to "keep watch" over themselves and the responsibilities of their work, making certain they were conforming to God's standards. They were also told to "feed the flock," so that the people in the congregation would be nurtured and guided in the right direction. They were told as well to protect the church from "savage wolves who will come in and not spare the flock." Let's take a closer look at these primary responsibilities.

## Three ministry responsibilities for elders
## 1. Give protection

In the New Testament, elders received the authority from the apostles to lead the local church, and then it was (and still is) their job to oversee and provide spiritual oversight for the flock. In Numbers 11, Moses was having trouble leading all the people, so God provided seventy elders to help him in leadership. "I will come down and speak with you there, and I will take of the Spirit that is on you and put the Spirit on them. They will help you carry the burden of the people so that you will not have to carry it alone" (Numbers 11:17). God took the Spirit that was on Moses and put it on the elders. In this way, Moses did not have to bear the burdens of leadership alone. The elders provided spiritual oversight for a smaller number of people.

Modern-day elders of the church have great concern for the spiritual well-being of the members. They work to bring out the best in the members under their care.

In the Old Testament, Jeremiah prophesied judgment on Judah's spiritual leaders who were selfish and did not care about the condition of the people. He said that they would be destroyed and that new leaders (shepherds) would come to tend the sheep (Jeremiah 23:4). Biblical elders understand that providing a safe place of spiritual oversight for the sheep will help the sheep to flourish.

It reminds us of the wild west in the United States. If, during a shoot-out, a sheriff told his deputy, "I've got you covered," the deputy knew he was protected. Elders keep God's people "safe" through prayer, sound doctrine and servant-leadership.

**Elders guard the church.** Part of the elders' work is to protect the church from false teachers. In Acts 20, Paul summons the elders of the church of Ephesus and gives them this warning. "Keep watch over yourselves and all the flock of which the Holy Spirit has made you overseers...savage wolves will come in among you and will not spare the flock. Even from your own number men will arise and distort the truth in order to draw away disciples after them. So be on your guard! Remember that for three years I never stopped warning each of you night and day with tears" (Acts 20:28-31).

In this charge to the church, Paul minces no words. Savage wolves will attack! There are those who are influenced by power and ambition who will distort God's Word and bring false teaching into the church. It is the elders' responsibility to guard and protect the sheep from wolves from the outside and false teaching on the inside.

*The Biblical Role of Elders for Today's Church*

It was seven years after Paul issued this warning to the Ephesian elders that false teachers did try to distort the true gospel. In 1 Timothy 1:3, Paul tells Timothy to confront these false teachers who compromised the truth. They were not to be allowed to continue their destructive teachings.

**Elders are responsible for the spiritual diet of the church.** Elders want to nurture the church with the Word of God so that people can grow and flourish. An unbalanced diet will make it hard for the believers to reach and maintain spiritual health. The elders see a need for teaching in a certain area and then ensure that the church receives that teaching. What spiritual vitamins are missing? Has the church had too much spiritual junk food?

Elders are aware of what is being taught outside of their circles. They are abreast of the trends in the body of Christ and they know what is best for their local church. They guard against excesses. They read books that reflect predominant teachings and sound biblical doctrine, so that they can better guide the flock. They spend quality time with the Father so that the input they give the flock is revelation from the throne room of God. Elders know how to "...correctly handle the word of truth" (2 Timothy 2:15).

**Elders lay their lives down for the sheep.** A shepherd will protect the sheep at all costs. He will put himself in harm's way to rescue a sheep from danger. In 1 Samuel 17:34-35, is found the story of David protecting his sheep. If a lion or a bear came and attempted to carry off a sheep, David would go after it, grab the sheep from the lion's mouth and slay the beast.

Elders don't run *from* problems, they run *to* problems in the church and help people in distress. The shepherds of the past always carried a horn of oil to doctor wounds of the sheep. Elders bring solutions to alarming situations and improve the quality of life for the people in their care. An elder's goal is to see the people of the church fulfill their destiny. In doing this, elders are extremely careful to point people to Jesus as the answer and not draw people to themselves.

**Elders are responsible to pray for the believers within their care.**
Perhaps the most important responsibility elders have is to pray for
those they give oversight to. Paul tells the church in Galatians 4:19 that
he prays as if he is "in the pains of childbirth until Christ is formed in
you." This diligent prayer includes both personal prayer "in the closet"
as well as the "prayer of agreement" with the other elders in the church.

Obviously, in large churches, the elders cannot pray daily for each
member. Wise elders will cover the key pastors and other church leaders in prayer daily, and then ask the pastors and other leaders to pray for
the leaders they oversee (cell leaders and other ministry leaders). The
cell leaders and other ministry leaders should be trained and encouraged to pray for every believer within their realm of oversight. This
way, everyone in the church is covered in prayer every day!

When Larry was serving as senior pastor of a cell-based church in
Pennsylvania, prayer was a key ingredient in seeing God's blessing released. Larry recalls, "One of the elders on the team sometimes drove,
late at night, to the homes of church members dealing with deep
struggles. He would park his car on the street outside their homes and
pray earnestly for spiritual breakthroughs.

"I am convinced that the prayers of this elder paved the way for
major spiritual breakthroughs in the lives of some of our church members. Many of God's people never even knew this elder was praying for
them."

**Elders teach the flock.** 1 Timothy 3:2 tells us, "Now the overseer
must be...able to teach..." We do not believe this means that an elder
must have the *gift* of teaching, although some elders do indeed have a
teaching gift according to 1 Timothy 5:17-18: "The elders who direct
the affairs of the church well...those whose work is preaching and teaching.*"

Rather we believe that "being able to teach" means an elder can
impart truth into another person. It means an elder knows what he believes and has an understanding of the scriptures so that he can teach
the truth from the Word to believers in the church. In this way, he guides

the church with pure doctrine and steers clear of heresy.

Paul's statements to both Titus and Timothy show the importance of an elder teaching the truth to keep pure doctrine in the church:

> He must hold firmly to the trustworthy message as it has been taught, so that he can encourage others by sound doctrine and refute those who oppose it (Titus 1:8-9).

> Preach the Word...correct, rebuke and encourage—with great patience and careful instruction (2 Timothy 4:2).

**Elders safeguard the church against false ministries.** Elders closely examine various ministries that could be influencing their flock, because Jesus said that a tree and its fruit always match.

> Watch out for false prophets. They come to you in sheep's clothing, but inwardly they are ferocious wolves. By their fruit you will recognize them. Do people pick grapes from thornbushes, or figs from thistles? Likewise every good tree bears good fruit, but a bad tree bears bad fruit (Matthew 7:15-17).

False teachers and their ministries outwardly appear righteous, but inwardly they are "ferocious wolves." Elders look at the fruit of a person's ministry and not just the external presentation. They are not enamored of the charisma with which a person speaks, but listen for sound doctrine and truth.

Elders are not carried about by every wind of doctrine (Ephesians 4:14). They do not accept human teachings and traditions when they contradict the Word of God.

Elders are able to think critically without being critical in their judgment of others. Thinking critically is not finding things you think are wrong and criticizing them. It is not poking holes in someone else's thinking.

Critical thinking happens when you take the time to pay attention to what is being said and done and think it through with care, trying to discover if there are assumptions being made that might not be true.

Elders listen and attempt to understand the words and actions of others, even though they may not agree.

## 2. Give direction

Elders are called to set the course for the church. They are responsible for the vision and direction of the church. As shepherds, they lead the sheep on the right paths toward rich pasture. Acts 20:28 exhorts elders to "...keep watch over yourselves and all the flock of which the Holy Spirit has made you overseers. Be shepherds of the church of God, which he bought with his own blood." *Giving direction* to the church by "keeping watch over the flock" involves a broad base of responsibility. It includes not only moving the church ahead with the vision God has given but also leading or ruling with God-given authority.

**Elders rule the church.** "Ruling the church" really means *to stand before, to preside, and to lead.* Elders develop a course in a particular direction and are responsible to the Lord for that course. They have this question at the forefront of their thinking, "Where is the Lord leading us as a church?"

There can be a danger in using the word *rule* when referring to the elders' responsibilities in the church. Although elders govern the local church, it is a spiritual role to be carried out with a heart of love and self-sacrifice as they lead by example as well as by legislation. Governing or ruling the local church is both a spiritual role and a management role.

Elders are shepherds and have God-given authority over the sheep in their care. They know the sheep who make up the flock and have a loving concern for them.

In the early church, Peter dealt with some elders who were "lording it over" those entrusted to them (1 Peter 5:3). He condemns their behavior. Being an elder is never about power but about servanthood and leading by example.

The following chart from Floyd McClung's book, *The Father Heart of God,* shows the difference between dominating leaders who try to lord it over God's people and those who rule as fathers in the Lord.

| Dominating Fathers | Fathers in the Lord |
|---|---|
| 1. Function as if they are the source of guidance for people's lives. | 1. Believe that God is the source of guidance and desire to help other Christians learn to hear His voice. |
| 2. Emphasize the rights of leaders. | 2. Emphasize the responsibilities of leaders. |
| 3. Set leaders apart and give them special privileges. | 3. Emphasize the body of Christ serving one another. |
| 4. Seek to control people's actions. | 4. Encourage people to be dependent on God. |
| 5. Emphasize the importance of the leaders ministering to others. | 5. Emphasize the importance of equipping the saints for the work of the ministry. |
| 6. Use rules and laws to control people and force them to conform to a mold. | 6. Provide an atmosphere of trust and grace to encourage growth.[1] |

Elders have chosen a life of service on behalf of others. They are servant leaders, not rulers or dictators. They are fathers in the Lord who understand that God leads His people by a theocracy rather than by a monarchy or a democratic rule. Let's look at the three types of rule to see the difference.

**Autocratic rule** is ruling with little or no regard for the input of others. It is a monarchy where one person "runs the show." A king rules a country. God runs the universe in an autocratic way because He is the King of the universe. It is only God who can dictate. No one, including elders, should have this kind of authoritarian power to wield authority. The desire for power should be a foreign concept to elders. Elders do not dictate; they direct.

**Democratic rule** is allowing the people to rule. In many parts of the world society is run by its citizens with voting power. Some churches use democratic voting to make decisions in the church. In this kind of rule, the people have the majority of the power, and final decisions are made by popular vote.

**Theocratic rule** is the third type of rule, which we believe is the biblical model. This is God ruling through His divinely appointed leaders. It is *God-rule* or *God-inspired rule*. Romans 8:14 states it this way, "...those who are led by the Spirit of God are the sons of God." How does God inspire an elder and his team to rule?

God inspires through His Spirit to the elder's spirit.

God inspires through the truth of His Word.

God inspires through the wise counsel of others.

Wise eldership teams will rule by listening to God through the voice of His Spirit, His Word and the godly counsel of others. Elders are answerable to their fellow believers and to God. They do not try to dictate what their congregation should do, but instead appeal to them to faithfully follow God's Word. The people in the congregation will then have a clear voice so there can be an atmosphere of "hearing together what the Lord is saying." Elders are humble servants who direct the church by genuinely manifesting the life of Christ to their congregations and to the world that is watching. In Chapter 7, we will go into more detail on this biblical model of God-inspired rule.

**Elders govern the church.** Elders are appointed by God and put in place to govern the church, which implies that they have authority as well as responsibility. Paul would not have warned the elders in 1 Peter 5:3 against "lording it over" others if they had no authority. Elders are humble servant leaders, but this does not imply that they are without authority in the church.

Hebrews 13:17 says, "Obey your leaders and submit to their authority. They keep watch over you as men who must give an account..." Paul writes to the Thessalonians: "...respect those who work hard among you, who are over you in the Lord and who admonish you" (1 Thessalonians 5:12). Elders are to be "shepherds of God's flock that is under your care..." (1 Peter 5:2). 1 Timothy 5:17 says that "elders who direct the affairs of the church well are worthy of double honor...." All these verses point to an elder's authority in the church.

Elders are God's stewards, overseers, and shepherds to lead the church. 1 Timothy 3:4-5 tells us that elders are to "direct the affairs of the church." This includes having the authority to handle the legal responsibilities of the church, or working with another in-house church team that is accountable to the eldership team in regard to legal matters. The eldership team needs always to make the final decision in these matters with a senior elder being the earthly final authority on the team.

**Elders make the final decision regarding the finances of the church.** The business affairs of the church are important because vision and finances go hand in hand. Usually where the finances go, the vision goes.

In Acts 11:27-30, Barnabas and Saul delivered a gift from the believers in Antioch for the church in Jerusalem. The gift was given to the elders, and the elders of the Jerusalem church were responsible to disperse this gift to those in need. (We will discuss finances and elders more thoroughly in Chapter 8.)

## 3. Give correction

Someone once said, "If you do not like problems, don't be an elder!" Every local church will have its problems that need to be addressed. In Acts 20:30, Paul issues the church a warning, "Even from your own number men will arise and distort the truth in order to draw away disciples after them." Sometimes people are led astray by ignoring the truth. Others may add to the truth or be divisive in the church. Still others may fall into and condone immoral life-styles. And still others may distort the truth. The end motivation of all these ploys is almost always to cast doubt on the present leadership and elevate their own authority over others to pull them away from that particular church.

Titus 2:15 encourages the church to "encourage and rebuke with all authority." Titus 3:10 says a divisive man should be "warned." Elders are the ones to bring correction when necessary.

When an elder brings correction, he responds as a father, not a grandfather. A grandfather who is not involved in the day-to-day responsibility for his grandson usually speaks in positive terms when he sees him. ("You can do it. I support you.") A father, on the other hand, who is directly responsible for his son, may become stern if necessary and say, "Son, we don't do that here." A father wants his son to learn and not make the same mistakes he made.

A father's goal is a loving investment in his son to see him become all he can be. He knows the benefit of discipline, but he must bring loving discipline that bears fruit. Not everyone will enjoy correction, nor is correction something that an elder is eager to administer. But elders are willing to take a risk by giving correction for the betterment of the individual and protection of the body. Of course, this must be loving correction and not humiliation. The final goal is to bring health and wholeness.

When Paul found out that the Corinthian church was tolerating open sin in their midst, he corrected them and instructed them to separate the offending party from the church (1 Corinthians 5). He chastised the Corinthian church leaders for their tolerance of this sin.

Paul encouraged Titus to warn divisive people that had an adverse effect on the church (Titus 3:10). Paul also instructed Timothy to correct those who were teaching false doctrines (1 Timothy 1:3). All of these are examples of correction, showing that elders are willing to reprove the church if necessary.

**The responsibility of the church is not to help people to have fun; it is to guide them toward holiness.** Jesus spoke these words about obedience at the end of His Great Commission. "And teaching them to obey everything I have commanded you. And surely I am with you always, to the very end of the age" (Matthew 28:20). Elders are leaders who give correction to the church and teach its members to obey God and live holy lives.

Holiness and obedience go hand-in-hand. Living a holy life is simply living as someone who belongs to God. It is living a life in obedience to His Word. Martin Luther wrote this rather straightforward message about obedience to God's Word: "You may as well quit reading and hearing the Word of God, and give in to the devil, if you do not desire to live according to it."

In his book *In Pursuit of Obedience,* Steve Prokopchak describes the connection between obedience and holiness this way, "Obedience is holiness and holiness is choosing obedience. Holiness is choosing to be separate from the world and its sin. Holiness is an attitude of the heart. Pursuing holiness is obeying God."[2]

One of the ways to discern if an elder is doing a proper job of eldering is to ask this question: "Is he teaching the people to obey all things commanded by the Lord?" Sometimes "teaching people to obey the Lord" involves loving confrontation. Avoiding problems in the church by looking the other way rather than facing them with honest and loving confrontation will ultimately hurt people in the church. Elijah admonished the people with the question, "How long will you waver between two opinions?" (1 Kings 18:21). For the church to be healthy, elders cannot put off dealing with problems in the church or be afraid to speak the truth in love.

## Questions for discussion

1. Name the three primary responsibilities of elders in the church.
2. Give an example of elders "ruling" in the local church.
3. How do elders bring correction to the church?
4. How do elders protect the church?
5. Should elders make the final major financial decisions in the church and why?

[1] Floyd McClung, *The Father Heart of God,* (Eugene, Oregon: Harvest House Publishers, 1985), pp.129-131.
[2] Steve Prokopchak, *In Pursuit of Obedience,* (Ephrata, PA: House to House Publications, 2002), p. 17.

# Choosing Elders

5

It is the Holy Spirit who ultimately calls elders in the local church. According to Acts 20:28, "...the Holy Spirit has made you overseers." The first step in becoming an elder is to know that the Holy Spirit has called you. If the Holy Spirit calls, you will be equipped for the task as you maintain a teachable spirit for further equipping. An elder is gifted with the ability to lead the church.

Notice God's charge of leadership to Joshua. This mandate could belong to every elder. "Have I not commanded you? Be strong and courageous. Do not be terrified; do not be discouraged, for the Lord your God will be with you wherever you go" (Joshua 1:9). God's call is clear, awe-inspiring and comforting—all at the same time!

Elders do not appear out of thin air. They are appointed to serve in their local church where they have already proven themselves and exhibited the qualifications of elders in their own lives. The leadership and congregation in the local church see that they are willing to fulfill the eldership responsibility because they recognize that the individual is already doing the work required.

Let us emphasize again that the individual should have a genuine desire to become an elder. He must know he is called by God to lead. Dick Iverson aptly expresses this truth when he says,

If a man is divinely called, he will also be divinely equipped.

It takes supernatural enablement to be a New Testament minister. Without this God-given equipment, no amount of preparation or schooling will do any good toward making men ministers.[1]

An elder must be called by God. He must be willing to serve, and desirous of using his gifts and talents for the local church. His motive is not for power or recognition; in fact, he realizes that "to win the approval of men" (Galatians 1:10) is a trait that is contrary to the character of a servant of Christ. He serves from the heart and does not care if he is noticed by men. An elder knows that to become great, he must become a servant of all (Mark 10:44). He cares for the people out of love for Christ and has a genuine desire to see the needs of the flock met.

## Authority to appoint elders comes from apostles

The initial appointment of elders in the New Testament churches was initiated by the apostles. Apostolic leaders, Paul and Barnabas, appointed elders in every church they established on their first missionary journey. According to Acts 14:23 "...Paul and Barnabas appointed elders for them in each church and, with prayer and fasting, committed them to the Lord, in whom they had put their trust." We also see that Titus is left in Crete to appoint elders in every church. "The reason I left you in Crete was that you might straighten out what was left unfinished and appoint elders in every town, as I directed you" (Titus 1:5).

In most cases the apostles did not settle down and assume responsibility for the local church, but yielded the responsibility for the local church to the appointed elders. These faithful and spiritually qualified elders had authority from the apostles to lead the church.

But how did the church appoint elders once the apostles had moved on? The New Testament does not give examples of elders appointing elders to perpetuate leadership, but it is implied that they are a vital part of the process. Raising up leadership in the local church is the elders' responsibility, along with the input and affirmation of the congregation. Tri-Lakes Community Church in Indiana explains how a pattern of selecting leaders in the New Testament church emerges:

> The selection of personnel to serve and represent the entire
> church involves the entire church in the decision-making pro-
> cess (Acts 6:1-7; 15:22; 2 Corinthians 8:18-19; Acts 14:23)...It
> seems that Paul and Barnabas gave direction to the process, but
> that the church was involved in the decision.[2]

We agree with this assessment. The selection of each elder should
be discerned through fasting and prayer. Wise elders listen to what God
is saying through their team of elders and through the congregation.
The appointment of elders is not a personal preference but a recognition of those the Lord has already chosen. For this reason, Paul said to
the elders in Ephesus, "...the Holy Spirit has made you overseers..."
(Acts 20:28). The Holy Spirit is the one who gives the desire in an elder
to shepherd the church. The church leadership and the congregation
recognizes this Spirit-given desire in the potential elder and recognizes
that the potential elder is morally and scripturally qualified.

After the leadership and congregation of the local church recognizes a new local elder, their recommendations should be taken to those
who give them oversight. For some churches this is an apostolic oversight team or denominational leadership. Other churches utilize a
presbytery of church leaders from outside the local church. These overseers are often involved in the actual commissioning and appointment
of the new elder.

## What about women in eldership?

In the body of Christ today, there are many interpretations regarding gender and leadership of the church. Some believe that the scriptures teach that both men and women can be called by the Lord to serve
in areas of church government, and others believe that the scriptures
teach that only men can be called by the Lord to serve in areas of church
government. Volumes of books and articles have been written on the
subject by theologians "proving" from scripture that both positions are
correct.

We personally believe that we are called by the Lord to focus on the Great Commission. Gender issues should not be allowed to divide us because the Great Commission is a major task and requires our full attention. We are of the conviction that we dare not become sidetracked by differing understandings on a woman's role in church government that would divide us and cause us to lose the focus the Lord has given to us. We need to honor one another, even though we may not have the same understanding from scripture regarding a woman's role in church government.

We believe there is no biblical or historical evidence that women cannot or should not be involved in ministering to the body of Christ. We affirm the need for the perspective and input of women in ministry and church life. We have licensed and ordained both men and women in leadership.

While the vast majority of governmental positions in the Bible were clearly held by men, there are instances of women in governmental leadership positions.[3] This biblical pattern is mirrored throughout church history. Because of this, we believe women can serve as elders in the local church.

It is important for each eldership team to discern the Lord's will on this matter for their own congregation. We generally allow the local church to decide if women should serve as elders based on their understanding of the scriptures.

In regard to this, there are two specific concerns to guard against. First of all, there has been a devaluing and demeaning of women throughout history. But God has never devalued women.

Genesis 1:27 says that God created "male and female." Both are needed and valuable to the Lord and to His people. Male governmental leaders need the female side of the Lord's wisdom that often comes through wives and other godly women in the church. The uniqueness in the way each is made complements each other. An elder team that is all male often needs female input in order to gain the full counsel of God. The influence and input of women is very important! Men in leadership should seek out the counsel and discernment of godly women in the church.

Second, if the senior elder and the eldership team of a local church believe a woman is called by the Lord to serve in an eldership position, and they can affirm her with faith and a clear conscience according to their understanding of the scriptures, then we believe she should be appointed. However, it should also be remembered that the scriptures teach us that whatever is not from faith is sin (Romans 14:23). So then, if a senior elder and his team do not have faith for a woman to serve on the elder team due to their personal conviction and interpretation of the scriptures, then she should not serve on the team.

We believe that the issue of women in leadership should not divide the church at large. Differences in churches should not prevent us from remaining in fellowship with those who take a different view.

## Elders in the local church should be sons

Elders should always be looking to build leadership with individuals that "act in the same spirit and follow the same course," as Paul described his relationship with Titus, the spiritual son he had trained.[4] If it is possible, an elder should be chosen from among the "spiritual sons" that have been trained and nurtured within the local fellowship. They should be those individuals whose hearts are joined to the vision and leadership that already exists in the local church. Wise leadership in the church will continually pray for spiritual sons and daughters to be added—people who are loyal, committed and have the same heart as the existing leadership.

The Lord will take those who are loyal and committed and anoint them, but He will not always take those who are anointed and make them loyal and committed. Spiritual sons are usually willing to do anything because they want to build the house—the local church. They are servant-leaders. They are vision-driven, not self-driven. They will use family language such as "we, us, our." A son will say, "We are not going to do that, because Dad wouldn't like it." A son has the father's

*The Biblical Role of Elders for Today's Church*

heart in mind. A son will always serve to build the house, not just serve in the house.

When the patriarch of a Jewish family dies, that family would never look to hire a father from across town to replace him. They would always look within the family to the next qualified candidate in the absence of the father. Churches today frequently look outside themselves for leaders and end up with hirelings who come to fulfill a job description yet do not have the same values as the rest of the family. A hireling may not truly care about the sheep, and will leave for greener pastures when things become difficult, (after he picks up his last paycheck of course) but a son has a stake in the family and will not quickly abandon the ministry.

A great example is David who risked his life when a lion and a bear came to attack the sheep. Those were his father's sheep. He was a son. He had a stake in the assets of his father. It was his family. He responded as if they were his very own, saying, "No bear is going to take my father's sheep!" He was a son who had ownership of the flock. He might get bitten or bloodied fighting the lion, but he was going to protect the sheep.

It was a natural progression then, for David to fight for the sheep of Israel when he faced Goliath. This was his family, and Goliath (a type representing the devil) could no longer be allowed to taunt the people of God. This is a key characteristic to look for in building a team of elders.

If there is a "son" in the local church family who is called to serve in leadership, it is not wise to look elsewhere. We should do everything we can to appoint a qualified elder from within the local church family.

Certainly, there are exceptions to this rule. A "next best" scenario was experienced when one of DCFI's Pennsylvania churches experienced the "stepping down" of their senior elder. While there definitely were qualified persons on the eldership team, no one felt a clear call from God to become the senior elder. Likewise, no one was identified to fill the vacancy from among the small group leaders or the congregation.

An apostolic leader from the greater church family stepped in temporarily to help with oversight, decision-making, and Sunday morning sermons. The local church team of elders along with the network of DCFI churches and the "apostolic council team" prayed for God's replacement.

It was clearly discerned that the Lord had someone from within the family who could step into this position. After months of asking God, a "son" came forward. Although not from the local church needing the senior elder, he was a recognized fivefold minister in DCFI's network of churches. So, in essence, he was considered "family." As he and his family prayed about the request from the apostolic overseer, the elder team, and the Lord, his answer was a Holy Spirit-inspired "yes."

Receiving a senior elder from the extended church family was the next best choice. Not just any leader would do; a son with like values, beliefs, and methods would best serve this congregation. We are grateful to God to be able to report that the transition has been a success since everyone involved was hearing from and obeying their heavenly Father. This local church has been blessed and is growing.

## Take time to build elders

We must recognize that in some cases, especially in new churches, it takes time to build leadership—often years. If it is premature for elders to be recognized and appointed in the local church, then we would suggest first drawing together *potential* leaders from among the body. These potential leaders can begin serving on a "leadership team" or an "advisory team" to the senior elder. From this team, elders can be identified and developed. The eventual selection of any of these leaders for eldership must be made only after prayerful consideration.

In developing elders this way, a word of caution is in order. Care should be taken to not defraud individuals by calling them "elders in training" or in any way indicating that they will definitely be future elders by serving on the team. On more than one occasion, we have observed a senior leader promising a position prematurely only to find that the "potential elder" was not ready. Tremendous hurt and rejection can occur if a senior elder makes this mistake.

In his book *Biblical Eldership,* Alexander Strauch gives this advice concerning the important process of developing and choosing elders:

> The church and its leaders must pray for spiritual insight, guidance, and unbiased judgment. They must desire God's will and God's choice, not their own. God said, of Israel, "They set up kings without my consent; they choose princes without my approval" (Hosea 8:4)...Sadly, too many churches expend the least amount of time and effort possible when selecting and examining prospective elders...Evaluating an elder's fitness for office should be done thoughtfully, patiently, and biblically. The scripture clearly states that no one is to be appointed to office in a hurried, thoughtless manner: "Do not be hasty in the laying on of hands..." (1 Timothy 5:22).[3]

## Elders need to be trained at entry level ministry

Elders start ministry at the entry level. Someone who wants to work as a stone mason, putting foundations in place for buildings, must first learn to mix mortar and supply the experienced masons. This seems like menial work that has nothing to do with laying blocks. But, the truth is that mixing the mortar teaches the aspiring mason about the proper consistency and properties of mortar, which will eventually help him to build strong and straight foundation walls for buildings.

We always recommend that anyone who desires to serve as an elder should first serve as a small group leader. This gives them an opportunity to learn how to lead in a smaller setting. It is best if they have been able to successfully train assistant leaders and have helped the group multiply into two or more groups.

## Affirmation and installment of elders

Over time trust and unity is built on an elder team—from enjoying good times together in seasons of blessing to persevering together during times of crisis and demonic attack—they overcome, experiencing victory and camaraderie. Adding a new elder to the team must be accomplished without violating this trust and unity. All of the existing elders, in particular the senior elder, should be in favor of adding the new person. If all are not in favor of adding the new elder, it is worth waiting so that relationships of trust and mutual respect are not violated.

A family that is considering adopting a child to add to their existing family will desire the approval of their other children before they move ahead with the adoption procedures. If the children were not included in this decision, imagine how they would feel!

Once a potential elder is recognized as called, qualified, willing and faithful in ministry, and affirmed by the existing elders, his name should be advanced to the small group leaders of the congregation for prayerful consideration. The small group leaders represent the next level of leadership. They should be in general agreement about the appointment of the individual. The congregation should also have the opportunity to give their input about the appointment by having the information in advance and being encouraged to contact the senior elder or one of the elders of the congregation with any possible concerns and godly advice.

Additionally, the senior elder should receive input from his apostolic overseer concerning adding a new elder. If the apostolic leader, senior elder and the elders team recommend the individual and there is general affirmation by cell leaders and the congregation, then the new elder is ready to be appointed to the office.

## The term of office for an elder

Exact procedures for appointing elders and their term of office are not mentioned in the New Testament. Every local church must use their

*The Biblical Role of Elders for Today's Church*

own discretion within the guidelines of scripture. It is probably safe to assume that most churches are looking for long-term commitment from elders. However, individuals must always be given the opportunity to come and go. If a church has Holy Spirit-inspired leaders with vision and dreams, there is bound to be flux. Any enterprise, be it business or government, will have transitions in its staff if it has talented and initiative-taking individuals.

Since elders are visionary leaders, their personal visions may extend and expand to other parts of the kingdom of God. Perhaps church planting or mission work is part of their vision for future ministry. To release an elder to accomplish the vision God has given him is a privilege to be encouraged. While the present elders team will surely suffer loss, the expansion of the kingdom of God is of higher priority. We need to hold our sons and daughters with an open hand.

Brian experienced firsthand the process of being released from an eldership team after serving as an elder for several years as part of his local church. He felt God was calling him to be on the local public school board, and this would involve a sizable amount of his time. The team graciously released him to serve the community this way. This also fit the church's vision for community transformation as a cell-based church reaching their community.

In a very practical sense, in order for an elder's term of office to be fruitful, regular evaluations of the senior elder and the team of elders should be performed. Elders should have evaluations by those giving apostolic oversight as needed (it is recommended that some type of evaluation be performed every year). This will help ensure that the team is united and functioning properly. The senior elder is responsible to conduct this evaluation in combination with the apostolic leadership, an evaluation team, or any combination. (See Appendix, pages 216-218, for a variety of useful evaluation forms which a senior elder and a team of elders can use for this purpose.)

## Handling transition in leadership

Steve recently encountered a church that was learning to cope with the transition of one of the key members of the team of elders. One of the DCFI churches that he oversees in the New England states had a very close team. One of the elders felt called to another state to work with a non cell-based church, not connected to the DCFI network of cell-based churches, to help them bring the cell structure to their fellowship. Initially he met with some resistance from the elders team because they had experienced such a strong, loving connection with one another. But after much prayer, the team realized that while this elder and the gifts that he brought to the team would be sorely missed, it was necessary that they release him to fulfill the call of God on his life. Often when we experience transition, we experience loss.

This does not make transition bad—we just have to be ready for it. Part of the purpose of conducting regular evaluations of senior elders and the team of elders is to anticipate transition in leadership and ensure that it is handled peacefully and properly—that is, without causing undue disruption to the flock. Transition should be handled in such a way as to not cause the sheep to scatter.

If godly, visionary leaders exist in our churches, it will not be uncommon that some of them will want to move around and start new churches or develop new visions that the Lord is initiating. This should be expected and anticipated by the senior elder, the elders and apostolic leadership. It is the responsibility of the senior elder and the apostolic leaders to precede transitional times such as these with leadership training and development. If new leaders are ready to take up the mantle of leadership, it will help the church remain stable during times of transition.

If the senior elder desires to transition, it is essential that the apostolic leaders have this information in advance. It is always advantageous for the new senior elder to be selected and trained from within the already existing team of elders. However, sometimes it might be necessary to appoint an interim senior leader, or perhaps the apostolic leader can step in for a period of time to allow for the elder on the team, who will become the new senior elder, to mature.

## Governmental elders vs. general elders

Every church in the body of Christ today has leaders—both those who are in church governmental positions and those who are not in positions of church government; nevertheless, they are leaders and influencers in the body of Christ.

Those individuals who give oversight to a local church are served well with a natural sense of leadership and government. Romans 12 mentions the motivational gift of leadership: "If it is leadership, let him govern diligently." A governmental elder has this gift of leadership and is appointed to the position as a local church elder. But a governmental elder is not the only kind of elder influencing churches today.

Not all mature Christians in the local church have a call or a gift to be involved in governmental oversight within the local church. These leaders in non-governmental roles may be given various titles to identify their function(s) within the local church. We have chosen to call these leaders "general elders in the faith." In his book, *His Rule in His Church,* Carlton Kenney describes such general elders who have a function of eldership but are not appointed to a position of eldership:

> ...[General elders] have "earned" [this function] with the people...by the very nature of gaining such credibility, the emphasis is upon age; it takes time to establish a testimony! Basically, they are like pillars in the church. Just their presence gives a sense of security and stability. It is natural that younger believers will gravitate to them and want to open their hearts for instruction.[5]

These functioning "general elders" are wonderful men and women of God who often function best, and are a great blessing to the body, as small group leaders, deacons or other ministry leaders.

Additionally, there are some general elders in the church who may have a gift of leadership but are not currently appointed to a position of eldership. This kind of general elder is not serving in the capacity of a governing elder of the local church for any number of good reasons. In some cases, he may be involved in a traveling ministry or may have previously served as an elder in the church. Larry is such an individual. He served as a local church senior elder for fifteen years but now has an extensive international traveling ministry which prohibits him from giving oversight to a local church.

General elders can offer spiritual insight, when consulted, that would help the existing, governing elders in decision-making. The governing elders need to be aware of this resource in their midst and be ready to consult them and draw from their wisdom as needed.

Churches of all sizes (especially larger churches) should find ways to utilize both governing elders and general elders. Some mega-churches, like New Life Church in Colorado, call their governmental elders "pastors" while calling their non-governmental elders simply "elders." The pastors or pastoral team has the governmental role and manages the day-to-day operation of the church. Although they function as biblical, governing elders, New Life chooses to call them "pastors." The leaders they specifically call "elders" are those in ministering or non-governmental roles:

> Our elders are ministering elders, not ruling elders. They do not have any corporate power. Their role is to help the senior pastor and his staff keep the church spiritually healthy.[6]

The terms may be different, but the result is the same. Whatever you call them, churches today need both biblical governing and non-governing leaders to help equip God's people so each one can find his or her place of ministry.

# Questions for discussion

1. How are church elders chosen in your church? Compare it with the examples we find in the New Testament.
2. What is your church's conviction regarding women in eldership?
3. What is the importance of building the church family with spiritual sons and daughters?
4. In your own words, explain the difference between governmental elders and general elders.

1   Dick Iverson, *Present Day Truths,* (Portland, Oregon: Bible Temple Publishing, 1975), p. 138.
2   Bylaws, "Article IV. Leadership and Decision Making," (Tri Lakes Community Church, Bristol, IN), p. 26.
3   Notes about women in church leadership: Priscilla, along with her husband Aquila, taught Christian doctrine to the learned Apollos (Acts 18:18-28). Women prophesied in the Corinthian church (1 Corinthians 11:5). Philip's four daughters also prophesied (Acts 21:9). God said He would pour out His Spirit so that both sons and daughters would prophesy (Acts 2:17). There was a woman apostle, Junia, whom Paul calls "noteworthy among the apostles" (Romans 16:7). In the Old Testament, the prophetess Deborah judged Israel for the Lord, and brought God's word to His people (Judges 4). These are some of the women who had leadership roles. They actively used the gifts God had given them— gifts of apostleship, prophecy, and teaching to spread the gospel of Christ and to build up the church.
3   Alexander Strauch, *Biblical Eldership,* (Littleton, Colorado, Lewis and Roth Publishers, 1995) pp. 288-289.
4   2 Corinthians 12:18
5   Carlton Kenney, *His Rule in His Church,* (Pineville, NC: MorningStar Publications, 1991), p.16.
6   Ted Haggard, *The Life Giving Church,* (Ventura, CA: Regal Books, 2001), p.204.

# Understanding An Elder's Field of Ministry

We live within the fertile agricultural area of Lancaster County, Pennsylvania with its lush green and golden fields of corn, alfalfa, barley and wheat covering the landscape. Whenever we fly over the area, we are amazed at the patterns that the fields of all shapes and sizes display with their unique colors and boundaries. Each of these fields represent a particular crop waiting to be harvested. This diversity of crops in carefully cultivated fields gives Lancaster County the distinction of producing more agricultural products and yielding more food than any other non-irrigated county in our nation.

In the same way, Christian believers have specific fields of ministry, unique to them, that have been assigned by the Lord. These fields, dotting the landscape of their lives, are their spheres of influence, responsibility and anointing.

Paul, the apostle, understood his sphere of influence and reminded the Corinthians that he was only to operate in the sphere God had appointed to him. He did not go around troubling churches founded by others. He only boasted of the Corinthian church because he was responsible before the Lord for them.

> We, however, will not boast beyond measure, but within the limits of the sphere which God appointed us—a sphere which especially includes you. For we are not extending ourselves beyond our sphere (thus not reaching you), for it was to you

that we came with the gospel of Christ; not boasting of things beyond measure, that is, in other men's labors, but having hope, that as your faith is increased, we shall be greatly enlarged by you in our sphere (II Corinthians 10:13-15).

Paul was careful not to take the credit or responsibility for another person's field of ministry. He knew his own sphere's "shape and color" and operated within God's authority and anointing for its oversight.

The Greek word translated *field (sphere)* is "metron" which is *a measure of activity that defines the limits of one's power and influence.* All believers have various spiritual fields that give them great opportunity to experience God's blessing and empowerment.

A married person has a field of ministry with his spouse. A parent's field of ministry extends to the family. A small group leader has another sphere of influence that includes the spiritual responsibilities he has for the small group members. Involvement in a local church gives one a sphere in which to experience God's blessing. One's community and workplace are yet another sphere. Everyone has several different areas in which they have the influence and power to decide what goes on within that field. A senior elder and a team of elders must recognize that the church they oversee is one of these fields of ministry for which the Lord has given them responsibility.

The authors of this book preach at different churches in different parts of the world nearly every week. We always attempt to remind ourselves that we are serving in someone else's field. We are helping a senior elder and a church leadership team build in their particular field. It is out of place for us to think that it is all about building our ministry. It has everything to do with helping them build what the Holy Spirit is already building in their field.

Sadly, over the years, many who claimed to be anointed and spiritual did not properly understand the limitations of serving within the field of another. Sometimes local church leaders have had to take months to "clean up" from various things that were said or "prophesied" by a visiting speaker that were not edifying to the church. This will not happen if we walk within our own fields of ministry and honor the fields of others.

## A ministry field has boundaries

Like the farm fields, clearly distinguishable by color, size and boundaries, ministry fields have certain boundaries and sizes. Elders must have a clear understanding of the boundaries of their fields. They should never presume to speak for another church across town. Their boundaries fall within their own local church.

An elder who wants to have prosperous fields of ministry understands that his field (his local church) has certain limitations and boundaries. These boundaries give protection to the field and must be carefully and prayerfully respected. When Larry was a farmer, he did not have the option of taking his tractor over to plow in his neighbor's field and then deciding which crops he would plant. That was not up to him. It was not his field! Larry also never contemplated going into his neighbor's field and planting seed. This would be counterproductive because Larry did not own that field and could never claim the harvest from it. Larry planted, cultivated and harvested crops that fell within his own property lines.

A police officer works within the boundaries of his jurisdiction. He can arrest only those criminals within the area of his legal authority. A parent has authority and responsibility for his own family's field. He cannot tell his neighbors how to raise their children because he does not have authority in their home.

In our locality, farmers often post "No Trespassing" signs at the edges of their property, meant to deter hunters from tramping across their fields during hunting season. In life, there are often disastrous results when someone trespasses on another's field. We have only to look at the divorce statistics in today's world to see the trail of devastation left when a married person steps across his or her marriage boundaries into someone else's marriage.

In Genesis 1:26, God gave Adam and Eve authority over the whole world, but they had to prove their stewardship in the Garden of Eden first. We know what happened when Satan came into Adam and Eve's field and they listened to his lies: they surrendered their authority to Satan. Pain and death fell on them and on the beautiful world God had made.

An eldership team cannot surrender their field to another. If a leader of another church feels he has a "word from God" for you, remember, it must be tested (I Thessalonians 5:20-21). Test it with the Word of God, with the godly advice of spiritual fathers the Lord has placed in your midst, and with the peace of Christ that rules in your heart (Colossians 3:15).

Several years ago when Larry was serving as the senior elder of one of DCFI's churches in Pennsylvania, a visiting Christian speaker gave a specific "prophetic" word to him and to the leadership team. In it, he described something he was convinced the Lord was leading our church to do. Part of the word involved meeting on a particular evening of the week at one of our church buildings. He was adamant that the meeting had to take place at that specific building on that particular evening. However, the building in question was already promised to another local Christian group in the area.

The leadership team prayed and considered his "word," and realized that in order to fulfill it, they could not keep their commitment to the other group, and it would be an issue of integrity not to keep their word. The leadership team thanked the speaker for sharing what he believed the Lord was saying and suggested to him that it could be a timing issue, and perhaps they could still do what he suggested at another time.

The next day, he called and gave Larry another "prophetic" word (which was actually a curse) for the church. He even used scripture to pronounce this curse. That evening Larry and his team called all of the local elders and ministry leaders together and united in prayer. Since this man was simply ministering in their area and did not have authority in their field, they knew he was not responsible for their field. It was a field that the Lord had given to them. They took authority over this curse and received the Lord's protection.

They avoided a potentially devastating "prophetic word" for the church by understanding their own particular field and its boundaries. A few days later, Larry spoke with a missionary friend who was serving in the home nation of this "prophet." We learned that this man had brought division in many churches in his homeland through "prophecies" that overstepped the boundaries of his authority. This was affirmation to Larry and the elder team that they had acted appropriately. What this man did was nothing more than spiritual manipulation. Thank God for a group of elders who were willing to unite in prayer and discover the truth. This type of commitment brings security to the local church body.

## Praying within a spiritual field

Another type of unhealthy control can even occur in prayer. For example, if an intercessor in a church begins to pray for his elders to "understand [a certain truth] like I understand it," he is attempting to change the elders rather than allowing God Himself to impress a particular truth on the elders' hearts.

Praying for things to go the way we think they should go rather than the way the Spirit leads the responsible person can be dangerous. If intercessors are not taught about fields of ministry, this kind of control becomes a type of "spiritual witchcraft." The scriptures teach that "...rebellion is as the sin of witchcraft (1 Samuel 15:23 KJV). We have ministered to many church leaders who were under tremendous spiritual oppression, because people in the church were praying according to their own agendas rather than praying for God's agenda. True elders, with maturity and experience, need to help leaders and other believers discern the source of this oppression.

## Authority in a field

One of the spiritual fathers the Lord has placed in our lives is Keith Yoder. In his book, *Healthy Leaders*, he gives clarity to a church leader's authority when he uses a triangle to illustrate three things that give a leader authority in his field or metron:

> One of the things that gives us authority and releases anointing in our metron is simply the *position* we have—our appointed role as elder, director, overseer, leader, etc. This is one side of the triangle. The position itself carries an anointing to fulfill the responsibility. A second side of the triangle is the aspect of our anointing that comes from the *gift* we have, whether it be the gift of mercy, the anointing of a pastor or the gift of prophecy. So the *position* we have gives us authority, and the anointing of our *gift* makes a place for us. The third dimension that is most crucial and is the foundation of this triangle is *fellowship* with God. Intimacy, prayer and communion with God releases the anointing within us that brings stability and support to the fact that we are in the leadership position.[1]

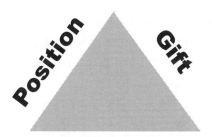

An elder can lead only those within his sphere of influence—those to whom the Lord has called him. If he stays within his field of ministry, he will have great authority and confidence. The fields are not for the purpose of limitation, but great grace is provided when we walk within the parameters God has given.

An elder will recognize the importance of defining his own territory. By this he can avoid infringing on the spiritual territory of another. Elders will work cooperatively and respectfully with existing efforts within their geographical region.

Evil powers take advantage when confusion exists and intruders are present in the field of another. When Satan deceived Adam and Eve in the Garden of Eden, he was trespassing in God's field. This is a demonstration of the fact that not everyone who enters our field is sent by the Lord.

If an elder leaves his field and steps into someone else's field, thinking he has authority there, he has stepped outside his proper authority. An elder cannot presume that the anointing and authority given him in one place is a general anointing to be used anywhere, any time. This is dangerous thinking, even when done in ignorance. When an elder moves out of his field of calling and anointing, it can open him to spiritual deception.

Elders will help their flock stay in their fields. This is one of the ways they can protect them. Paul thoroughly understood fields of ministry. He often appealed to those in authority when he was in their field. In Acts 22:25, he appealed to the Roman guards, stating that in their field he should not be beaten because he was a Roman citizen. So, when an elder understands his field and respects others' fields, he may be kept from getting beaten up by the enemy!

Natural fathers know their field of ministry involves helping their children stay in their fields because it is a way they can protect them. Steve recalls when his fourteen year old son said that he could not wait to leave home. Apparently he felt this way because within his father's field, there was disagreement concerning appropriate television programming. However, it was not time for Steve's son to leave the protection of his home. In fact, Steve's son is now 24 years old, and Steve has yet to see his departure!

## Grace for a field

Along with the authority an elder has within the boundaries of his field, a portion of grace is also given to do the job. *Grace* is often described as *the free unmerited favor of God on the undeserving and ill-deserving*, but it also can be defined as *the desire and the power to do God's will.* It is like a divine energy that the Holy Spirit releases in our lives. It helps us to victoriously accomplish a task within our field of ministry.

How do we know that God gives a person grace to operate within his field of ministry? Ephesians 4:7 also uses the word *metron.* "But to each one of us grace has been given as Christ apportioned it." Here the word *apportioned* is a translation of the same word *metron* found in II Corinthians 10:13. So, it would follow that for each metron or field of ministry, a special grace is given.

Since we all have different-size fields, God apportions grace in varying amounts according to what we need. If elders get out of the specific field of ministry to which they are assigned, they get out of God's grace, and that is not a good place to be!

Elders will caution their flock to remain in their specific fields of ministry and thus remain in the grace of God. Did you ever wonder why some elders have large churches and others have smaller ones? Simply stated, God gives some senior elders grace for larger churches, and others grace for smaller ones. The size of a church is not the issue; the issue is obedience and training and releasing those within our care.

Larry attended a leadership conference of about 500 Christian leaders several years ago, where at the evening service, the moderator asked a church leader to stand up for recognition. This man was at the time leading a church of 50 people in Dallas, Texas, but he had served as a leader in various churches in several states over the years.

The moderator then asked every man in the auditorium to stand who had been influenced by this pastor. Men stood up all over the auditorium! Larry was deeply moved and sensed the Lord's still small voice say, "That's success."

Success does not necessarily have anything to do with the size of a church or ministry. Success is loving God enough to obey Him as a humble leader and servant, raising up spiritual sons and daughters (John 14:15).

## A field yields fruit

When an elder is cultivating his field, it will yield fruit: "Lord, you have assigned me my portion and my cup; you have made my lot secure. The boundary lines have fallen for me in pleasant places; surely I have a delightful inheritance" (Psalm 16:5-6 NIV).

A word of caution is that just because an elder has been effective in one part of the world, he should not automatically presume he will get similar results in another part of the world. Elders must continually seek the Lord for His direction and be sure they are in God's field during each season of their lives.

Rather than limit us, boundary lines allow elders to be fruitful in their spheres of influence. The fields to which God assigns them are protected, secure places of learning. Within the boundaries of our fields, we will receive rich blessings because we are where the Lord wants us to be.

This does not imply that we will not face hardship and trials as we obey God in our fields. Sometimes, even if we are in the right place, we will experience times of unfruitfulness. But if the condition persists, we must examine ourselves and our field(s). Our fields should yield fruit.

## God determines and expands an elder's fields

Fields of ministry are areas in which God gives church elders stewardship. It is only the Lord who can determine and expand these fields. Only He can open up the doors and develop the right fields for each elder (Psalm 75:6-7).

God gave the apostles Paul and Peter different fields (see Acts, chapters 17-21). Paul's call and anointing was to reach the Gentiles, and Peter's call and anointing was to reach the Jews.

These lines were so clearly drawn that Paul confronted Peter when Peter crossed over into his field (Galatians 2:11-13). In Antioch, Peter was temporarily helping Paul, but since Peter still carried with him the old notion that Gentiles could not be accepted without circumcision, he allowed his human prejudice toward the uncircumcised Gentiles to undermine what God was doing at Antioch. Paul rebuked Peter for this because he knew God had given him the authority to reach the Gentiles. Peter was interfering in his field.

Later in the scriptures, we see that Peter readjusts his thinking on the Gentile matter. God had to expand Peter's thinking because his field of ministry was so closely focused on the Jews. Peter speaks favorably of Paul's work in Acts 15:7-11. Peter learned not to infringe on the ministry fields of others, but to submit when he was in their fields.

We see many examples throughout the New Testament of this kind of submission. Although Paul gave clear oversight to those in his field, when he came to Jerusalem, he submitted to James, the lead apostle in the city. Paul knew he was in James' field (Acts 15). He clearly understood the need to come under authority himself. His field of ministry existed within another field. When fields of ministry coexist in this way, there is unity and respect for each other.

An eldership team must be responsible within their present field. Build it, and God will enhance it. Allow God to promote. With an elder's calling, timing is everything. Ecclesiastes 8:5-6 indicates that there is a proper time and procedure for every matter. David is the classic example—he was called and anointed to be king, but there already was a reigning king. David did not seize or attempt to overthrow the existing authority. He allowed God to promote him at the proper time.

He chose David his servant and took him from the sheep pens;
from tending the sheep he brought him to be the shepherd of his

people Jacob, of Israel his inheritance. And David shepherded them with integrity of heart; with skillful hands he led them (Psalms 78:70-72).

David allowed the Lord to promote him. Sometimes when we teach this concept, it sounds a lot like a business principle. It is true that many successful businesses have adopted this kingdom principle of promoting those that are faithful in the area that has been assigned to them. This was in the Bible long before modern business owners recognized it as an effective principle.

## Delegate authority in a field

An elder can temporarily delegate to others the authority granted him by God. This is similar to when parents are away from home, and they ask the oldest child to be responsible for the house. This child has received delegated authority for his parent's field.

1 Timothy 1:1-4 describes how Timothy was assigned a portion of Paul's authority in Ephesus, even to the point of bringing correction to false teachers and doctrines. An elder may assign authority to small group leaders to lead a small group, and small group leaders work within the field they are assigned. They do not take authority in other areas of the church. This would cause confusion.

It is only the Lord who empowers us and gives us the anointing to rule our fields. In Matthew 10:1, Jesus gave authority to His disciples. He was opening up a new field for them. He did not send them out without first giving them the delegated authority. With this delegated authority, they would operate in His power and love to change the world.

Elders must allow God to assign them fields through His delegated authority with the expectation that He will expand these fields as they are faithful. All the while, elders must remember that they have *stewardship* of the field, *not ownership*. A teller at a bank does not own the money she handles day after day, but she is a steward of it. Our God owns all spiritual fields. In the long run we are simply stewards.

If an elder becomes discouraged when someone leaves his field, this is a symptom that he is taking ownership rather than stewardship. For instance, if some of the people in the local church move on to another church, the elder must realize that God brings people into his field for a season, and God can lead them away. Ultimately it is God's field, and these are His people. The people do not belong to the elders. We must get a broader picture of the greater body of Christ and rejoice, rather than be threatened, when "our family" (those we have mentored and trained) moves on to other fields (churches and ministries).

## Don't plow in another's field

In the mid 1970's a movement called the "shepherding movement" was popular. Good discipleship principles were sometimes overshadowed by unhealthy one-on-one relationships where leaders required those under their authority to get their approval before making decisions such as dating, marriage, and even visiting relatives during holidays! In some cases, families were split apart and lives were turned upside down.

This movement led to unbiblical obedience to human leaders, and in some cases, leaders twisted the biblical principle of accountability by stepping into others' fields and attempting to make their decisions for them. Occasionally, believers moved halfway across the country to follow their leaders.

Many of these individuals found themselves in what could be called "unholy covenants." While a holy covenant is a promise on the part of God, an unholy covenant is made with a person or group that is above and beyond the Holy Spirit's leading.

Elders must not make decisions for members of their flock or ask them to make unholy covenants. Asking believers to stay at a certain church their entire lifetimes because they are "in covenant" with the leadership is both unholy and unhealthy. Elders will never seek to control their spiritual children in this manner. Elders should not cling to their flock if the Lord calls some to serve elsewhere. Elders should release and help individuals find their most fruitful field. James 4:13,17 tells us, "...you who say, 'Today or tomorrow we will go to this or that city'...instead, you ought to say, 'If it is the Lord's will, we will live and do this or that....'" We must allow our spiritual children the freedom to go when God calls them elsewhere.

As elders, it is important to discern the right time for someone to leave and the right time for them to stay. Sometimes the timing is misperceived. A part of raising children is to release them at the appropriate time. It would be evil and manipulative to attempt to pressure them to stay or leave at the wrong time.

## Elders do not tolerate the enemy's activity in their field

Paul had a sense of responsibility for the Corinthian church (II Corinthians 11:28-29). Elders must be responsible and stand in the gap and intercede for their spiritual children. Ezekiel 22:30 gives a picture of prayer warfare as a believer standing in the gap between God's mercy and man's need. God has given an elder the authority to intercede in this way.

As an eldership team leads the flock, they need to stand in the gap for them and refuse to allow the enemy to rob them when sin creates a gap between them and God. Intercession restricts and destroys satanic strongholds and the evil forces of the enemy, allowing the Holy Spirit to bring godly influences into our spiritual children's lives.

An elder does not tolerate the enemy interfering in his field. Through prayer and intercession and declaring God's Word, he rises up in faith and throws the enemy out! God has given an elder authority in his given field!

In his book, *The House of the Lord,* Francis Frangipane, senior pastor of River of Life Church in Iowa, tells what happened when churches in his city came together in warfare prayer for their city. "Violent crime decreased by 17 percent in Cedar Rapids and FBI files confirm that it became the safest city of more than 100,000 people in the United States.

These significant breakthroughs will happen when Christians stand in the gap and take back those areas that the enemy occupies. Satan can only occupy those areas where humanity, through its sin, has allowed him."[2] Christians have the authority to stop the enemy's activity in their field. When elders come together to pray regularly in a specific region (their field), the strongholds of the enemy will fall.

During the past twenty years, church leaders have met regularly to pray for our area of Lancaster County, Pennsylvania. A few years ago, on the front page of our local newspaper, it was reported that crime had dropped 28% in Lancaster city in the previous year.[3] It is our belief that this statistic has a direct correlation to the time spent in unified prayer for Lancaster.

## Take possession!

By way of summary, elders must recognize what their fields are and faithfully work within them. These fields have certain boundaries of size and shape. Elders must rise up in faith and possess these fields the Lord has entrusted to them!

An elder-led church is a team-led church. As with any team, however, there is a primary leader of the team, along with those in supportive leadership roles, and other team-players. As an example, a basketball team has a head coach, a coaching staff, a captain and players. In the home, there is a husband as the head of the wife, the wife as a supportive leader, and the children as the team players. Each leader knows his field and his role of leadership in that field.

Larry has different roles of leadership in different settings. When he is in the field of DOVE Christian Fellowship International, he is the primary leader. When he attends his local church, he is a team player. When he serves with a regional leadership team of his county, he is a supportive leader.

Elders will take possession of their fields, working faithfully in God's grace and respecting others' fields around them. They will walk in His grace and produce a diversity of crops in carefully cultivated fields.

This will give them the distinction of yielding more fruit than they could ever have imagined!

As elders work in their fruit-bearing fields, it is paramount that they know how to make wise decisions. In the next chapter, we will learn how elders make godly decisions and impart biblical decision-making principles to their flock.

## Questions for discussion

1. Reviewing what you have just read, what is a field of ministry?
2. What do you see as your primary field(s) of ministry?
3. What is the danger of "plowing in another's field"?
4. How can an elder take the responsibility to protect his field?

---

[1] Keith Yoder, *Healthy Leaders,* (Ephrata, Pennsylvania: House to House Publications, 1998), p. 62.
[2] Francis Frangipane, *The House of the Lord, (Lake* Mary, Florida: Creation House, 1991), p. 56.
[3] Brian Christopher, "City Crime Rate Plummets 28 Percent," *Intelligencer Journal,* September 11, 1999, p.1.

# Decision-Making Principles

Did you know that you can make the right decision, but make it in the wrong way? If leaders make decisions without involving their people in the process, it devalues the people.

If we understand how Christ designed the family to make decisions, we can understand how the church is to make decisions. The church is a family. The church must reflect God's creative design of the family. Christ designed decision-making to operate within the church as it does within the family.

That is why it is so important for elders to learn how to make wise judgments in decision-making involving the entire team and the congregation. Leaders of all kinds must lead as spiritual fathers and mothers, humbly working together with others to make solid, biblical decisions. In this way, elders honor and bless all those they serve.

Let's look at the first century church and see what they did when faced with a crisis in Acts 15. From this chapter, we learn how elders can make decisions that honor the Lord and values members of the church family.

The early church found itself in a controversy. Does this sound familiar? Church groups today have disagreements over everything from theology to the color of the carpet. But at some point, a decision must be made.

Who makes the decision? How is it made? In Acts 15, we see a clear model for decision-making in the church. Good leaders will combine the strengths of the three decision-making principles found here. These principles are (1) God speaks through a leader (2) God speaks through a team and (3) God speaks through His people.

## A model for decision-making

In this particular church crisis in Acts 15, a group of Pharisee believers from Jerusalem visited the church in Antioch and objected to the Gentiles coming into the church without submitting to the Jewish rite of circumcision. Paul and Barnabas were sent to serve on a council at the Jerusalem church along with the other apostles and elders to resolve this matter because of the heated debate that ensued in the church:

> So, being sent on their way by the church, they [Paul and Barnabas] passed through Phoenicia and Samaria, describing the conversion of the Gentiles; and they caused great joy to all the brethren. And when they had come to Jerusalem, they were received by the church and the apostles and the elders; and they reported all things that God had done with them. But some of the sect of the Pharisees who believed rose up, saying, "It is necessary to circumcise them, and to command them to keep the law of Moses" (verses 3-5).

As the apostles and elders came together in Jerusalem to consider the matter, there was much dispute. Peter rose up and said to them:

> Men and brethren, you know that a good while ago God chose among us, that by my mouth the Gentiles should hear the word of the gospel and believe. So God, who knows the heart, acknowledged them by giving them the Holy Spirit, just as He did to us, and made no distinction between us and them, purifying their hearts by faith (verses 7-9).

Peter reminded these Jewish believers that they were saved by faith and faith alone just as the Gentiles were. Paul and Barnabas testified next:

*The Biblical Role of Elders for Today's Church*

Then all the multitude kept silent and listened to Barnabas and Paul declaring how many miracles and wonders God had worked through them among the Gentiles (verse 12).

After Peter, Paul and Barnabas had their say, James, the lead elder and apostolic leader of the Jerusalem church, spoke up. The early church leaders trusted James to hear what the Lord was saying to them because they were in his "field" of authority and responsibility.

First of all, James reviewed what he had heard from various leaders throughout the meeting together. Then he quoted from the scriptures. Finally, He spoke up in favor of accepting the uncircumcised Gentiles:

Therefore I judge that we should not trouble those from among the Gentiles who are turning to God (verse 19).

The apostles, elders and the whole congregation agreed and decided to send delegates to Antioch and throughout the churches that had been planted to report this decision with an "acceptance letter." A church doctrinal issue was resolved! What can we learn from this story, and how was such a volatile issue of the early church doctrine resolved?

## Principles to make father-like decisions

It is quite possible that this early church issue was resolved because God's leaders followed proper, biblical decision-making principles. As we look at this story carefully, we see three principles of godly leadership and decision-making. Surely the combined strengths of these three decision-making principles can help us make wise father-like decisions at any level of leadership.

Again, the three principles are very simple: God speaks through a leader, God speaks through a team, and God speaks through His people.

Trouble often comes when one of these principles is given greater precedence than the others. It causes church eldership to lead in a lopsided manner, often making poor decisions. These three principles are meant to complement each other as each level of leadership works together in relationship with the others.

To help us better understand the dynamics between all three principles, let's think for a minute about the options a natural family has if they utilize one or more of these principles while planning a vacation.

Let's say the Mancini family wants to make a decision about where to spend their summer vacation. Who should make the decision? Should the father make a decision to go on a fishing vacation without taking into consideration the rest of his family? Should the family discuss the issue thoroughly and then hopelessly give up the idea entirely when no one can agree? Should the children vote and decide by majority where to go? Or is there a better way?

Read the following decision-making principles, and then decide.

## 1. A primary leader—episcopal government

First of all, let's look at the biblical principle of "God speaking through a primary leader." God always calls and anoints someone to lead the way and speaks through this leader. James was the head elder and the apostle at Jerusalem who held this role.

Although God may speak His vision and direction through many, someone is appointed by the Lord to be the primary spokesperson for the vision. He has a responsibility that is a bit greater in seeing the vision fulfilled than the others on the team. You could say James was the *father* or *primary vision carrier* for the group he was leading. He was the one who took responsibility and with discernment heard what the Lord was saying through the entire team and made the declaration of what He believed the Lord was saying to the church.

When a primary leader, called by God, takes his role as the leader of a team and recognizes that God speaks through him, this is often called *episcopal government*. Practiced properly, the advantages of this kind of leadership are obvious. Someone needs to take headship of a team, hear what the Lord is saying through the entire team, and make the final decision. Without someone in headship, many situations requiring a final decision come to an impasse.

Both the Old and New Testament give numerous examples of this leadership principle of one leader leading the way (Adam, Noah, Abraham, Joseph, Debra, Gideon, David, Jesus, Peter, James, Paul): the list goes on and on. Although Moses worked closely with a leadership team (Aaron and Miriam), he was clearly anointed by God to lead the children of Israel. When Moses realized that someone needed to lead the way after his departure, he asked the Lord to appoint a man over the congregation, and Joshua was appointed to lead the way (Numbers 27:16).

In the New Testament (Acts 13:1-4) we read about Barnabas and Saul being sent out with a team as missionaries to evangelize and plant new churches. By verse thirteen, the Bible says Paul and his companions went to the next city. Paul had already become the clear leader— the primary leader of the team.

In the corporate world, we often call the head leader of a corporation a Chief Executive Officer (CEO). The CEO is responsible for the vision and general oversight of the company—what goes on within its doors, how it will grow and its overall image. He has authority to make the decisions that affect the future of the company. That leadership is usually equated with power, position and prestige.

Similarly, primary church elders also have positions of authority and are responsible for the people placed within their care. However, they have a servant-leadership understanding that is not to be equated with power and prestige.

In the church, the opposite of a servant-leadership understanding is a clergy-laity mentality. A clergy-laity mentality expects the clergy to do all the ministry because they are in authority while the laity is inactive, taking on a spectator role. This kind of thinking stunts effectiveness and maintains a distance between leaders and the rest of the church body. Elders who lead biblically know they must lead as fathers so the people see the need to participate actively to advance the kingdom of God and do not become complacent.

Although the primary elder needs to declare a clear vision for the church, as part of that vision he must recognize the importance of helping each person fulfill the call of God on his or her own personal life. Elders who lead as fathers will encourage their flock as they would their children to fulfill their dreams and visions. They help their children to hear from God and make their own decisions rather than handing them decisions already made.

When primary elders choose to lead humbly as servants, people following them will be encouraged and trained, by example, to do their jobs with the same spirit—namely, that of a servant. In this way, they can participate fully in the life of the church.

A misguided CEO often *uses* people, but an elder *serves* people. A true elder's rights actually decrease as he takes his position of authority, and his responsibilities increase. His rights decrease because Christian eldership does not involve power and prestige but servanthood. Servanthood is to be the mark of an elder who is deeply committed to the development of others. Servant leadership takes its example from Christ, the master leader, who demonstrated that He "…did not come to be served, but to serve…" (Mark 10:45).

In a family, fathers should be willing to serve by making final decisions: "For the husband is the head of the wife, as also Christ is head of the church; and He is the Savior of the body" (Ephesians 5:23). In every team, there is always someone the Lord places as the primary leader within that team. In the case of the husband and wife, the Bible says the husband is the head of the wife. He's the one who is called to love his wife the same way Jesus Christ loves His church and gave His life for it. He is also the one who, in times of crisis, is responsible to make the final decisions in the home.

A few years ago, Larry and his wife LaVerne came to an impasse in making a decision regarding whether or not one of their children should be enrolled in a public school or a Christian school. They prayed and waited before the Lord for an answer but could not clearly hear the voice of the Lord. Finally LaVerne told Larry, "Honey, you are the head of our home, and I believe you will hear what the Lord is saying in this situation. I will honor your decision." It turned out that the decision Larry felt God was leading them to make was the right one.

A godly elder never throws his weight around as a leader. Paul, the apostle, a respected leader of the early church, set the example, not as a boss, but as a servant called by the Lord to be a spiritual father: "Nor did we seek glory from men, either from you or from others, when we might have made demands as apostles of Christ. But we were gentle among you, just as a nursing mother cherishes her own children" (1 Thessalonians 2:6-7). Paul's letters to the church were written from a loving spiritual parent's perspective, as he modeled the life of a servant to those he spiritually fathered.

On the opposite side of the spectrum, what can happen if the primary leader called by God has abdicated his God-given leadership role of authority and responsibility? If God's appointed leader does not lead the way, someone else (who is not God's appointed leader) will fill the leadership vacuum. This opens the door to confusion. This situation may occur if an elder shrinks back and abdicates his decision-making role in an attempt to please others and gain approval.

Having said all this, there is a downside when people lead solely through the principle of episcopal decision-making, because they can become autocratic. In fact, it can become dangerous. Abuses of this kind of leadership may breed the Jim Jones-type cult leaders, husbands who abuse their wives, or those who believe they have a right to tell others what to do in a way that violates the other person's individual authority and responsibility before the Lord.

Authority and responsibility must work hand in hand. One cannot claim all authority without accepting all responsibility. That would be authority abuse. As well, one cannot be given all responsibility and be stripped of any authority. That is responsibility abuse.

When an elder leads entirely with this style of decision-making without listening to his team, abuses can occur. That is why it is important to also add the next component of decision-making—working together with a team.

## 2. God calls a team to work together—presbyterian government

Although James was the clear leader in Acts 15, it is important to see that as a primary leader, James did not make decisions alone. The other apostles and elders met with him, and they worked together as a team to make a decision. In this way, they were all able to confirm James' final decision as he listened to what the Lord was saying through the entire team. The other apostles and elders were honored because they were involved in the process, and their input was valued. The Lord speaking through a team of leaders who discern His voice together is sometimes called *presbyterian government.*

In families, the Lord has called husbands and wives to submit to each other. God wants husbands and wives to be in unity and work as a team: "Submitting to one another in the fear of God" (Ephesians 5:21).

We see this team leadership modeled many times in both the Old and New Testament. Elders rarely worked alone, but with a team of leaders who served with them. Moses, Aaron and Miriam worked together as a team in Exodus. Acts 16:4 speaks of *apostles and elders*. In I Peter 5:1, the plural term *elders* is used again. In Titus 1:5, Paul exhorts Titus to appoint elders in every town. Paul and Barnabas appointed elders in every church (Acts 14:23) and worked with them as an eldership team.

Why is it so important to work together as a team? A senior elder has only so many gifts. According to the Bible, no matter how spiritual we think we are, "We know in part and we prophesy in part" (1 Corinthians 13:9). A team of elders will fill in the gaps for the senior elder's limitations. A senior elder has only a portion of the Lord's wisdom.

A senior elder and his team will listen to what the Lord says through everyone on the team. Then the senior leader will receive the grace to discern what the Lord is saying through the entire team.

When a plane is in flight, the pilot, copilot, and flight attendants all work together as a team. Everything proceeds like clockwork. But this is not true for the whole flight. During take off, landing and times of turbulence, it is the pilot who has to take clear leadership, and everyone on the plane is glad that he does!

A wise senior elder recognizes that the Lord speaks through each of the team members, and discerns what the Lord is saying through the team (Acts 15). Then he makes the decision and the others on the team affirm his decision. The down-side of solely applying this form of government is when a team of elders cannot come to a consensus, the forward motion of the church may become paralyzed.

When God called Larry to start a cell-based church over two decades ago, as a leader he had little concept of how to make decisions. He admits, "I knew God had called me to start an 'underground church,' but I did not want to take the reins of the group and lead as a senior pastor. So I insisted that our entire team of leaders, including me, would be coequal. In this way, I thought we could all have a say and would not need a head leader." In his book, *House to House*, Larry recounts the confusion that ensued.

> It's funny to recall, now, but with six of us leading, we discovered on one Sunday morning that we couldn't come to a decision about who should preach the Word in our celebration meeting. Since none of us were giving clear leadership, no one preached! It would be fine for no one to preach if the Lord was truly leading in this way; however, when it is by default, it causes confusion and stress among the body of Christ. This type of leadership structure will either cause a move of God to stop, or it will slow it down until there is clarity regarding God-ordained leadership...Within the first year, this "leaderless group" came to the difficult realization that there was a need for clear, delegated leadership among us. Although we continued to believe

that team leadership was important, we recognized the need for "headship" on each leadership team.[1]

The abdication of Larry's leadership led to a devastating gridlock when a final decision had to be made. As a leader, he had to discover that he needed to assume responsibility and receive God's anointing to lead the team, rather than back off and cause the entire church to become frustrated in making decisions.

## 3. God speaks through His people in the local church—congregational government

Wise parents will listen to their children before making decisions that will affect the family. Elders will take the time to hear the heart's cry of their spiritual children in the church because they love them, believe the Lord speaks through them, and they want to see them fulfill their destiny in God. Someone once said, "If you listen to the whispers, you won't have to endure the screams."

It is implied in Acts 15 that James and the apostles and elders listened to *the people* in the congregation at Jerusalem before they made a final decision. In Acts 6:1-7 leaders whom we sometimes call *deacons* were chosen. Who chose the deacons? Scripture says *the people* chose seven men, and the apostles appointed them. Wise elders will listen to what God says through His people. Elders must value the input of the people they serve!

It is a godly principle to receive input from those you serve before making a decision that affects them. Before an important decision is made, wise church elders will publicly share the facts and receive godly input so as to leave no room for doubt and discontent among the congregation.

Some churches rely heavily on the practice of hearing what God's people are saying and then voting on the situation. This is sometimes called *congregational government.* The only problem with applying only this type of  decision-making process is that when you take a vote, someone nearly always loses. Applying this type of church government alone is not the best method for making decisions in the church. With this style of leadership, the elders who are praying and fasting for a specific situation can have their "votes" canceled by a group in the church who are focused on personal preferences rather than the voice of God.

The healthy biblical pattern for church government and decision-making is theocracy—God speaking through chosen elders He has appointed. However, elders need to recognize that the people of God are also hearing from the Lord and need to be honored by listening and taking into prayerful consideration what the Lord is saying through them.

Biblical decision-making should come through fasting and prayer and spiritual discernment (Acts 13:1-3) that involves healthy aspects of all three leadership principles. This will bring us balanced decision-making with the eldership team listening to what the Lord is saying through the body. The senior elder listens to what the Lord is saying through the eldership team. With the input of the body and the elders, the senior elder speaks what the Lord is saying, and the others affirm the Lord's direction.

## Head, shoulders and body—balanced decision-making

As an elder constantly acknowledges the Lord, he must make an effort to focus on all three decision-making principles in order to make balanced decisions. There are strengths in all three, and if an elder combines these strengths, he will experience tremendous unity in his sphere of influence.

Sometimes the analogy of "head and shoulders and body" is used to show the combined strengths of all three principles. This analogy helps to explain further how an elder works together with a team of elders and the congregation to hear what the Lord is saying.

In Psalm 133, David is singing a song about unity. At this point in biblical history, the tribes of Israel were united under one head. The blessing of this unity is described as the fragrant holy anointing oil poured upon the head of Aaron, the high priest. It was so plentiful that

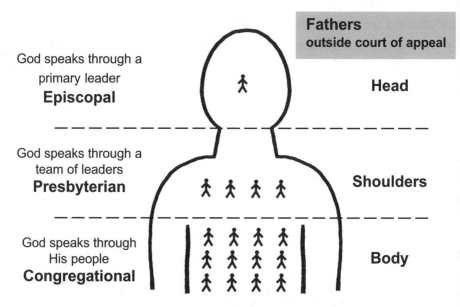

God speaks through a
primary leader
**Episcopal**

God speaks through a
team of leaders
**Presbyterian**

God speaks through
His people
**Congregational**

**Fathers**
**outside court of appeal**

**Head**

**Shoulders**

**Body**

it ran down his face onto his shoulders and down the garment of his body. In a similar fashion God pours out His wisdom on the head, which then flows to the shoulders and on to the body.

> How good and pleasant it is when brothers live together in unity! It is like precious oil poured on the head, running down on the beard, running down on Aaron's beard, down upon the collar of his robes. It is as if the dew of Hermon were falling on Mount Zion. For there the Lord bestows his blessing, even life forevermore (Psalm 133).

Using the analogy of a head, shoulders and body regarding balanced decision-making, the head (senior elder) of every team needs to be properly attached to the shoulders (the others on the team) and the body (the people) through a God-ordained relationship of trust and affirmation. If the head is appropriately attached to the shoulders (through relationship, trust, servanthood, prayer and proper communication), and the shoulders properly support and affirm the head, there will be unity, and God will command the blessing "life forevermore" as indicated in Psalm 133. As a team flows in unity, the life of God flows out of the team.

The shoulders are part of the government but are not the head. They constantly lift up and support the head. They share the burden of leadership and carry the load. This allows the head to concentrate on looking, hearing and leading the body in the right direction.

God gives His grace and anointing to the senior elder of the team to hear what He is saying through the entire team. However, if the head is stretched too far from the shoulders (the senior elder is not honoring the team) and makes decisions in an autocratic style, the shoulders (the team) and the body (the people) will experience a "pain in the neck." By the same token, if the head is forced down into the shoulders (by the team not honoring the head), the body will again experience a "pain in the neck."

If there is a right honor and appreciation between the head and shoulders, then the head is able to turn on the shoulders smoothly and without pain. The head is able to respond to suggestions and connection from the shoulders. The shoulders will do this respectfully.

We believe that many times, the Lord will give vision to a senior elder, but the timing is in the hands of the team and the people. It takes time to pray and share so that all three gain a sense of godly stewardship for a decision. Returning to the analogy of the family, Steve discovered after many years of marriage that he frequently has "the vision" for something and his wife Mary carries "the timing." While this has not always been the case, it is a scenario that they have repeatedly encountered.

Unless there is trust established between team members and team leaders, decisions cannot be made effectively. When brothers "dwell together in unity" (Psalm 133:1-3), the Lord commands a blessing, but it takes time to build trusting relationships.

## Senior elders and teams work together to make biblical decisions

In order for biblical decision-making to be effective, the members of the team must be convinced that (1) they are called to serve on the team, (2) others on the team are called with them, and (3) the senior elder is called to serve in his role as the leader of the team. The senior elder must also be fully convinced that every member of the team is called to serve in the role they are in. This is why regular (perhaps yearly) evaluations are so important. It gives everyone the opportunity to express what the Lord is saying to them at the present time. (See Appendix for evaluation forms, pp. 216-218)

## Acknowledge the Lord first

The key to all decision-making is simply knowing that only the Lord can give us wisdom for making decisions. We cannot lean on our own understanding as the writer of Proverbs admonishes us in Proverbs 3:5-6: "Trust in the Lord with all your heart, and lean not on your own understanding; in all your ways acknowledge Him, and He shall direct your paths" (NKJ).

We must live in the constant reality that Christ is in our midst, waiting for us to ask Him for wisdom and for direction. Jesus tells us clearly in Matthew 18:19-20: "Again, I tell you that if two of you on earth agree about anything you ask for, it will be done for you by my Father in heaven. For where two or three come together in my name, there am I with them."

We must continually acknowledge Christ in our midst. Some eldership teams become so familiar with each other that they no longer continue to acknowledge the Lord, and they stray from a place of desperation for God and listening to His voice. They are led more by marketing schemes and the latest management style of successful companies. We believe we can learn from the business world, but we need to be sure we are listening to the voice of the Father first and foremost.

## Guard our hearts from selfishness

James warns us to guard our hearts from selfish ambition in decision-making in James 3:13-17:

Who is wise and understanding among you? Let him show it by his good life, by deeds done in the humility that comes from wisdom. But if you harbor bitter envy and selfish ambition in your hearts, do not boast about it or deny the truth. Such 'wisdom' does not come down from heaven but is earthly, unspiritual, of the devil. For where you have envy and selfish ambition, there you find disorder and every evil practice. But the wisdom that comes from heaven is first of all pure; then peace-loving, considerate, submissive, full of mercy and good fruit, impartial and sincere.

The Lord is concerned that our attitudes be pure before Him so that the decisions we make are not based on selfish ambition, for this would lead to demonic activity in our midst. Many eldership teams encounter demonic activity, and they are not even aware of it. It is easy to spot. Just look at the fruit. Is there peace, submission, mercy and consideration for the feelings of others—or is there bitterness, envy and selfish ambition? Being right is not the most important issue. Having the Spirit of Christ is the real issue. We can make a bad decision, but if our heart is right, the Lord will direct our paths and turn our bad decision around for good (Romans 8:28).

## Avoid the rule of the negative

On an eldership team, the leaders will submit to one another and try to reach a unanimous decision, but this is not always possible. If we were bound to always require a unanimous decision, then if in a team of five people four agree and one disagrees, the one "negative" vote would by default carry the decision. We can avoid this "rule of the negative," by the senior elder of the team being responsible to discern what the Lord is saying through the team and making the final decision within his field of ministry. If a team believes a unanimous decision is necessary, in effect, the dissenting member is leading the team rather than the senior leader.

Did you ever try to come to a consensus about selecting a movie to watch that the whole family will enjoy? "Our family would not watch any movies if we had to unanimously decide what to watch," admits Brian. "Everyone has a different view and cannot totally agree. So I allow the kids to speak and give their input, and then I make the final decision as the father."

Obviously, there are certain major decisions for which the senior elder may believe he needs a unanimous agreement. In those cases, the Lord gives the senior leader the grace and perseverance to wait to make the decision until there is complete agreement.

## How spiritual fathers provide an outside court of appeal

It is important to note that while we combine the best principles of "a leader leading the way" as he "works through a team" who "listen to those whom they serve" to make decisions, the senior elder and the eldership team should have additional spiritual fathers who provide input and accountability for them. In some denominations, this someone is called a bishop, district superintendent, or other denominational leader. In new apostolic movements (see Appendix D), these are the apostolic overseers who serve as spiritual fathers to church elders.

Since the senior elder does not have "absolute authority," but "final authority, " there must be a court of appeal. By being accountable even for the final decision, a leader avoids the absolute authority trap. This applies to all levels of leadership.

For example, a small group leader in a local church may receive this kind of accountable "outside court of appeal" from his church eldership. The church eldership team receives its outside court of appeal from the apostolic leaders who give the team oversight. It is important to note that total agreement is needed regarding who the spiritual fathers are that provide this court of appeal. If there is not complete agreement, in a time of crisis there will not be faith and trust in the court of appeal which is necessary for them to be effective in bringing resolution.

Elders and churches without an outside court of appeal, will often find a sense of insecurity within their ranks and will try to meet this need by setting up some type of accountability team within the church. This could be a church board, the church elders, a board of deacons, or a pulpit committee. A team like this, providing accountability and oversight for the senior leader of the church, is like young children trying to help their parents through a problem in their marriage by providing accountability for them! They may be sincere, but they simply do not have the grace from the Lord to help their parents. It is not their field of authority or responsibility.

We are grateful to the Lord for a team of spiritual fathers who are outside the DOVE Christian Fellowship International family who speak into our lives and into the lives of the other leaders on our international leadership team.

## Biblical theocracy—The church has ruling elders

The practical outworking of using head, shoulder and body government for a local church means that the elders make the decisions regarding the direction of the church. Another term to describe this is that the church has ruling elders.

We have found that the church's bylaws have to be written to reflect this. The bylaws are the governing document of the church. It is important that this document reflects the style of leadership with which you want to function. Shortcuts in this area have held back many local churches. Simply stated, the elders have to be the legal officers of the corporation and the senior elder should be the chairman or president of the corporation. The sample bylaws in the Appendix (page 250) are written in this way.

Let us explain how biblical head, shoulders and body government can function while fulfilling the legal requirements of governmentally recognized church bylaws. It is quite simple. For a decision to be made, it requires a two-thirds majority of the elders, including the senior elder within that majority. What this means is that the senior elder cannot take the church a different direction from where the rest of the elders want it to go and the elders cannot take the church a different direction from where the senior elder wants it to go. It forces them to talk through defining the vision and working together. It also eliminates the possibility of one elder holding up the church from moving forward. If there is a deadlock of opinions, then the outside court of appeal (the apostolic leadership) is called in to help resolve the dispute.

Church bylaws and the spiritual decision-making policies are to be compatible, or elders will potentially experience great pain if they come to an impasse on decision-making. A friend of ours, after serving as founding pastor of a church for 15 years, was removed from his church by a woman who was in charge of the "board of trustees" in the church because she disagreed with the vision the Lord gave him. Most people in the church were shocked to discover that their church's bylaws and policies allowed for such an action. Only bylaws that reflect a  biblical church government will stand the test of time.

## In conclusion

If the natural tendency of a senior elder  is toward the episcopal model of leadership, he needs to trust the Lord for grace to honor his team and listen to the people within his sphere of influence. If the elder's natural tendency is towards the presbyterian model, he needs to be sure he is giving clear leadership during times of crisis, or he will frustrate the team. If the elder's personal leadership understanding leans towards the congregational model, he needs to give clear leadership and honor his leadership team by processing decisions in prayer and dialogue with them.

The senior elder often finds that his greatest emotional need is *affirmation* from the team members. Elders on a team need to affirm the call of God on their senior elder's life. Those who serve on the team often find that their greatest emotional need is for the senior elder to give them *relationship and communication.* Wise senior elders will be intentional in "sharing their hearts" with their team. This helps to provide an atmosphere of trust, relationship, openness and security (1 Peter 5:1-3).

An elder must understand that without a New Testament church government, he cannot give clear scriptural leadership to the church. He must be sure his church constitution and bylaws reflect a New Testament pattern of church government. More instruction on New Testament church government and constitution and bylaws is available in *Helping You Build Cell Churches*, a comprehensive manual for pastors, cell leaders, and church planters.[2]

In summary, the team is called by God to support the senior elder. The senior elder protects the team. The senior elder discerns what the Lord is saying through the others on the team. Both the senior elder and the team listen to the wisdom that comes from the people. They are all connected by relationship and accountability. There are outside spiritual fathers to appeal to, and this brings security to everyone. No one is depending on their own wisdom, but all are trusting the Lord, who is all wisdom.

## Questions for discussion

1. Which of the three decision-making principles have you experienced most frequently?
2. From your life give an example describing how the application of biblical decision-making helps you become a more godly spiritual leader.
3. What is the greatest emotional need the senior elder has? Who can be used of God to meet that need?
4. What is the greatest emotional need the team of elders has? Who can most effectively be used of God to meet that need?

---

[1] Larry Kreider, *House to House*, (Ephrata, Pennsylvania: House to House Publications, 1995), pp.6-7.
[2] Brian Sauder & Larry Kreider, *Helping You Build Cell Churches*, (Ephrata, PA: House to House Publications, 2000).

# How Elders Function Together

## 8

God has designed the local church to be a place where believers can flourish, love and obey God, love their families and fulfill their destinies. The elders are responsible to guarantee that this kind of protection, guidance and nurture is found in their "pasture." They are responsible to provide a safe place for believers to enjoy the relationship between the Lord and His people that is found in Psalm 23.

The Lord Jesus is the Chief Shepherd of His church (1 Peter 5:4). He is not an administrator who is remote and uninvolved in the details of the lives of His people. Instead, He is a Shepherd who cares for the sheep and lives among them. The Lord is concerned for His children and desires to guide them just as a good shepherd cares for his sheep. Let's read Psalm 23 as a picture of what the local church should look like. You could say the elders (or stewards) are the keepers of this garden, maintaining this lush place of protection and prosperity.

*The Lord is my shepherd* An elder lovingly helps people find guidance and direction in the local church.

*I shall not be in want* An elder makes sure that people find provision in the local church. He finds great pleasure in seeing his sheep contented with their needs met.

*He makes me lie down in green pastures* It is almost impossible to make sheep lie down unless four requirements are met, according to Philip Keller in his book, *A Shepherd Looks at Psalm 23.*

1. Owing to their timidity they refuse to lie down unless they are free of all fear.

2. Because of the social behavior within a flock, sheep will not lie down unless they are free from friction with others of their kind.

3. If tormented by flies or parasites, sheep will not lie down. Only when free of these pests can they relax.

4. Lastly, sheep will not lie down as long as they feel in need of finding food. They must be free of hunger.[1]

An elder creates an environment in the local church that provides a place of safety and security. It is a safe place where people flourish because they can be themselves in a family-like atmosphere.

*He leads me beside quiet waters* An elder makes sure people find refreshment in the local church. It is a place of peace and security. We live in a chaotic world. Satisfying relationships with other believers in the church give us encouragement.

*He restores my soul* An elder ministers to men and women of God, who are pounding the pavement and doing the work of ministry. There should be renewal and refreshment in the local church. Life has a way of wearing us down. We need the help of fellow believers to overcome problems and frustrations. We need help to rise up from a fallen position, be restored, and run into the arms of Jesus.

*He guides me in paths of righteousness for his name's sake* Sheep are creatures of habit. People are too! An elder sees to it that his flock is moving ahead on the path that God wants them to travel. The elder leads the local church with the vision, mission and plan God has given them.

*Even though I walk through the valley of the shadow of death* An elder encourages everyone to keep walking on with God even when times may be difficult. He knows that the only way to gain higher ground in our Christian walk is to climb up from the valleys of discouragement and defeat.

*I will fear no evil for you are with me* An elder protects the people of God through prayer and intercession and through exposing heresy and wrong teaching. The people of God are taught to overcome their fears and live a life of faith.

*Your rod and your staff, they comfort me* An elder provides both encouragement and discipline as needed. A shepherd's rod is a long slender stick with a hook on one end. It is used to draw sheep close to the shepherd and guide them in the right way so as to be kept safe from harm.

*You prepare a table before me in the presence of my enemies* An elder prepares teaching from the scriptures—spiritual food that stops the accuser in his tracks, destroying the lies of the enemy.

*You anoint my head with oil; my cup overflows* An elder lays hands upon the believers and offers the oil of healing and blessing, so it overflows into the church body. A shepherd sometimes rubs oil on rams' heads during mating season. When the rams attempt to butt heads, they bounce off one another. Jealousies and rivalries seem ridiculous when the oil of the Holy Spirit is poured on our lives.

*Surely goodness and love will follow me all the days of my life* An elder brings blessing through his servant-leadership, modeling the fruit of the Holy Spirit. The sheep will be productive because they receive the support of their shepherd.

*And I will dwell in the house of the Lord forever* A healthy elder who loves the people of God causes them to love the church and live a life of obedience. The flock will be satisfied and long to remain in the presence of the Lord.

## Elders must function as a team

The importance of elders functioning in unity cannot be overstressed. The basic commonalities for any team to function collectively include: healthy God-given relationships, common vision, common values, and common procedures. First of all, let's look at God-given healthy relationships.

There are many horror stories of leadership teams that have fractured. A church that was going through some relational leadership problems encouraged their senior elder to take a vacation, and generously sent him to Hawaii. While there, he got a call from one of the elders who informed him that he had taken two thirds of the congregation and started a new church. The remaining congregation was torn apart and never recovered.

Why do teams, initially called of God to work together, sometimes separate in disillusionment, hurt and anger? For one thing, the church is a very real target for the devil and his demons. We must be on guard and keep our relationships honest and healthy. Churches split apart when leaders are in disunity in their relationships. Matthew 26:31 tells us plainly "...strike the shepherd, and the sheep of the flock will be scattered." If the protective trust relationship of our spiritual leaders is broken, the sheep become susceptible to danger. Guarding relationships on the eldership team is top priority.

Team members must feel valued and secure in the team environment. They must all realize they have a job to do, and no one can do their job better than they. Senior elders will do all they can to create a team environment that encourages each member to function in their particular gifts. A senior elder should never feel threatened if others on the team are more gifted in certain ministry areas.

The author of this little motto is unknown to us, but the message is loud and clear. "The best leader is the one who has sense enough to pick good people to get done what he wants done and has self-restraint enough to keep from meddling with them while they do it."

From a place of security and love for each other, it will be easier for the team members to function as they should—with common vision, common values and common procedures.

Elders must have common vision. This means they must all know where they are headed. But they must also have common values. Values are those things you believe so deeply that you would be willing to die for them. It takes a period of time to serve with someone to begin to see what he really values. In addition, there must be common procedures. Common procedures are the practical methods needed to carry out the vision. You must all be in agreement concerning how you will carry out your God-given vision. If any of these areas are missing, the team of elders will find themselves struggling to function as a team. The following is a list of how elders should function together.

## 1. Function with prayer

Unity comes from praying together. Prayer is a powerful means of supporting each other and a spiritually bonding experience. This is one reason it is important for husbands and wives to pray together. Remember the disciples that were disputing about what position they would have in the kingdom? They all dropped their desires for position and their ambitions in the prayer meeting in the upper room at the day of Pentecost.

When elders come together in prayer, it dissipates personal agendas and helps everyone focus on what God's agenda is for the local church. Many times direction is given prophetically by the Lord while the elders are praying together and seeking God's direction. Vision that is birthed in prayer is seldom second-guessed later.

## 2. Function with vision

Colin Powell says leaders must be driven by a vision. "Find ways to reach down and touch everyone in a unit. Make individuals feel important and part of something larger than themselves." God wants to give His people "vision"—something that is larger than themselves.

Each local church should formulate a clear mental portrait of where God is leading them as a church. Solomon gave us an understanding of the importance of vision when he said, "Where there is no vision, the people perish" (Proverbs 29:18 KJV). If a local church has no common vision, the people will not have clear  direction or purpose. They will live according to their own scattered visions, and confusion becomes the result.

Common vision is essential for the success of any team and its local church. The senior elder is the "primary vision carrier," and he carries the vision in his heart with a burning desire to see it become a reality. He has the final authority in setting the broad parameters of the vision, but many others will help bring greater clarity to the vision. Only an insecure leader thinks he sees all the vision and that all vision will come from him.

Vision always precedes reality, so it is important to take the time to "write the vision" so the eldership team can run together (Habakkuk 2:1-4). A vision needs to be written down so you can come to an agreement about the wording, which sharpens the vision. A vision can then be given to the congregation, so together all the saints can fulfill it. A written vision also helps hold us accountable to prayerfully fulfill it.

An exercise to help develop a vision statement is included in the Appendix, page 249.

## 3. Function in holiness

The Old Testament high priest was commanded to wear priestly garments, one of which was a turban with a gold plate engraved with the words, "Holy to the Lord."[2] As new covenant priests, we need to have holiness engraved on our thoughts. We should never grow weary of maintaining an intimate relationship with Christ and with fellow believers. A team of elders not only desires to exercise a greater love for God but also a greater love for others on the team.

With a variety of people and their different ways of looking at situations, conflict is often inevitable. Conflict is not unhealthy. It is a natural element of working together as a team. What becomes unhealthy is unresolved conflict that is allowed to taint the team's ability to be productive.

Sin must be confronted if conflicts are to be resolved. Sin (especially rebellion) divides and opens the door for more sin.[3] Divisiveness is a sin. The team must be encouraged to focus on the nature and holiness of God. The fear of the Lord eliminates personal agendas and helps the group to come into oneness in order to seek God's agenda.

If at the end of any meeting an elder senses that something was misunderstood or uncomfortable between himself and anyone else on the team, he should always make a point of talking through any possible misunderstanding with that individual. This practice will make sure relationships remain intact, genuine and functional.

## 4. Function in diversity

Diverse personalities, diverse cultures and races, diverse ages, and a variety of gifts both spiritual and natural should be welcomed on a team of elders. A diverse team reflects the character of God. In Acts 20:1-6, we see a cultural and religious diversity on this team of elders. Some were of Gentile background and others were of Jewish. In Chapters 13-20 of Acts, it can be seen that teams varied in both size and gifts.

Unity does not mean uniformity. Furthermore, we should not think unity is a nebulous concept that we either have or don't have. People can be taught how to walk in unity. When conflicts arise, Matthew 18:15-17 dictates how they can be resolved. (For more on resolving conflicts on a team, see Chapter Ten.)

Unity should be built around common values, not common personalities. Sometimes a senior elder may be tempted to have people placed with him on the team who are similar to him in personality. This is a mistake! A diversity of personalities helps to round out the team.

## 5. Function with inclusiveness

Elders should realize that fulfilling the Great Commission is more important than minor doctrinal differences. Church leaders want to "major on majors and minor on minors." They desire to be inclusive in making decisions. The first step in clear communication is for an elder to listen and respect what he hears and take it seriously. All team members should be respected, understood, and their input valued.

As a senior elder, Ron often told the other elders on the team, "If you always agree with me, I do not need you." He was not saying that they should be disagreeable, but that he needed leaders around him who would see things that he could not. All the elders on the team should speak what God is saying to them so the senior elder can get a complete picture of what the Lord is saying.

## 6. Function under authority

If an elder cannot come under authority, he should not be in authority. Understanding authority does not mean anything until we have to give something up—our own authority. Jesus applauded the Roman centurion who fully understood authority. The Roman centurion knew he had authority if he stayed under authority. He did not say, "I myself am a man with authority," but instead, "I myself am a man under authority, with soldiers under me" (Romans 7:8). In his book, *Understanding Leadership*, Tom Marshall explains it further:

> The centurion knew that he had authority over his 100 men as long as he himself stayed under authority. His men obeyed his orders unquestioningly, because they knew that if they disobeyed the centurion, his superior would back him up, and his superior's superior would do the same, all the way back to Caesar on his throne in Rome. All the power of Rome stood behind the centurion, as long as he stayed under authority. If he stepped out of that obedience, he lost all his authority.[4]

Elders are those exercising authority themselves, so it provides safety to be in obedience to those in apostolic authority over them. Elders should recognize, desire and value apostolic oversight. In Acts 15:2 an argument in the Antioch church led the elders there to turn to the apostles in Jerusalem for help. They knew they needed to access delegated authority to help resolve the matter.

## 7. Function joyfully

As God calls elders, He calls them to a place of responsibility and rejoicing. Celebration should be included in the function of the team of elders. God has created us with a need to celebrate! The Bible is filled with feasts and festivals. We are right to celebrate those things that are special in our lives and ministry. An environment should be created that is open and fun and allows healthy productive interaction. Being on a team of elders should be enjoyable. Close, meaningful relationships within a team of elders are essential for the success of the team.

It is advisable for elders to do other things together besides ministry. They could watch a movie together, go to dinner together, play sports or attend a sporting event together, go camping for a weekend together with their families, or any other activity that allows the team to get to know each other without the pressure to complete a task.

Proverbs 17:22 says "a cheerful heart is good medicine." Sometimes the most healthy activity elders can do together is to laugh! An elder team that plays together can work together more effectively. Laughter often helps to diffuse the intensity of a situation. It actually places a leader in a better position to hear the word of the Lord for that situation.

## 8. Function with discernment

Elders are fighting against the powers of darkness. They must discern the tactics of the enemy that are specifically aimed at them. They must saturate their minds with the truths of God's Word to discern what is of God and what is not (Ephesians 6:12; John 8:32). There is a protective role given to elders to watch over the church. It is their field. They should not open the door to everyone who comes along. They need to first get to know them.

Steve has shared this principle frequently with senior elders and eldership teams. On one occasion, a senior elder shared the following story with him. A well-known television evangelist was coming to his town and was "available" to speak at his church. Wisely, the senior elder agreed to first meet him for lunch.

At lunch, they each enjoyed quite a bit of small talk and the evangelist's stories. At one point, the television personality asked the senior elder, "So, tell me about your church." The DCFI senior elder proceeded to reveal to him that his church, among other things, was "cell-based." The evangelist interrupted him with, "That will never work!" and then went on to share more of his "success" stories.

A wave of relief came over the senior elder realizing that he could have invited a man to speak at his church who disagreed with a central value of his church and may have spoken publicly against this value. The senior elder was happy he had heard from God before inviting disruption into the church family.

Elijah heard from God and warned the king of Israel about the plans of the enemy against Israel. Elders must hear from God and be fore-warned of disruptive teaching that could come into their church.

## 9. Function as learners

Elders should never stop learning. Elders will stretch their minds; they will read books with which they may not always agree. They will share what they are learning from the scriptures.

Senior elders should ask questions so they can get past the surface communication and "hear" the hearts of the other elders. A primary way to lead people is to ask questions.

A team of elders should go on retreats regularly. Something happens when you get away from the normal routine and begin to relate to each other in a different setting. The elders team could also go to a conference where they learn and discern together. A team may be surprised how unity and commitment will grow as they bond together at times like these.

## 10. Function with good communication

The senior elder should make sure he is communicating to the team all of the information they will need in order to make wise decisions. Without clear information, decisions will be off-balance. When communicating with the team, a senior elder should say the same thing in as many different ways as possible so he is sure to be understood.

The elders should be affirming of each other. Elders will disagree, and speak openly and honestly in private, but once a decision is made by the group, everyone should stick with the decision in speaking publicly. Sound a sure, steady, unified note.

When it comes to dealing with problems in the church, elders can set the tone of right communication by talking only about that which edifies others (Ephesians 4:29). Do not gossip about someone's problems on the team or in the church. An elder does not correct the whole church or the whole team when only one person is the problem. Go to the individual. If additional light needs to be shed on a situation, for instance, communicate only that information that is necessary to address the problem.

## 11. Function with good planning

Elders can develop good planning and administrative skills and be spontaneous, visionary, Bible-quoting, Spirit-filled individuals! Being open to hearing God's voice and doing what He says also means planning for the mission God lays before them. Good planning will avoid confusion and increase unity in the church. Nehemiah gave clear job descriptions as they built the wall (Nehemiah 4:13-14). Good management builds unity. Communicate clearly with people when they are not doing their job. Implement regular evaluations. Common procedures are essential for the success of any team.

## 12. Function with delegation

Delegate as much as possible to others. Moses went up to the mountain to be with his heavenly Father and delegated the administrative and pastoral responsibility to Aaron and Hur (Exodus 24:14). An elder will work himself out of a job! Remember, people learn by doing. Of course we should not delegate responsibilities to anyone. We should delegate to FAITH Christians, that is those who are Faithful, Able and available, Intimate with God (they love the Lord), Teachable, and Holy (those who live lives of purity).

## How often should elders meet together?

The elders need to meet together regularly to maintain vision, unity, faith and momentum for the church to keep moving forward. Keep in mind that a lot of the elders' time can end up being spent in problem-solving. The first priority of the elders must be prayer, setting vision and implementing that vision so the church can move ahead. Keeping these priorities in first place will make problem solving easier.

There should be some meeting times when the elders meet with the department heads and/or church staff to hear what these people are sensing from the Lord. It is also important for those individuals to really hear the vision directly from the elders. There might be others from the church who are asked to join for part of an elders meeting to share vision, concerns or revelation they are getting from the Lord. This is especially important if there are fivefold ministers functioning in the fellowship who are not elders.

To facilitate all of the above, we would suggest that the elders meet at least twice a month. Perhaps one meeting a month could be made sacred for only prayer and the other could be used more for problem solving and inviting people in to meet with the elders. Obviously, whenever elders meet, it is paramount that they pray!

We suggest that the senior elder should meet individually with the other elders (and spouses when possible) every one or two months to maintain and enhance relationship. The senior elder needs to see his relationship with the elders on the team as a top priority.

## Elders weekend retreat

The elders should make every effort to get away for a weekend retreat at least once a year to build relationships, pray and keep seeking the Lord for vision for the church. Being away from the home base has a way of generating team spirit and camaraderie in a relaxed setting. The best time might be the last part of the year, so the elders have a fresh sense of what God is speaking as they approach the task of setting the church budget for the next year.

Several of us have had the privilege of taking senior elders and eldership teams on a weekend retreat. Let us walk you through some guidelines that we feel will help a senior elder serve his team in a powerful, life-giving way.

Make an outline for the time away with your team. Second, prepare a list of prayer requests and concerns for an extended time of prayer. Third, begin praying. Pray in the Spirit, praise, worship (sing acappella, to a guitar, or a worship CD), pray loudly and with enthusiasm, pray silently and on your face before God. Bring with you a map of your area, your county, your state or region and pray over it. Pray over a map of the world. Pray over your missionaries, pray over prospective areas where you want to plant new churches in the future and pray over cell groups. Pray over every area of the church—the children, youth, worship, small groups and outreaches. Pray, pray, pray!

Next, take time for evaluations. Evaluate every ministry of the church. Ask yourselves, "Where are we being effective and where do we need to become more effective?" Consider going through the "senior elder and elder evaluation questions" found in the Appendix, pages 216-218. When evaluating the past year, look at both the positive and negative. Discuss what is working and what needs improvement. This will keep the session from focusing too much on only the negative.

Following this time, take a close look at the finances and church budget. Are there any areas of concern? Take the time to evaluate all of the equipping ministry taking place. Is it forming the life of Christ in the church family, equipping them for service?

Begin to turn the corner, after the time of prayer and evaluation, to vision. Where is God taking you as a team, as a local church? What do you need to bring to a close, and what or who do you need to utilize for future equipping?

Close your retreat by giving anyone an opportunity to share reflections about your time together. Then have a time of prayer and communion. Consider feasting together after a time of fasting.

## Elders must have the authority to make financial decisions

The old detective's adage "to follow the money" holds true here. Where the money goes the heart goes and visa versa. There is no doubt about it: how the money is spent will dictate what the vision of the church will be. So, if the elders do not have final decision-making powers over the finances of the church, they will not be able to lead the church effectively. We see in the New Testament at the end of Acts 11 that the elders were responsible for the finances.

> During this time some prophets came down from Jerusalem to Antioch. One of them, named Agabus, stood up and through the Spirit predicted that a severe famine would spread over the entire Roman world. (This happened during the reign of Claudius.) The disciples, each according to his ability, decided to provide help for the brothers living in Judea. This they did, sending their gift to the elders by Barnabas and Saul (Acts 11:27-30).

When there was an offering taken for the church in Judea, it was sent to the elders to decide what to do with it. In the New Testament, the elders had financial decision-making powers.

The elders should set the budget for the church because this sets the vision for the church. This does not mean that the elders should write all the checks and read every bank statement. The execution of the elder's budget can be delegated to others in the church who serve in a deacon role by carrying out the elders' vision. Clearly, for any major financial decisions in the church such as building projects, we highly recommend that the elders receive input from the congregation before any final decisions are made.

## Elders must talk unashamedly about finances

Have you noticed that many times when the topic of money or finances comes up in church settings, there seems to be an icy chill that spreads across the group? Have you ever wondered why it seems like every time an offering is taken, you feel like you want to quickly exit the building? Why do we feel this way? What is this uncomfortable feeling? Is it from God or the devil?

We have come to believe this icy chill is not from God. It has been identified as the spirit of poverty—sent from hell to strip the church of one of the tools it needs and God wants to supply (money).

In his book *Prosperity with a Purpose,* Brian Sauder, states that *El Shaddai,* the God of more than enough, wants us to prosper.

> Money or material things are simply tools that the Father has given us to accomplish our mission...Giving has the power to break the back of materialism. As long as we teach, exhort and practice giving, the nasty hands of materialism will never be able to get a grip on us.[5]

Brian goes on to say that money is simply a tool God gives us to complete the job He has assigned us to do. Our job is called the *Great Commission.* If we closely examine the Bible, we find it talks about natural riches as well as spiritual riches. What good are all the spiritual riches in the world if we don't have the natural riches to get them to the people who need them?

The church has to change its way of thinking in the area of finances, and the elders need to lead the way. How will our thinking change? By comparing our thoughts to the Word of God. We need to renew our minds to embrace what the scriptures say about finances. Money is a good thing that God wants to give us to help accomplish His mission for us.

Elders need to unashamedly teach about tithing, giving and offerings. This topic should be taught on a regular basis at least four times a year. Elders must not allow the people of God to suffer under the spirit of poverty. If elders don't teach the biblical truths of financial blessings, the people will not walk in them and the church will suffer financial lack. The people of God should be given regular opportunities to give offerings in addition to their regular tithes.

## Elders should not set their own salary level

Senior elders or elders who receive a salary from the church should never set their own salary level. A "support guidelines group" can be selected from mature Christians in the church. This group's function is to establish and review salaries, pension plans, and other benefits. Their research should include investigating other local church salary packages and local business salaries, as well as gaining knowledge of the average income levels within their geographical area. It can also be helpful for some of the "support guideline members" to have business experience. However, we would not recommend that everyone who serves on this group be a business professional because those outside the business world might bring an important perspective that business professionals will not have.

This group should also consider input from the apostolic oversight of the local church in setting the senior elder's salary. The senior elder needs to be involved in the process of evaluating performance and setting salary for staff members of the church. The apostolic oversight provides an outside court of appeal if any financial problems or irregularities occur. In addition, we wholeheartedly recommend that each local church have a financial review performed each year.

### Questions for discussion
1. Why is functioning in unity so important for a leadership team?
2. In what ways do the members of your team feel valued and secure?
3. How do healthy elders relate to church finances?

[1]  Philip Keller, *A Shepherd Looks at Psalm 23,* (Minneapolis, Minnesota: World Wide Publications, 1970), p. 35.
[2]  Exodus 28:36
[3]  Romans 16:17; 1 Corinthians 1:10
[4]  Tom Marshall, *Understanding Leadership,* (Chichester, England: Sovereign World Ltd., 1991). p. 104.
[5]  Brian Sauder, *Prosperity With a Purpose,* (Ephrata, PA: House to House Publications, 2003).

# The Elders Team: Called to be Armor Bearers

9

An article printed in "Focus on the Family" *Physician* magazine called attention to the loneliness and discouragement of church leaders: 80% of church leaders and 84% of their spouses feel discouraged or deal with feelings of depression, while more than 40% of church leaders and 47% of their spouses suffer from feelings of burnout.[1]

David was a righteous man "after God's own heart" and the anointed king of Israel. Yet even as God's chosen, he found himself one day crying out to the Lord from the dark cave of Adullam (Psalms 142:1-7). The battle before him was greater than he felt he could handle. It seemed like a desperate and hopeless situation, and there was no one at his right hand to help him. There was no one to stand with him. David felt as if no one cared for him.

This is the picture of many church leaders today. They feel like they stand alone, and they are discouraged. There is a feeling that they are in church leadership by themselves, and there is no one who feels what they feel, who hurts the way they hurt, and who bleeds the way they bleed.

Fortunately, it was never part of God's plan for a leader to stand alone. The wonderful blessing of a healthy team of elders is the way it provides the senior elder with close working relationships. The other elders on the team rally around the senior elder to surround, serve and help him bear the responsibilities of leadership. The Lord is raising up teams who will stand alongside their leader and not shrink back. These teams are willing to go to the battle and not break rank nor be intimidated by the odds against them.

On May 31, 1889, in Johnstown, Pennsylvania, relentless rains poured down. The old South Fork Dam was at risk, and the telegraph officer at the top of the mountain could only hope the people of Johnstown could hear his repeated warnings through the heavy rains. At 3:10 PM, the dam broke. A wall of water, 60 feet high, traveling at 40 miles per hour, swept down through the valley, taking with it everything in its path.

The wall of water took everything, that is, until it came to the church on Franklin Street. There it split into two walls of water, and the five buildings standing behind the church were undamaged along with the church which stood firm.

Most of Conemaugh Valley's history ended on that tragic Friday when over 2,209 people died. It was a horrible tragedy.

Nevertheless, it is a fascinating fact that the church building and the ones behind it still stood strong. This is a picture of a team of elders holding on and not breaking rank. An elder and his team can withstand the force and pressures they face when together they stand firm. They are committed and sold out to the vision of their church and the people to whom the Lord has called them. The senior elder does not have to cry out, "Does anyone care for me?" He will have those who stand with him as armor-bearers, burden-bearers and cup-bearers to bear the load. They will help him remain steadfast in times of trouble, uncertainty and seemingly insurmountable odds.

## Three "bearers" that every senior elder needs and successful senior elder has[2]
## Armor-bearer

An armor-bearer is a servant, one who supports his leader by helping the leader's God-given vision come to pass. He is called to walk alongside his leader as a humble, faithful, trustworthy and loyal servant. In many ways he is like the shield, taking the hits of the enemy that were meant to kill the vision and plans of his leader. He is an intercessor who stands in the gap for his leader. A motivating force in a armor-bearer's life is one of compassion. David became Saul's armor-bearer because he loved him: "David came to Saul and entered his service. Saul liked him very much; and David became one of his armor-bearers" (1 Samuel 16:21).

We find a great story of an armor-bearer's loyalty and support in 1 Samuel 14. The Israelites were outnumbered, inadequately armed and discouraged. The Philistines had assembled their army to attack with its 3,000 chariots, 6,000 horsemen, and soldiers like the sands of the sea. Jonathan spotted a Philistine outpost on a cliff and turned to his armor-bearer and said, "Come, let's go over to the outpost of those uncircumcised fellows. Perhaps the Lord will act on our behalf" (1 Samuel 14:6).

Notice how Jonathan phrases that challenge. "Perhaps" the Lord will act. What a seemingly foolish thing to do—attack on a hope that "maybe" the Lord would intervene. But Jonathan was fearless. He saw the threat and was up for the challenge. Would his armor-bearer follow him? Would he leave the protection of their six hundred man army and venture out alone to attack a Philistine garrison in support of his leader?

The armor-bearer's unselfish answer shows he was thinking of Jonathan and not himself, "Do all that you have in mind," his armor bearer said. "Go ahead; I am with you heart and soul" (v. 7). The armor-bearer stood by his leader and committed his life to a divine "maybe," and the rest is history. The armor-bearer climbed up the cliff after Jonathan, and they started killing the Philistines. Suddenly panic struck the entire army and the ground shook. The Philistines were in confusion and started killing each other with the Israelites chasing them in hot pursuit!

A leader of a team needs armor-bearers who are willing to follow him into battle, supporting him fully. The resulting teamwork of a leader and his faithful supporters causes a mighty impact. The armor-bearer did not merely watch Jonathan's back defensively. He offensively fought side by side with Jonathan. It is probable that Jonathan only knocked some of his opponents down; the armor bearer, in support of Jonathan,

*The Biblical Role of Elders for Today's Church*

had to finish the job. Eldership teams that march into the fray with their senior elder, supporting him fully, are successful teams.

A leader does not necessarily need to actually hear the words, "I am with you heart and soul," but he does need to see them put it into practice. Ted Walker, senior elder of Christian Life Church in North Little Rock, Arkansas, says that when he mentions to his eldership team that there is a prayer walk in their city with several other churches, his team does not say, "Good idea, we are behind you, brother," and then they forget to show up. All the leaders turn out to show support. If Ted says, "We are going to meet to pray at 9 PM Saturday night for the Sunday service," he simply shows up, and sure enough, all the leaders appear. Their actions show they are loyal armor-bearers, willing to serve their leader and rally around him. They can be counted upon for the battle.

Being loyal armor bearers means the team respects and supports their leader. It does not mean they cannot question him. Every senior elder knows that in order to grow spiritually, he must conscientiously welcome suggestions and criticisms from the team. One elder noted that "what makes Christians effective in the ministry as individuals or as a group is not the strengths that they have on their own, but the weaknesses that cause them to rely totally on God and others. It is not the power that we have within us, but the power that He places within us that makes us effective warriors for the kingdom of God."

A team of elders must be willing to go through times of testing. The pervading attitude should be, "We look forward to seeing how the Lord will bring us through this one! It will be exciting and we will grow and be strengthened as we walk through this test."

Leaders are looking for those who stay with them when the going gets rough. In 1 Samuel 30, David and his men faced a devastating personal loss of their families while they were at battle. The men who had pledged themselves to David turned against him. But David "strengthened himself in the Lord," and God told him what to do.

Sometimes it may seem as if all hell has broken loose against a senior elder and his team. The team that will stand is the team that rallies behind their leader even when the situation is bleak.

## Burden bearers

Senior elders need help from their team and others in the church to fulfill God's will for their congregation. They need others to help them bear the load.

A story is told about Dr. Albert Schweitzer at Lambarene, on the banks of the Ogowe River. It was about noon and the sun was beating down mercilessly as a group walked up a hill with Dr. Schweitzer. Suddenly the doctor strode across the slope to where an African woman was struggling with a load of wood for the cooking fires. The 85-year-old doctor took the entire burden and carried it up the hill for the relieved woman. When they reached the top of the hill, someone asked Dr. Schweitzer why he did things like that, implying that in that heat and at his age he should not. Albert Schweitzer pointed to the woman and said simply, "No one should have to carry a burden like that alone." [3]

King Solomon knew it was God's will to build the temple, but he also realized he could not do it by himself. In 2 Chronicles 2:7-10, King Solomon appointed burden-bearers to build the temple. These people were skilled in doing a job so that the king's vision could be completed.

As a leader, Moses was trying to carry his burden alone. It took the wise insight of his father-in-law, Jethro, to point out the fact that others "will bear the burden with you" (Exodus 18:22).

A burden-bearer, whether he is another elder on the team or someone in the congregation, is one who notices when the senior elder is distressed or overworked and helps to relieve those burdens. He sees when a wall of the church building needs paint or offers to comfort family members when a member of the church is having surgery and the senior elder is out of town. A burden-bearer truly understands that when we "carry each other's burdens," we fulfill the law of Christ (Galatians 6:2). They are the unsung heroes who work behind the scenes to serve. A burden-bearer's great pleasure comes from serving Jesus by serving the senior elder.

*The Biblical Role of Elders for Today's Church*

A burden-bearer goes to the Lord first in prayer for personal problems and situations in the church before he even bothers the senior elder about it. He knows that he and the rest of the people in the church must be taught to "carry their own load" (Galatians 6:5). Depending upon a senior leader to solve all the problems will result in a weak church. Elders on the team know they are ministers as do the people in the congregation.

## Cup bearers

Nehemiah was a cup-bearer to the King of Persia (Nehemiah 1:11). Cup-bearers were like modern day butlers who anticipated the king's every need.

Cup-bearers were so attentive to the king's needs that they even endangered their own lives to serve him. A cup-bearer tasted the food before it was served to the king to be sure it was not poisoned. He put his life on the line to help meet the physical needs of his king. He was the most trusted person in the king's court.

They were the kind of men found in 2 Samuel 23:15. King David mentioned that he longed for a drink of water from the water at the well near the gate of Bethlehem. The problem was the Philistines' garrison was at Bethlehem. This did not deter the three men (cup-bearers) who overheard King David's desire. They broke through the Philistine lines and brought back the water for David. They sacrificed greatly so the physical needs of the king would be met.

When David was handed the water, he refused to drink it. He was so humbled by the nature of the men's sacrifice that he poured it out on the ground before the Lord. He knew that their sacrifice was more than just serving his need for a drink of water. They had crossed a boundary of serving. David, in his wisdom, knew he needed to give a sacrifice in holy gratitude to the Lord.

## Ten keys to building trust on a team of elders

How do people become bearers? On what is the relationship built? One of the key relational foundations for a strong team to develop is trust. Below are some indicators of how trust between team members is built.

## 1. Elders build trust by knowing they are called to the right place

In John 6, Jesus spoke a message to those following Him that caused many to desert Him. They just could not understand it. Many said, "This is a hard teaching. Who can accept it?" (verse 60). These are words He spoke: "I tell you the truth, unless you eat the flesh of the Son of Man and drink his blood, you have no life in you. Whoever eats my flesh and drinks my blood has eternal life, and I will raise him up at the last day" (John 6:53-53). After many disciples had left Him, Jesus turned to the Twelve and asked if they wanted to leave too. Peter gives his famous response, "Lord, to whom shall we go? You have the words of eternal life" (verse 68).

One of the very first steps in building trust on a team of elders is to know *the Lord has called you there* and to know *to whom you are called.* Peter had settled in his mind that He was called to Christ. There was nowhere else to go. It didn't matter if someone else was having more success for the moment. It didn't matter that their numbers were diminishing. What mattered was that he was called and because he was called, he was not going anywhere!

## 2. Elders build trust by being committed to the work

It is not possible to be a lazy servant of Christ. Jesus said, "My Father is always at his work to this very day, and I, too, am working" (John 5:17). There is a story told of a pastor who went to his office early every morning and pulled on a pair of work boots. He wanted to remind himself that he was there to work hard and diligently.

Are you aware that it takes more commitment to play on a school's athletic team than it does to be a part of a local church? Ron's son, a football player, has to be at every practice preparing for the real game. He has to give it his all. For many weeks before the actual games start, it is practice, practice, practice. No excuses for tardiness or absenteeism. Once games start, he has to be on time, fully suited up, and full of energy and team spirit. Everyone on the team has to be committed to the team or they get cut from it. He does all this, regardless of whether he knows he will play at a particular game.

Now, what if we used that same measuring stick in the church? What if we would say that to be a part of our church, you have to be at every pre-service prayer meeting, every Friday night prayer, every single service that is open for the congregation?

"Wait just a minute," you say, "church is not a football team and you cannot demand commitment."

You are exactly right! However, when you made Jesus the Lord of your life, you gave Him your whole life. When the Lord "planted" you in the church you are attending, you committed yourself to its vision and values, as well as to the leaders of that church. As a member of the entire team, you are committed to faithfully carrying out its mission.

Commitment cannot be demanded, but you should be willing to give it. Commitment and faithfulness to our local church should cause us to want to pay a price to be there. Elders lead by example in demonstrating their commitment.

## 3. Elders build trust by being loyal

Armor-bearers are both loyal and faithful. Loyalty and faithfulness go hand-in-hand. The combination of these two character traits is powerful.

Some people are one or the other, and that spells trouble. A dog may be your most loyal friend and faithfully greet you as you enter your home after a day at work. But if he responds to everyone with that same loyalty, he will allow a burglar to come in your house and take everything you have! A dog like this is loyal, but not faithful.

A team member can faithfully show up at every meeting and event of the church, but if he is not loyal enough to jump into the fray when spiritual battles need to be fought in the church, he will allow Satan to tamper with God's people and his leader. Elders' teams stand together in both loyalty and faithfulness. Elders are a team that loyally fight together against the enemy of the church. They do not fight with each other!

There is a story from the Vietnam War that tells of a platoon coming under a surprise attack. They fell back to a safe zone, but one of the men was wounded and lying out in the open field. His friend told the commanding officer, "I must get my friend."

The officer said, "I absolutely forbid you to run out there; it is too dangerous." But the young private ran off into the field, amidst the fire and explosions, to pull his best friend to safety. He arrived back to the safe zone with his friend, and the officer looked down at the man, now dead. He asked, "Well, private, was it really worth it?"

The young man, with tears in his eyes, responded, "Yes sir, it was. The last words he spoke to me were, 'I knew you would come.'"

This is the kind of loyalty God wants to place within a team of elders. The enemy will attack. Can we remain steadfast and loyal when the pressure is on?

## 4. Elders build trust by being disciplined

Elders will not be loyal or committed without discipline. Discipline is what keeps us going forward when our emotions are saying something different. Discipline is what causes us to "order our steps" and face our fears. Paul saw himself as a runner in a race and pressed on toward the goal of knowing Christ. He knew that he could be distracted by this world's temptations and worries, but he determined to press on. "Not that I have already obtained all this, or have already been made perfect, but I press on to take hold of that for which Christ Jesus took hold of me" (Philippians 3:12). Such determination is necessary to go where God has called us and to press into Him.

Elders press on to receive and achieve, to fulfill what Jesus Christ has destined for them. It will not just happen. There is a pressing into Christ and a pressing on in the Spirit to fulfill all that Christ has for them. It takes discipline. Discipline is what gets us up in the morning when our bodies say, "I need sleep." Discipline keeps us fasting when our stomachs cry for food. Discipline keeps our thoughts and emotions on track when circumstances around us would dictate otherwise.

## 5. Elders build trust by fighting the fight of faith

A warrior knows in his heart that he will not go anywhere in God without a fight! He is ready to fight the spiritual battles that must be fought to see God's kingdom advance in the church, in individual lives and in the community. Elders with warrior hearts are those who do not run away in the heat of battle. They can be counted upon to run straight into the battle. "He runs at me like a warrior" (Job 16:14). An elder knows that just as Jesus had to pay a price to advance the kingdom of God, he will pay a price too.

In Matthew 11:12, Jesus gives information about the nature of those who are committed to Christ. He says the kingdom of heaven is taken hold of by warrior-like people who turn from sin to Christ and continue to resist Satan in a fight of faith by the power of the Spirit: "...the kingdom of heaven has been forcefully advancing, and forceful men lay hold of it."

A senior elder can gratefully say to his fellow team leaders: "God has called me here, and He has called me to you. No matter how intense the spiritual battle gets, no matter what the devil throws at us, I will not leave. I will not leave even if I do not get my own way. I will not leave if I have unmet expectations. I can only leave if the Lord tells me to leave by giving me new marching orders, and if He does, it will be confirmed by others around me." This kind of elder knows that if God has called him, he will succeed and fulfill God's vision, plan and purpose.

## 6. Elders build trust by getting to know the senior elder's heart

It is easy to trust someone when you know his heart (the opposite is also true). Trust does not mean "performance-based trust" that is contingent on the senior elder not making any mistakes. Trust is when the team believes that to the best of the senior elder's ability, he will do what is right and obey God.

The importance of knowing a leader's heart, even though it seems like he may be making a mistake, unfolds in 2 Kings 10. Jehu was the King of Israel and determined to kill Ahab's descendents and eradicate Baal worship during his reign. He meets with Jehonadab and asks him if he is in one accord with him in his mission. Jehonadab replies in the affirmative. Jehu takes his hand and helps him into his chariot and says, "Come with me and see my zeal for the Lord" (verse 16). He predicts that his zeal for the Lord will rid the land of idol worshipers.

Later, however, Jehu calls the people together and seems to contradict himself. He says, "Ahab served Baal a little; Jehu will serve him much" (verse 18). If Jehonadab had heard those words, he would have had reason to question Jehu's integrity.

Jehu then summons all the prophets of Baal to assemble in one place and offer a great sacrifice to Baal. Now if Jehonadab had not known Jehu's heart, he may have decided that Jehu had "gone off the deep end!" Why would he say one thing but do another? Jehu's true motive, however, was to ambush the prophets of Baal, which he did, destroying the worshipers and temple of Baal in one sudden attack!

When we know someone's heart, we do not misunderstand his words and actions. When another person comes with an accusation that is totally out of character for the person we trust, we believe the best. One elder says it like this, "Because I really know my fellow elders, I can quiet the accusing voice of the devil when he tries to play with my emotions and lie to me about someone's motives on the team." Getting to know each other's hearts takes time. That is why it is important for a team to go beyond the normal "church business" and spend some quality time together as leaders. Elders need to get to know each other's hearts.

## 7. Elders build trust by communication

Elders build trust by sharing with each other. Senior elders encourage their team members to communicate their dreams and aspirations. The team gets to know each other when they share exactly what they are thinking. When the senior elder communicates clearly and honestly, the rest of the team learns to trust the senior elder because they know they are getting all of him.

Elders do not keep hidden hurts as ammunition that goes off when the wrong buttons are pushed. This builds mistrust and causes others on the team to question whether the senior elder is being completely honest.

Senior elders do not take the ideas and dreams of others and fashion them into their own without giving due credit. The team will begin to withhold their thoughts and ideas for fear the senior elder will take advantage of them. Senior elders are careful to build a solid infrastructure of trust and confidence with clear communication so that the team can walk in unity.

## 8. Elders build trust by walking in unity

The true test of any relationship is, "What do we do when the pressure is on?" Can we stay put under fire? Unity is really a decision to "be one." It comes from the perspective of thinking "we are one" versus "we need to agree to be one."

Most people think in terms of working a problem out with another person in order to have unity. But when a believer makes Jesus the Lord of his life, the Bible teaches that he becomes one with Him and also with every other believer. So when a believer understands Ephesians 4:3 which says, "Make every effort to keep the unity of the Spirit through the bond of peace," he realizes that he is in unity already; that is why he can work through the problems in order to maintain what is already there.

The corporate anointing increases as the church, and ultimately the team of elders, walks together in unity. In wartime, nations put aside their differences to fight the bigger enemy. We have seen this enacted with the tragic terrorist events of September 11, 2001, in the United States. If nations who disagree on major things can lay aside their differences, how much more should people in the church lay aside their pet doctrines and minor differences to fight the larger enemy! When we are in settings where unity is threatened, we must ask ourselves this question: "Are we really trying to help others grow in their relationship with Jesus Christ or are we just trying to get them to see things our way?"

Jesus prayed in John 17:21-23 that we would be one just as the Father and He are one. Jesus' prayer was for us is to be in unity with one another.

The blessing the Lord commands over those who choose to walk in unity is life. The blessings of the life in God will be poured out on the team. They will find that the anointing of God increases as they walk in unity. Not only will their anointing as a team increase, but the corporate anointing of the congregation will increase as well.

## 9. Elders build trust by putting others first

First and most importantly, an elder loves others with the unconditional love found in John 13:34-35. His shepherd's heart goes far beyond the Golden Rule of "doing unto others as you would have them do unto you."

When Jesus walked with His disciples on this earth, He taught them the Word of God along with the "Golden Rule." However, just before He left, He said He was giving a new commandment.

Jesus' new commandment was to "love others as I have loved you." The new commandment challenges and moves us far beyond the old commandment of loving others like we want to be loved. Now we are commanded to treat others as Christ has loved and treated us. This takes us to a whole new level. It moves us beyond our personal preferences and causes us to esteem others as more important than ourselves. At this point it is not what is important for me, it is what is best for the team. How can the team advance into the greater things of God?

With the old commandment, you are still the center of your universe, and everything depends on *your* human capacity to love. When you move away from being the center of your universe, you are challenged to love unconditionally like Jesus loves. An elder will unselfishly put others first (Philippians 2:2-7).

An elder keeps focused with his eyes on the vision (1 Corinthians 3:1-4). The main goal is not to preserve life or position; it is to advance the kingdom of God. It is not the building of our own ministries that should consume us; it is advancing God's kingdom. Floyd McClung wrote an article on "passion" that stirred our hearts. He said, "I can tell when I have lost my passion for Jesus when I make decisions based upon what it will cost me vs. the glory that Christ will receive."

One elder put it succinctly when he said, "I am here on earth to see the kingdom of God advance. I am part of a leadership team that desires to see our church fulfill its God-given mandate to plant churches. I am sold out to that vision and can trust the others on the team because they have taken their eyes off themselves and have the same purpose. I am not building my own ministry. I am working to see God build His kingdom and stretch forth His habitations. I want to see lives changed, and I can only give myself wholeheartedly to that task when I take my eyes off myself."

## 10. Elders build trust by not comparing themselves to others on the team

God requires different things of different people. Elders build trust on the team when they do not compare themselves to others on the team. Keeping mental notes of successes and failures of others on the team begins to sow seeds of unhealthy competition. Selfish striving, jealousy and mistrust are born in that seedbed of wrongly focused thoughts and emotions.

According to 2 Corinthians 10:5, we need to "take captive every thought," by bringing all our thoughts into alignment with God's will. In "Special Ops" training in the military, trainees perform special water operations to train the mind and body to respond in that element. To train in the water, their hands are tied behind their backs and they jump into water that is over their heads. Two things are learned in this training exercise. 1) It cures the fear of water because you learn how to control your breathing by coming up for air at the right times. 2) It teaches you how to control your mind. If your mind tells you that you need air, you will need air. If you can control your mind by focusing on the task in front of you, you can go much longer without air.

Elders should go through the kind of "Special Ops" training that teaches us to allow the Holy Spirit to control our minds. If we could allow the Holy Spirit to control our minds and emotions, we could eliminate a lot of headaches and heartaches. Romans chapter eight teaches this principle clearly by insisting that the Holy Spirit within us must control our mind and emotions. Change occurs as the Spirit overrules our flesh. When we allow the Holy Spirit to control us, we will not be tempted to compare ourselves with each other.

Paul says in 2 Corinthians 10:12 that he did not dare to compare himself with other leaders like some false prophets were doing. "We do not dare to classify or compare ourselves with some who commend themselves. When they measure themselves by themselves and compare themselves with themselves, they are not wise." Healthy elders know comparison is not wise. They will build trust on their teams by welcoming each team member's gifts as unique and useful for the team.

## Questions for discussion

1. What does an armor-bearer do on a team of elders? Burden bearer? Cup bearer?
2. Describe ways in which you can build trust on an elders' team.
3. How can you be an armor-bearer in your local church?

---

[1] *Physician* magazine, (Focus on the Family, September/October 2000).
[2] Much of the information on "armor bearers, burden bearers and cup bearers" is gleaned from a message that Ted Walker, senior elder of Christian Life Church in Arkansas (one of DCFI's partner churches), teaches on the subject.
[3] Woodrow Kroll, *Lessons on Living From Moses*, "Burden Bearers," (www.backtothebible.org).

# Resolving Conflict on the Team

**10**

You may have heard the story where one elder pulled out a gun and shot another elder at a church leadership meeting. Obviously this is an extreme example, but the truth is that conflict does happen as elders meet together. Elders will disagree with one another and have differences of opinion. These conflicts may leave individuals feeling hurt, ignored, confused, isolated or threatened. Unresolved conflict is compounded when members on the team become stubborn and selfish and refuse to love biblically. The Bible gives us insight into resolving such conflict. If handled biblically, conflict can become a real asset instead of a liability.

Conflict often provides a time for teams to get to know each other better as they reveal their unique ways of thinking and feeling. Healthy teams will encourage the members to air their opinions freely and openly. Disagreements are an opportunity to demonstrate understanding, respect and acceptance of others, thus strengthening relationships. Conflict allows us to recognize our deficiencies and invite the Lord to correct them as we grow spiritually.

Bill Hybels, pastor of Willow Creek Community Church in Illinois, admits that they expect conflicts on their church leadership teams.

> The popular concept of unity is a fantasyland where disagreements never surface and contrary opinions are never stated with force. We expect disagreement, forceful disagreement. So

instead of *unity*, we use the word *community*. The mark of community—true biblical unity—is not the absence of conflict. It's the presence of a reconciling spirit.[1]

Hybels gives the excellent advice of reminding leadership teams that they have a biblical responsibility "to take the high road of conflict resolution." The high road, of course means conflict resolution according to God's Word. The first step is going directly to the person involved (Matthew 18:15-17). Confronting and discussing the situation privately often gives an opportunity for quick resolution, lessening the chance for misunderstandings and animosity to grow.

Eldership teams need to be prepared to handle conflict because conflict will occur. Teams that realize conflicts are inevitable can persevere. God tells us that we will have problems in this world (Philippians 1:29). Unresolved conflict, however, will destroy teamwork.

 In this chapter, we take a look at steps we can take to resolve conflict on a team. If conflict cannot be resolved, in the next chapter, we will discuss further disciplinary measures that may be needed to bring healing and complete restoration to the individual(s).

## Areas of possible conflict on an elder team
## Who is in charge?

An egalitarian spirit on a team defines everyone as being equal in authority. This is simply not true. We believe it is essential that every team have a leader.

First of all, as elders meet, God is in charge! The team must cooperate with the dealings of God as He molds and prepares each one to grow into Christlikeness. Earlier, we talked about the head, shoulders and body principle of leadership where one leader acts as the leader for the team. He is the "head," although all the while being firmly attached to the shoulders (the team) and the body (the congregation).

A team needs to clearly understand this headship within the position of senior elder and cooperate with it. 1 Chronicles 11 lists David's mighty men. These men were powerful warriors having accomplished

*The Biblical Role of Elders for Today's Church*

great exploits in battle. The Bible doesn't indicate that David was a more powerful and fierce warrior than the other mighty men. There were probably better fighters on David's team, but one thing is clear: David was called to lead that group of warriors, and each of the warriors was convinced of it. Senior elders are the leaders and equippers on the team, even though some of the team-players may be much more gifted. A senior elder does not have to be the best at everything, but he must be respected as the leader.

Selfishness on teams will lead to power struggles. Power struggles endanger the unity of the team and eventually trickle down to the congregation.

## Vision

Vision for a local church must come from the senior elder and team. A new church must take the time it needs to know and understand what their vision is. Everyone on the team should wholeheartedly agree with the vision and believe it is the vision God has given them for the church. If the vision for your church is not clear, you will probably eventually have conflict on your leadership team.

As leaders of an international group of churches, our team begins praying for vision every June for the year to come. By September, the vision is finalized, and in October we begin working on the budgets. God-given vision takes time. We must be hearing from the visionary of visionaries—the Lord.

Vision is a most critical matter in the life of a church. Habakkuk 2:2-3 says,

> Write down the revelation and make it plain on tablets so that a herald may run with it. For the revelation awaits an appointed time; it speaks of the end and will not prove false. Though it linger, wait for it; it will certainly come and will not delay.

Vision is always about the future. It is about something not yet achieved or experienced. It is the stretching of reality beyond anything you are currently experiencing. When vision does not materialize as you expect it, sometimes frustration develops around that lack of realization of the vision. James 5:8-11 gives us four things to keep in mind while vision is developing and unfolding.

<sup>8</sup> You too, **be patient** and **stand firm**, because the Lord's coming is near.

<sup>9</sup> **Don't grumble against each other**, brothers, or you will be judged. The Judge is standing at the door!

<sup>10</sup> Brothers, as an example of patience in the face of suffering, take the prophets who spoke in the name of the Lord.

<sup>11</sup> As you know, we consider blessed those who have persevered. You have heard of Job's **perseverance** and have seen what the Lord finally brought about. The Lord is full of compassion and mercy.

Verse 8 tells us to be patient. The nature of vision is beyond reality. That's why it is called vision; it is forward thrusting, compelling, and pulling us into the future of what the Lord has for us. Elders on a team must be patient with each other and with the Lord as they prayerfully seek His vision. You must wait for it, and take the time needed to formulate a clear mental portrait of where God is taking the church. Even if it takes a long time for it to become a reality, patience waits until the timing is right. Impatience has resulted in the premature birth of many visions—before they are developed properly or fully.

The second part of verse 8, tells us to "stand firm." The New King James version says "establish your heart." The team must be of one mind, not only patient for the vision to be revealed, but standing firm and believing that the vision is indeed going to come to pass. Abraham stood firm and believed God when it seemed impossible, according to natural circumstances, for the vision of Issac's birth to be fulfilled. Because Abraham stood firm, it was accounted to Him as righteousness.

Settle the vision in your heart. If the Lord spoke it, it will come to pass. Sometimes you may not personally see the vision to its completion, but you will witness its beginning.

Verse 9 says, "Don't grumble against each other." When waiting for vision to be fully realized, the tendency is to try to figure out what is taking it so long. Our next tendency is to try and place blame on something or someone, "This vision is not becoming a reality because so and so is not praying enough or not pulling their weight." When elders begin to grumble against each other, the enemy can really come in with strife and division.

Verse 11 tells us to "persevere." We must hold on, keep believing and keep trusting. Just as the Lord's intentions for Job were fully realized because he endured, so your vision will become a reality if you persevere and do not lose heart. You will reap if you faint not!

## New elders added to the team

When new elders are added to a team, other members can feel threatened by the new gifts they bring to the table. The additional personalities and leadership styles may bring out areas of insecurity even in an established team.

Ron served exclusively with a senior elder for a couple of years in a local church. They were a team of two, and their bond became strong as they walked through the joys, trials and tribulations of the growing pains of their church. Soon growth necessitated the addition of another elder to the team to help with the leadership needs of the church.

Before long, and much to Ron's chagrin, he noticed a disturbing phenomenon invading his thoughts and feelings. If he noticed the senior elder talking to the new elder and he was not included, Ron felt left out. He wondered, "Shouldn't I be in on that conversation? Maybe they could use my input? Why didn't they ask me to join in?" Finally, Ron realized that he was allowing his insecurities to get the best of him. He realized that the new elder was an asset to the team and brought new insights and gifts to the team.

Ron made a decision. He chose to reach out to the Lord and receive His unconditional love. Before long, Ron experienced God's peace and security in the situation. It was a maturing time for Ron as an elder.

## Unmet expectations

Times of conflict give the opportunity to clarify our expectations of others. We may need to modify our thinking based on our expectations of others on the team. We must guard our hearts from picking up an offense when our personal expectations are not met.

As senior elders, we must be careful of what we speak. What happens if we speak vision over people's lives concerning what we see in them, and it does not come to pass in the time frame they expected? They will be hurt and disappointed. Proverbs 13:12 tells us, "Hope deferred makes the heart sick." We need to be careful that we do not set in motion expectations that cannot be met and lead to conflict.

## Communication

Conflict gives the opportunity to define our rules of interaction in an attempt to strengthen our relationships. Teams must learn how to air feelings openly and freely. True communication gives the opportunity to draw close to one another in intimate self-disclosure. Clear information is a key to making proper and wise decisions. We can recognize our deficiencies and brainstorm about ways in which to correct them. It is a time to talk and communicate openly and honestly, reducing hostility, anger, or misunderstanding in relationships so we can be challenged to grow.

C. Peter Wagner says, "Whatever is assumed will be forgotten." An eldership team cannot know by osmosis what the others are thinking. It is important that each elder on the team speaks what God is saying to him. In this way, the entire team can get a better picture. If the team always agrees with the senior elder, he does not need them. He can agree with himself! All the elders must speak what God is saying to them so that the senior elder can get a more complete picture of what the Lord is saying.

## Personality differences

Every team should carry out some type of individual and team personality profile to understand how everyone's unique personality has been created in God's image. Understanding the diversity in personalities will help in understanding each other's strengths and weaknesses. We have found the *DISC Relationship Profile*[2] and Bobb Biehl's *Team Profile*[3] to be very helpful.

When we are convinced that God has called each person as a member of the team, we are also convinced that each one has something unique to offer to the team. There can be no competition, because others' gifts and personalities bring wholeness to the team. When we understand others' strengths and weaknesses, we can build as a team, capitalizing on strengths and providing support where others are weak.

## Failure and mistakes

Failures and mistakes will occur on a team. All men and women of God are first of all men and women. Everyone, including servant leaders, will make mistakes. The question is, "Can I handle your mistakes the same way I want you to handle mine?" We can either rise up in judgment or bow down in intercession. The choice is ours as to how we will respond.

The founder of Operation Mobilization, George Verwer, gives this sound advice to leaders having to deal with hurts and problems in the church, "Get more familiar with the pain, and don't let it be such a big deal." We are going to have pain. We are going to misunderstand and be misunderstood. We will be hurt at times. We will make mistakes. When we nurse our hurts and dwell on our mistakes, we allow ourselves to be hurt again and again. Although we must face the pain, we cannot dwell on it. Healthy leaders will forgive themselves and others so they can move on to the victory season of their lives. When we remain in the pain and the hurt, we will stunt our leadership growth. But when we face the pain and deal with the hurts, we will grow as leaders. It is our choice.

One of the key building blocks of the kingdom is relationships. It should not surprise us that the enemy very often attacks in these relational areas. Paul said in 1 Corinthians 6:7, "It is an utter failure that you go to court against one another." The world deals with problems by going to court and then passing judgment. The kingdom way is taking it to our heavenly Father, and trusting him to sort it out. God has ordained the family as the place to find healing for strained relationships. The local church family is therefore the place to do it. When elders are in conflict the apostolic leaders (or "fathers") the Lord has placed in their lives will help them work out the conflict.

## Control

When one or more team members try to manipulate or force the group in a certain direction, other members will sense their attempt at control. This kind of unhealthy control communicates to others that there is only one acceptable decision to make. If this pressure is resisted, comments surface like "Why are you holding up the process?" or "Everyone else seems to agree...." This is nothing short of manipulation and must be avoided. It is unhealthy and a dead-end-street for the team.

Each person's input must be freely allowed and accepted without judgment from others. No one person on the team is to be singled out as having less value or more value. Unhealthy control stems from insecure leaders. These are leaders who do not invite a difference of opinion because they interpret that difference as disagreement and disunity with their leadership. This closes the door for healthy dialogue and opens the door for ongoing control.

Leadership teams that do not practice healthy open communication will suffer from a high turnover rate. When ongoing, unhealthy control is felt and observed repeatedly, members will "jump ship" and move on.

## Steps to resolving conflict

Now that we have examined various areas of possible conflict, let's look at some systematic principles to resolve conflict. Remember, conflict is not necessarily bad. Elders are often strong leaders who have been fruitful in ministry and other areas of life because of boldly following what they believe is right.

Elders on a team should learn to defer to each other. They must patiently learn to listen, forgive, receive, rebuke, correct, and submit to each other. But even with these patterns in place, conflicts will occur. Sometimes the conflicts are about a specific subject, and other times they may be about personalities and needs. James 4:1 reveals that our conflicts come from our desires. We are wanting something different from what God desires. No matter what their origin, when conflicts occur, an elder's response should be to discern the reasons behind the conflict and the needs of those involved. The following principles apply to resolving conflict within a team of elders as well as resolving conflict in the local church.

## 1. Gain agreement that a problem exists

First, we must listen to each others' views on the subject at hand so it is clear as to what the conflict really is about. Define what issues are involved in the conflict and for whom it is a conflict. Pray for discernment to be able to detect any possible hidden issues in the disagreement.

In approaching the problem situation, we should begin by asking questions to draw the other(s) out. Statements tend to push people apart. Instead, ask questions. Try to understand the other's point of view. Try to find out what is behind each opinion. This helps another person see that you are willing to accept responsibility if you have contributed to the conflict.

Dialogue should use these kinds of phrases: "When you...I feel...because..." For example, "When you speak in that tone of voice, I feel like you are devaluing me because you are treating me like a child." This lets the other party know how you feel when the conflict is occurring.

Let the other person know how you react to the conflict. Listen for the feelings and emotions of the other and reflect on them with empathy and understanding. This creates an atmosphere of being cared for and listened to. It reduces defensiveness and focuses on the process involved rather than on the issues.

## 2. Identify the consequences up front

Ask yourself, "What is the worst possible consequence if this conflict is never addressed and resolved?" One thing you should be able to agree on immediately is that if the conflict goes unresolved, it may lead to divisions on the team. This helps warn the group that the conflict should not be allowed to fester or remain unresolved.

Paul addressed dissension in the early church by appealing for them to make an adjustment so that unity could prevail. He encouraged them to take immediate measures to repair their disagreements before strife tore them apart. "I appeal to you, brothers, in the name of our Lord Jesus Christ, that all of you agree with one another so that there may be no divisions among you and that you may be perfectly united in mind and thought" (1 Corinthians 1:10-12). When conflict is resolved, the team will reap the benefit of "perfect unity."

## 3. Pray together in faith asking the Lord for wisdom and solutions

Pray and ask the Lord to help you discern the reasons behind the conflict and what to do about it. "If any of you lacks wisdom, he should ask God, who gives generously to all without finding fault, and it will be given to him" (James 1:5). Praying is a powerful way of seeking agreement. Sometimes the solution is revealed during the prayer time.

Solutions do not always occur readily, but we have experienced the immediate, mighty power of prayer in solving a conflict before any other intervention had to be implemented. One time Ron was at the airport about to fly to another nation to help a church leadership team resolve a breakdown on the team. The flight was overbooked, and he was offered an additional free trip to the same location if he waited another day for the flight. Ron immediately got on the phone and called the eldership team. He suggested that he could come one day later than expected, and the next time, he would have a free ticket to visit them, if they could wait the extra day to see him.

Ron fully expected them to agree to a one-day delay, but instead they pleaded for him to come on the scheduled flight. They did not want another day to pass before they received some help. Ron sensed the urgency of the matter and realized that the Lord really wanted him to be there at the allotted time.

He arrived on schedule and immediately met with the team that was gathered in the senior elder's living room. Ron felt they needed to come into the presence of God before they discussed anything. It was a wonderful time! Some prophetic words were spoken, and it was clear that God was moving in people's hearts. Ron had instructed them ahead of time to write down their grievances. At the end of the prayer time he said, "Okay, you know why I'm here. Go ahead and read your concerns to me."

The first individual took out his paper, unfolded it, looked at it, and then refolded it. "In light of what just happened, these concerns are really insignificant," he said.

Why did he no longer see the "problem" as significant? It had "disappeared" in the light of God's wonderful grace and forgiveness! Sometimes what seems major and insurmountable, becomes minor in the presence of God.

The presence of the Lord brings situations into right perspective. It washes off the junk that the devil tries to attach to our spirits and sets us free to humbly forgive and defer to each other on a team.

## 4. Mutually agree on an action

Too often we spend most of our time on the conflict and forget to pursue possible solutions. Make a list of any proposed action (solution). Then pray over the list and pick an action (possible solution) that everyone agrees with. Believe in faith for a win-win solution as you approach possible solutions together. "Do two walk together unless they have agreed to do so?" (Amos 3:3). Will the proposed action allow a healing process to begin with no one being blamed? Does it provide for an end of the conflict with no recurrence? Will it result in better understanding by all parties with all feelings being respected? Remember there is power in unity, and when we can agree on an action, the blessings of "life" the Lord promises in Psalm 133 will flow into the situation.

## 5. Follow-up and measure progress

Allow for a period of evaluation to determine if the resolution is successful in averting similar conflict(s). Set a specific date to meet and review the resolution and determine to alter the resolution if it is not working.

Once a conflict has been resolved and all the parties feel like they have been listened to, cared for, and understood, then it is time to "let go" of the conflict. The team and individuals involved should put the conflict behind them and forget it. Don't bring it up in the future. God does not remember our sins to hold them against us, and we should do the same.

## 6. If the conflict cannot be resolved, appeal to authority

God is a God of restoration, and the goal of any conflict is always restoration. If an eldership team finds themselves at an impasse, an objective outsider can be brought in to help them resolve the issue. For an eldership team, those objective outsiders are the apostolic persons to whom they are accountable.

Watchmen Nee said, "Everywhere I go I look for someone who is in authority and I submit to him. You do not have authority unless you are under authority." Every person has authority and is under authority.

A conflict between elders that cannot be resolved goes to the apostolic leaders who give the eldership team oversight. They have the God-given authority to bring resolution. "Obey your leaders and submit to their authority. They keep watch over you as men who must give an account. Obey them so that their work will be a joy, not a burden, for that would be of no advantage to you" (Hebrews 13:17).

## Questions for discussion

1. Discuss the statement, "True biblical unity is not the absence of conflict; it's the presence of a reconciling spirit."
2. What kind(s) of conflict do you most often experience on your team of elders? How do you resolve it?
3. How is understanding and agreeing with the vision so critical to the life of the church?
4. What are the basic steps to resolving conflict?

1 *Building Church Leaders Notebook*, Theme 6: Handling Conflict, "Conflict Above Ground," an interview with Bill Hybels, (Christianity Today International).
2 *DISC Relationship Profile*, (Minneapolis, Minnesota: Carlson Learning Company, 1995).
3 Bobb Biehl, *Team Profile*, (Lake Mary, Florida: Masterplanning Group International, 1998).

# Discipline and Restoration

11

The Lord God we serve is a God who, through discipline, desires to reconcile and restore. As previously discussed when we looked at an elder's responsibilities, giving correction to church members is a vital part of the role that all church elders play. Church members need to be confronted when they are openly sinning.

Likewise, when it is the elders who need correction, those who are responsible to give oversight to the elders provide that correction. In this chapter we will discuss the need for discipline and how the Lord uses it as a means of His love, both for church members and elders.

## The need for discipline

Discipline is an essential element of healthy and vibrant growth. This is true in the natural realm as well as in the spiritual realm. We only need to look around us to see the fruit of undisciplined lives. Along with a lack of discipline comes a lack of personal integrity and responsibility. Rather than accepting responsibility for actions, there is a tendency to project blame and pass on responsibility.

This unwillingness to accept responsibility for our actions began in Genesis with Adam and Eve. "It was her fault!" "It was the serpent's fault!" It is always someone else's fault. The abdication of personal responsibility becomes a scapegoat for one's own weaknesses, thus allowing personal self-preservation and victimization of others to prevail.

There are various types of discipline, but they all have the same purpose—to shape our hearts and lives so that we are brought into conformity with the image and likeness of Jesus Christ.

Him we preach, warning every man and teaching every man in all wisdom, that we may present every man perfect in Christ Jesus. To this end I also labor, striving according to His working which works in me mightily (Colossians 1:28-29).

Mankind was designed by the Lord to have limits and for correction to occur when those limits are breached. We can easily see this in the Garden of Eden. Limits were both in the garden itself and in the command not to eat of the tree of the knowledge of good and evil. When the limits of the command were broken, discipline occurred. Christians are given freedom and limits. These freedoms within their corresponding limits are there to serve us in the discipline (shaping) of our lives.

The Father God has the right to discipline our lives because we are His. The fact that He disciplines us at all is a proof that we are His children (Hebrews 12:1-13). Since we are His children, we need to recognize, be thankful for and submit to His discipling (shaping) process.

The two general categories of discipline are *positive* discipline and *punitive* discipline. *Positive discipline* helps shape our hearts and lives to reflect the person and glory of Christ Jesus through correction, warning, reproof, rebuking, teaching, training in righteousness, prayer, personal ministry, deliverance, relational accountability, friendship and discipleship. *Punitive discipline* shapes our lives through direct application of governmental authority and consequence. This is the kind of discipline we are addressing here and specifically the discipline that must happen when biblical discipline of church leadership is required.

If the positive discipline of the Lord is not heeded, we will come under the punitive discipline of the Lord. Punitive discipline comes because of unbelief, rebellion, stubbornness, pride and hard-heartedness without repentance. It comes because the positive discipline of the Lord has not been heeded time and time again (Proverbs 5:12;15:10).

## Discipline for church members

In his book *Due Process*, Dan Juster states that if church members yield to behavior contrary to God's law and are not disciplined, it destroys love and community in that church.

> A congregation cannot allow one to profess to be a true believer in Jesus and yet live in gross sin or foster serious, basic, doctrinal error. Secondly, to allow these professing believers to remain connected to the congregation in a limited way, without real commitment, is to discourage the commitment of the whole community. It is time to build communities of faith that seek to reflect the kingdom ideals taught by Jesus and by the apostles. It is time to stop building a weekly rally as a substitute for true body life. A "McDonald's drive-in" religion is not biblical. A radio or television "church" is not a church![1]

Church members may need corrective discipline for any number of reasons. When a member enters into sin in a way that threatens his own spiritual life and those around him, he and the church must be protected. The church needs wise and decisive action from its leaders in such a case. In addition, other church members must understand their own role in the process of corrective discipline and restoration. Some areas that may require decisive discipline of church members are

- Unresolved offenses between members
- Drunkenness
- Moral impurity
- Extortion
- Covetousness
- Active, aggressive divisiveness
- Idolatry
- Racism
- Quarrelsome or abusive behavior
- Unbiblical divorce

Although much of the church and society in general seem to be operating in a mind-set opposed to restrictions and discipline, God expects the church to exercise discipline over its members. In so doing, it must guard against harshness and condemnation toward the one being disciplined. The general attitude on all sides must be aimed at restoration of the fallen member, purification of the church, and in the end, glorification and honor of God.

> Brethren, if a man is overtaken in any trespass, you who are spiritual restore such a one in a spirit of gentleness, considering yourself lest you also be tempted (Galatians 6:1).

Matthew 18:15-17 should be followed whenever accusations are brought against a church member. If Matthew 18 is violated and information is made public prematurely, 1 Corinthians 6 should be used. According to 1 Corinthians 6, a council of judges should hear the issues, evidence, testimony and render a decision. This should be done swiftly. Clear records should be kept of dates, times, evidence, discipline carried out, and specific sins confronted—but only if these records will be maintained with strict confidentiality.

God's leaders must use discipline wisely and firmly to help the church grow "in the midst of a crooked and perverse generation." Otherwise, the church will lose her ability to act as salt and light for a fallen world. We can all thank God that He has given us clear instructions in the Bible on how to deal with sinning church members and leaders.

## Biblical discipline of elders

The scriptures make it clear that God expects purity of heart and holy living in all of His people, especially those in church leadership due to their high visibility and responsibility. Elders are expected to live blameless lives, above reproach.

Biblical discipline of elders is an important part of church life and if administered properly will help keep the leaders of the church above reproach. It was once said that what the parents do in moderation, the children will do in excess. Leaders set the example for the flock. They must therefore live by the standards the Word of God puts forth.

Elders must be Christ-like in their life-styles and conduct. It is especially important because an elder is set apart for the spiritual task that the Lord has assigned to him. It is to be taken seriously. There is a higher standard for a leader. When elders fall into sin, the integrity of the church is called into public question.

No one rejoices when there is need for corrective discipline of an elder. However, it is a duty which must be performed when other, more positive methods to cause growth and maturity have failed. Most leaders would prefer not to discipline a fellow member of the team. Wherever the fault may lie, the need for corrective discipline is an indication of failure and disobedience, not of success.

Wise elders enter into a corrective discipline situation with compassion and understanding along with a firm resolve. While the need for such discipline may be disappointing, a positive outcome is at the heart of every elder's discipline. What elder does not want to see a fellow elder cleansed and restored into a protected, united, healthy church?

No elder's discipline should be initiated without the input or involvement of apostolic overseers. Outside accountability ensures that discipline is indeed needed and is administered correctly. In a natural family, parents help bring resolution and determine if one child needs discipline when a family feud occurs. Likewise, an apostolic overseer can objectively see the difference between sin issues and personality conflicts and help discern the appropriate course of action in regard to the discipline of an elder.

## Areas that may warrant discipline and restoration

There are various areas of sin an elder may commit that may require a process of discipline and restoration. These sins threaten his own spiritual life and those around him, and he and the church must be protected. They fall into the general categories of moral failure, irreconcilable disputes, disorderly conduct, and apostasy.

- Immorality / adultery
- Sexual abuse
- Sexual harassment
- Physical abuse
- Abuse of power (control, manipulation, intimidation)
- Misuse and abuse of finances
- Abuse of privileges
- Divisiveness
- Advocating heretical teaching
- Participation with an effort to subvert other leadership
- Slander, especially of leadership
- Marital discord / unbiblical divorce
- Intense family conflict
- Irreconcilable disputes
- Disorderly conduct
- Apostasy
- Racism

Some of these areas would require immediate removal from eldership if proven to be true, while others, if acknowledged and repented of, would not require removal but instruction, monitoring and careful observation to make sure that heart changes have been made.

In some areas, such as child abuse issues, we recommend that a church have a clear written policy dealing with both avoidance and protection as well as how to deal with any allegations.

After discipline, the goal should be to restore the fallen leader in "a spirit of gentleness, considering yourself lest you also be tempted" (Galatians 6:1-2 NKJ). With Christ, redemptive restoration can be achieved, ministries can be resurrected, and the church can move forward in health. Apostolic leadership will help the local church walk through the following steps.

## Process of discipline and restoration for leaders
### Discovery

Discovery happens when others become aware of the situation needing disciplinary attention. Fellow elders should  immediately seek the Lord for wisdom and discernment, praying for a full disclosure of the truth concerning all that is going on. There must be a commitment to openness, honesty, transparency, and genuine vulnerability by the over-sight team leading this process.

Even at this early stage, begin written documentation of the process and continue documentation until the end. Remember that this is a time of gathering information, not establishing guilt. This documentation is extremely important. It will help everyone recall the process accurately and it will provide, in writing, a history of the team's communication throughout the process. This is especially advantageous in situations where legal counsel becomes necessary or where the issue could be a crime.

## Assessment

Now is the time to start the process of discovering the truth concerning the issue(s). Pray that everything that needs to be uncovered is uncovered. You are not only looking for the truth of the situation but at the same time discerning the heart condition of those involved. This will be important to the judgment process.

This is the information and fact-finding process. Look for the truth and accurate facts, not senses or suspicions, or emotion and accusations.

## Judgment

At this point, take all assessments and information into consideration with prayer and fasting and make a judgment. This includes the heart issues as well as the specific nature of the events involved. By "heart issue" we mean, "Is the person teachable and walking in humility, admitting his failure?" Or, is he walking in pride and/or denial? Is his heart arrogant and hardened, or is it repentant and pliable?

Seek outside legal counsel if needed. Consider other available resources to assist in dealing with the issue redemptively as you prepare for the discipline process.

It is appropriate to now render a clear decision. If it is discerned that discipline is necessary, move to the next step.

## Consequences

Biblical standards require that a leader "be removed from leadership and undergo a process of restoration and counseling," according to Dan Juster.

> To simply say, "I repent, it's under the blood and God has forgiven; I am continuing in leadership," makes a mockery of biblical standards. Yes, God forgives. However, a truly repentant person is concerned more for the glory of the Name of God. He gladly receives discipline so that God's Name might be honored. The truly repentant will not see his gifts and calling as more important to God than the issue of upholding His standard of holiness and thereby glorifying His Name.[2]

Lay out the strategy of the discipline process. What action is warranted? Specific people should be assigned to work through the discipline process. Follow through on the discipline with updates to those responsible.

Church discipline is a lot of work, and all of that work must flow out of a heart that is full of Christ's love. We must be committed to seeing God's redemptive purposes fulfilled in each other. Remember that the goal of any discipline is healing and restoration, not punishment or humiliation. It is at this step that the implementation of discipline actually begins.

It is important to note the difference between punishment and discipline. Punishment is paying a price deserving of the mistake. Discipline is taking action to bring about change and restoration to a fuller, more productive and abundant life.

## Reconciliation with full restoration

After following through with the disciplinary process successfully, there needs to be the same amount of prayer and commitment to the restoration process. Closure does not happen without restoration and healing.

There must be genuine repentance before the restoration process can begin. In 2 Corinthians 7:10-11, Paul identifies two kinds of sorrow. There is a genuine sorrow for sin that leads to repentance, and there is sorrow only for the consequences of sin.

> Godly sorrow brings repentance that leads to salvation and leaves no regret, but worldly sorrow brings death. See what this godly sorrow has produced in you; what earnestness, what eagerness to clear yourselves, what indignation, what alarm, what longing, what concern, what readiness to see justice done. At every point you have proved yourselves to be innocent in this matter.

Contrition is not repentance. Contrition is feeling guilty about being caught or exposed, but it does not change the heart. If the heart is not changed, the thought and behavior will not change. While contrition may cause one to admit wrong, genuine repentance will move the spirit, soul and body to change.

When this occurs, there will be plenty of evidence that will stand the test of righteousness and godliness. Depending on the intensity and severity of the actions of a Christian leader, the process in going through these steps may vary.

It is important to note, however, that having come to a point of judgment concerning the sin of a fallen leader and having taken a proper course of action, elders are not through with their responsibilities. There will need to be a clear assessment of the damage to God's people in the congregation.

The assessment should include asking where we may have missed something along the way that could have prevented the situation from going so far. Were there warning signs, procedures, or structures in place that helped this occur and that we missed or tended to overlook? If so, how and what do we need to change? What preventative steps can we take that will diminish the risk of this occurring again?

Do not assume that once the fallen leader has gone through discipline and restoration there is no longer any concern. In reality, it may be only the start of the real work. If the leader had been on salary with the church and his job is terminated, a financial plan may need to be worked out. Leaving him financially destitute will not facilitate restoration.

## How and to whom is all this communicated?

In 1 Timothy 5:20, the church is given instructions regarding the discipline of leaders. When sin is confirmed "those who sin are to be rebuked publicly, so that the others may take warning."

Elders must not cover up or remain silent about the sin of other elders. Communicate enough to let people know that there is a situation that you are dealing with but without revealing the personal details.

In determining who should be informed, the level of responsibility determines the level of communication required. You need to communicate with those the situation has affected.

Again, the goal is healing and restoration, not humiliation. Communicate to those who are a part of the individual's sphere of influence. If that individual is an elder, his sphere of influence is the local congregation. If the individual is a worship leader, his sphere of influence is the local congregation. If he is a small group leader, his sphere of influence is the small group, not the entire congregation.

When serving in the U.S. military during the Vietnam conflict, Steve was taught the "need to know" principle; that is, he was given the information if it was determined that he needed to know it.

How was the "need to know" determined? It was determined by whether or not you were either a part of the solution or a part of the problem. If either of these were true, you were then classified as having the need to know.

Why is this principle so important? Too often the body of Christ engages in sharing information with those persons who literally are not part of the problem or the solution. This spreads information horizontally with persons who cannot affect change.

We must be careful that everything we do is done in a way that honors the individual as well as the body. "No discipline seems pleasant at the time, but painful. Later on, however, it produces a harvest of righteousness and peace for those who have been trained by it" (Hebrews 12:11).

Discipline must be looked at as a catalyst to spiritual growth or change. After going through discipline, we should be able to say that we have renewed our faith and trust in God and have grown spiritually.

*See Appendix (pages 221-238) for more on "Guidelines for Discipline and Restoration for Church Members" as well as "Guidelines for Discipline and Restoration for Fallen Leaders."*

## Questions for discussion

1. Discuss the difference between positive discipline and punitive discipline.
2. What is the goal of any discipline?
3. Give an example of a time the disciplinary process was successful and a person was restored to fellowship in your church.

---

[1] Dan Juster, *Due Process*, (Shippensburg, PA: Destiny Image Publishers, 1992), p. 121.
[2] Ibid, p. 67.

# Apostles, Elders, Fivefold Ministers and Deacons

"When leaders lead, the people freely volunteer!" This observation in Judges 5:2 (TLB) meshes perfectly with the pattern and precedent the apostles set in the first century church. As servant-leaders, they humbly walked in their God-given authority, training elders, who in turn trained others to function in their gifts and grow spiritually. The people were eager to follow the example of the apostles and elders because they led as humble fathers.

The leaders did not stand over the people, but led from among them (1 Peter 5:1-3). They followed our Lord's teaching of leading by example in humble, sacrificial service. This is God's desire for every kind of leader. Leadership is characterized by a servant's heart. Biblical elders are service-oriented. They must never link their authority with hierarchical structures.

Jesus set the example. He came not to be ministered to, but to minister (Matthew 20:25-28). In John 13:1-17, Jesus washed the disciples' feet, modeling servant leadership. In the New Testament, both the leaders and the people were in active service in the kingdom of God and servant-leadership was established as the standard.

How do the various kinds of leaders in the church interact together to lead the church? Let's first define the different levels and categories of New Testament leadership.

## Three levels of New Testament leadership

At the grass roots level are the **ministry leaders or small group leaders** who give spiritual protection and training to those they oversee in the local church. They may be cell group leaders, youth leaders, worship leaders, Sunday School leaders or any other church department leader. These leaders train and teach God's people to become functioning members of the body of Christ and eventually become leaders themselves. Leaders of this type can generally be considered to have a "deacon" role.

**Local church elders** have been chosen by the Lord to lead the church. They have a responsibility from the Lord to give oversight to the local church and "watch out for the souls" of the believers in the flock. They give spiritual protection, oversight and training to the small group leaders and other ministry leaders in the church.

**Apostolic leaders** have been chosen by the Lord to give spiritual protection, oversight and training to local church elders. In this book, we have not yet clearly defined the role of apostles in contemporary Christianity, so let's take a look at how they function.

At the beginning of a new church, before the elders have been qualified by their faithful service, the apostles have the responsibility of establishing the church as they lay a firm foundation for the church.

In 1 Corinthians 1:1, Paul boldly declares he is "called to be an apostle of Christ Jesus by the will of God." Then he speaks of this foundation in 1 Corinthians 3:10: "By the grace God has given me, I laid a foundation as an expert builder...." This is an excellent definition of an apostle. Apostles are builders. They plant a church by laying a spiritual foundation and raising up spiritual sons and daughters.

How do they lay this kind of foundation? The apostles help the people learn who they are in the Lord, and the people also learn to hear the voice of God. They begin to understand the gifts they have and start to become spiritually mature. It is from  this body of believers that elders eventually emerge, those who have been gifted with the grace to lead the local church. Apostles have the responsibility of establishing churches on sound doctrine and appointing elders to carry out the ministry in the local congregation. Their job in the New Testament was to establish a church and appoint elders and then they often moved on. Their job was usually itinerant, and they generally worked themselves out of a job!

An apostle has been given the spiritual gift of an apostle to do this work. If an individual has the calling on his life to plant and oversee churches and does it over a period of time, he is functioning in his spiritual gift as an apostle. Planting and overseeing churches is the main thrust of most apostolic ministries. C. Peter Wagner, the author of the book *Churchquake!,* defines the spiritual gift of an "apostle" as "the special ability that God gives to certain members of the body of Christ to assume and exercise general leadership over a number of churches with an extraordinary authority in spiritual matters that is spontaneously recognized and appreciated by those churches."[1]

Paul never called himself "Apostle Paul" as if it were a title. As we already mentioned, he speaks of himself as "...an apostle of Christ Jesus...." He considered himself to be a father to the church. He was a father because he had raised spiritual children in the church.

There are different kinds of apostles mentioned in the New Testament. We could call them the Paul-type apostle, Timothy-type apostle, James-type apostle and Titus-type apostle.

The Paul-type apostle is one like Paul who had a vision burning in his heart to establish a family of churches. He is sometimes called an *overseeing apostle*. He gives leadership to an entire family of churches that he starts and oversees. The Lord brings others alongside this kind of apostle to fill in what is lacking in his gifts so that the vision can be fulfilled.

Timothy was an apostle who served on Paul's team. He was more pastoral in nature and is the kind of apostle who prefers to serve on a team. He built on the foundation that another person had laid. In many of Paul's letters to the early church, he mentioned Timothy as a co-writer of the letter.

A James-type apostle has a heart for leadership in a city or region. He prefers to stay in this area and rarely travels to wider circles. James spent most of his time in Jerusalem and gave oversight to the elders there. This kind of apostle builds apostolic regional centers which become the resource center for many others.

The Titus type apostle is one who has a call to his own culture or nation. Titus claimed an island (Crete) for the kingdom. This was his nation, a people group to whom he was called.

Whether we are a small group leader, elder or apostle, we must recognize who we are, who we are supposed to reach and what our boundaries are. We all are called to make disciples (spiritual children) and reproduce ourselves so the kingdom of God continues to be built.

Obviously, larger churches need more than three levels of leadership within their infrastructure. However, even in the hierarchy of leadership in large churches, there are still three main leadership levels: ministry leaders (perhaps various levels), elders, and apostolic leaders. In many mega-churches, the senior pastor has an apostolic call on his life, and he then submits to other apostles in the broader church family.

## Categories of New Testament leadership

During the years of church history recorded in the book of Acts, the simple organization developed into a wider range of leaders. Initially, the only leaders were the apostles (Acts 2:42). When the care for the poor became too much for this small group of apostolic leaders (Acts 6:1-4), "deacons" were appointed to care for the poor so the apostles could devote themselves to prayer and the teaching of God's Word. As the apostles moved on, "elders" gradually took their place (see Acts 11:30).

Elders and deacons exercised leadership in local churches, while many of the apostles, prophets, evangelists, teachers and others moved about from congregation to congregation to minister. Some leadership gifts are equipping in nature, and some are governmental. Let's look at the difference.

| Governmental Leadership | Equipping Leadership |
|:---:|:---:|
| (Acts 15) | (Ephesians 4:11-12) |
| apostles | apostles, prophets, evangelists, |
| elders | pastors, teachers |

## Governmental leadership (oversight)

Not all the leaders in the early church held positions of governmental leadership. Only the apostles and elders held those positions. In Acts 15, 2 Corinthians 10:13 and 1 Timothy 3:1, we see such apostles and elders. Governmental leaders have a sphere of authority and responsibility. The elders and apostles held those positions in the church.

## Fivefold leadership (equipping)

Another category of New Testament leadership appears in Ephesians 4:11-12, where we see equipping leaders mentioned: apostles, prophets, evangelists, pastors and teachers. These leaders, who are often called fivefold ministers, were equipping leaders who were not necessarily responsible for a particular local church but nevertheless were church leaders. What is the difference?

If you cook in a restaurant and teach others to cook, you are using an equipping gift, but if you own and manage the restaurant, you are exercising a governmental gift. If you play a guitar and teach others to play, you are in the equipping category, but if you manage a band, you are in a governmental position. Similarly, the fivefold ministry leaders equip and teach believers in churches, but they do not have the responsibility for church oversight (government).

The fivefold leaders in the New Testament seem to mainly have a traveling emphasis and were responsible to equip the saints to minister to others and to encourage the body of Christ. They exercised an equipping gift rather than a governmental gift.

These fivefold ministers traveled translocally between the churches preaching the Word of God and helping to equip the believers with their particular gifts (Acts 15). We have found that most fivefold ministers have a mixture of gifts, not just one. For example, someone may be an evangelist/teacher or a pastor/evangelist. These vital fivefold ministry leaders equip and minister to individuals both in small groups and at the congregational level.

Governmental and fivefold leaders work together. Both apostles and elders (governmental) along with apostles, prophets, evangelists, pastors and teachers (fivefold leaders) are needed and must work together for the church to come to maturity. None should disregard or devalue the other.

The apostolic gift brings fivefold leadership and governmental leadership together. Since the apostolic gift is both an equipping gift and a governmental gift (Ephesians 4:11-12; 2 Corinthians 10:13-17), the apostolic brings both types of New Testament leadership together.

Many elders also have Ephesians 4 fivefold ministry gift(s). However, the primary reason they serve as elders is not because they have fivefold ministry gifts, but because they have the calling of eldership. It is advantageous for fivefold translocal ministers to serve in eldership for a season (if possible) so they can experience local church leadership before they begin to minister translocally. *(For more on how fivefold ministers can be utilized in the local church, see Appendix: "Releasing Fivefold Ministers" by Ron Myer, pages 255-268.)*

## Accountability for elders

In the Old Testament, God's people consisted of twelve tribes and a multitude of clans and families. You could say that the Lord continues to see His church as composed of believers in spiritual families. God's kingdom is made up of "tribes" (local church families) for the protection of both leaders and God's people (2 Corinthians 10:13-17). Each spiritual family (local church) is connected to the entire body of Christ by the tribe to which they are joined. No local church should be unconnected and uncovered. Senior elders and eldership teams in the local church need to have apostolic oversight and protection. These apostolic leaders are there to give them oversight and encouragement.

There are those who reject this kind of accountability because they have had negative experiences in the past with church oversight. This does not mean we should "throw the baby out with the bath water." God is raising up healthy families of churches all over the world. True apostolic leaders will have a father's heart to serve and protect local church leadership. If church leaders do not have proper apostolic oversight, they should fast and pray and ask the Lord to bring them proper oversight. It is important not to move too quickly but to wait on the timing of the Lord.

A New Zealand friend told us of a wonderful move of God in their home several years ago. Many were saved and the new church grew quickly as dozens were saved. Soon they recognized a need to have some oversight and started looking for an apostolic type leader to help them. They wanted to be accountable to someone for this new move of God. They found an "apostle" who agreed to come in and serve them. However, instead of protecting and training the flock, he created dissension and all kinds of strife in this young church. Too late, the elders of the church realized that this man did not have their best interests at heart, and the church was devastated. The scriptures warn us to look out for false apostles.

God wants to raise up apostolic fathers and mothers with whom local church elders can have relational oversight. Elders need to know and trust those who give them protection, direction and correction.

## Kingdom clusters

The diagram on the following page outlines a pattern of relationships for healthy church leaders on each level of church leadership in the local church. The Lord is building His church through relationships! Every leader should have those over him in the Lord with whom he is in relationship, and those under him in the Lord whom he is called to mentor and serve.

If we pursue and honor the relationships God gives to us, we can experience the unity Jesus Christ prayed for in John 17.

# Kingdom Clusters
## A Pattern of Relationships

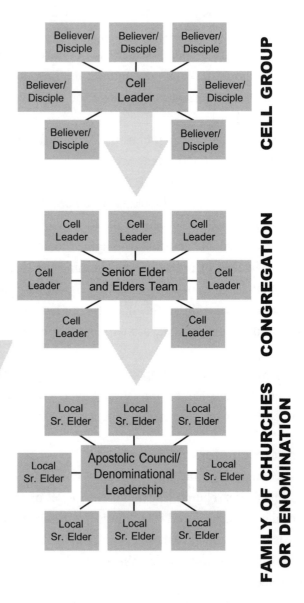

*The Biblical Role of Elders for Today's Church*

## The role of deacons

The word *deacon* comes from *diakonos* in the Greek, meaning *a servant of the people, a waiter, attendant, servant or a minister.* Jesus, as Head of the church, gives us the best example of a "servant of the people" because He had the attitude and spirit of a servant. Deacons are those who set an example of serving and ministering in the church.

The first deacons mentioned in the New Testament appear to be in Acts 6 when a problem of food distribution presented itself in the church. Too much of the apostles' time was being taken up with distributing food to the widows, and they did not have enough time to pray and minister the Word.

> So the Twelve gathered all the disciples together and said, It would not be right for us to neglect the ministry of the word of God in order to wait on tables. Brothers, choose seven men from among you who are known to be full of the Spirit and wisdom. We will turn this responsibility over to them and will give our attention to prayer and the ministry of the word (Acts 6:2).

It is not that the twelve apostles were not willing to serve. They just knew that they had the huge task of discipling many new Christians and they did not have time to also administer all the work in the local church. As the church grew in numbers, some people in the church needed to be overseeing the church by "teaching the Word of God" in order to safe-guard the church from heresy, and others needed to be taking care of the specific ministries in the church.

Consequently, the early church appointed deacons to take care of the day-to-day activities of the church. In this case, the deacons were placed in charge of administering the work of distributing food.

A deacon's role is not limited to serving people's physical needs, however. We should note that out of this food distribution ministry, Stephen and Philip emerged. They both had an evangelistic ministry that did spectacular miracles among the people.[2]

We often think of the small group leaders or cell leaders in our church as serving in "deacon-type roles." These important ministry leaders lead and serve their small group, training and equipping individuals to grow spiritually. It is often from these small groups that potential elders receive their training and experience to later lead out in church oversight as elders.

Both elders and deacons were addressed by Paul in his letter to the Philippian church, "To all the saints in Christ Jesus at Philippi, together with the overseers and deacons" (Philippians 1:1). This again tells us that both the elders and deacons had roles of leadership in the church.

Yet again in 1 Timothy 3, we see that both elders and deacons served together in the church. The difference between elders and deacons was one of function. It seems that the elders were to concern themselves more with the ministry of the Word and prayer as they led the church, while the deacons were to deal with other supportive church ministry aspects.

So we could say that the elders oversee the local church while deacons primarily administrate different ministries in the church. The deacons are meant to help the elders implement their task. In some churches, rather than supporting the senior leader who should be leading the church, deacons take on that governmental leadership role, and chaos occurs. A church senior leader once told us, "We have a board of deacons who actually run our church. They make final decisions and often override my opinions." He laughed uneasily, "We are a deacon-possessed church!" This kind of oversight role was never meant for deacons.

## Character qualifications of deacons

The character qualifications of deacons are similar to the character qualifications of elders. They are both to be mature believers with proven character. They should be full of faith, full of wisdom and full of the Spirit, along with possessing a good reputation. These servant leaders are qualified personally, spiritually and domestically as described in 1 Timothy 3:8-13, Titus 2:2-7 and Acts 6:3;16:1-2.

It is interesting that in the qualifications for elders in 1 Timothy 3, the qualification of "being able to teach" is mentioned for elders, but it is not mentioned as a qualification for deacons. Of course, this does not mean that the deacons cannot teach; it probably is making this distinction between the role of deacons and that of elders whose primary responsibilities were to "teach the Word" as they gave oversight to the local church.

Deacons are to be full of the Holy Spirit and spiritually mature because they have learned to walk with God over a period of time. They do not serve for the sake of recognition or because they have large egos. They serve because they are answering the call of God on their lives.

The problem of food distribution which prompted the need for deacons in the early church did not just require mature people who were willing to serve. Deacons certainly were not just those who could move furniture, bake a cake, or make soup or perform other physical acts to help meet the needs of others. They were full of the Spirit and wisdom and faith (Acts 6:3,5). Inner character qualifications like being blameless, not greedy, of honest report, and not being double-minded were necessary to get the job accomplished. Why were these so important?

It seems that more was at stake than simply distributing food. The problem in the Jerusalem church was not just to get nutritious baskets of food to the widows. The real reason the Greek widows were not being given food was because they were considered second-class citizens. The Grecian Jews felt ostracized and started complaining bitterly about the problem. So the deacons really had to be wise men who could deal with the prejudices of the day and the bad attitudes that came with it. Deacons needed to be courageous individuals who were not afraid to lead by making wise and godly decisions in times of crisis.

God's wise plan is for each duty found within the local church to be given oversight, equipping, and accountability through servant-leaders. While the titles and the roles may be different, each works together to build the church into the glorious bride for whom Christ is returning.

## Questions for discussion

1. Briefly explain each of the five ministry gifts mentioned in Ephesians.
2. How should elders relate to apostolic leaders?
3. In your own words, describe the difference between governmental leadership and equipping leadership.
4. Describe the responsibilities and importance of deacons in the life of the church.

---

[1] C. Peter Wagner, *Churchquake!,* (Ventura, California: Regal Books, 1999), p. 105.
[2] Acts 6:8; 7-8

# Investing in Spiritual Sons and Daughters

**13**

Don Finto, who served as the senior pastor of Belmont Church in Nashville, Tennessee, for many years, has a great passion to father younger men in ministry. His relationship with one of his more famous "spiritual sons," singer and musician Michael W. Smith, is described here:

> For the last 20 years—starting before Smith cut any records—Finto has laughed, cried, worshiped, prayed and traveled together with Smith in a father-son type of relationship.
>
> "I could write a book about Finto," Smith says. "He's my daddy in the Lord. I don't think I'd be where I am today if it hadn't been for Don."
>
> Finto now serves as a pastor to pastors. "I am an encourager," Finto admits. "I can often see more in people than they can see in themselves, and I want to call it forth in the name of the Lord."
>
> The effect on Smith has been profound. "I've saved all my letters from him, all the little note cards," Smith says. "He has encouraged me in so many ways—my self-confidence and who I am in the Lord—pulling stuff out of me that nobody ever was able to pull out." [1]

This is the kind of mentoring of leaders we need in today's church. The potential for spiritual parenting is enormous. In his book, *The Cry for Spiritual Fathers and Mothers,* Larry Kreider says that spiritual parenting helps potential leaders to find their identity and purpose in life and brings them to maturity.[2]

When elders practice spiritual parenting, the result is that the church begins to function like a family. God's intention is to empower spiritual parents who are willing to nurture spiritual children and help them grow in their Christian lives. This is a fulfillment of the Lord's promise in the last days to "turn the hearts of the fathers to the children, and the hearts of the children to their fathers..." (Malachi 4:6). The Lord wants to restore harmony among spiritual fathers and their children, so fathers can freely impart their inheritance to the next generation.

All believers, including potential leaders, need help to grow spiritually. We cannot do it by ourselves, just as natural infants cannot thrive if left on their own. Babies need the care and nurture of parents just as believers need the practical input from loving spiritual fathers and mothers who delight in seeing their children reach their full potential. Elders must invest in divinely-appointed spiritual parenting relationships to reproduce what God has invested in them and train the next generation of leaders.

It was the lack of mature leadership in the Corinthian church that stunted the believers' spiritual growth. Unequipped to grow up spiritually, they struggled to find their identity. They did not know who they were in the Lord.

When believers lack spiritual fathers and mothers to model God's fatherhood, they often struggle, feel spiritually alone and lack identity. Because they did not have their identity in Christ, the Corinthians sought it through their favorite leader: "I am of Paul...I am of Apollos..." (1 Corinthians 3:4). Paul chides the Corinthian church for its lack of maturity, making it plain that, while other people do have a role to play, it is clearly only God whom they should ultimately follow. He is the source of every good thing. Wise spiritual parents will always direct their spiritual children to Jesus.

Deficient of true spiritual fathers to model fatherhood, the Corinthian church was mired in spiritual immaturity. What they really needed were spiritual fathers and mothers to pay close attention to them so they could be nudged toward maturity. They needed spiritual parents to sow into their lives, expecting them eventually to become spiritual parents themselves. The goal was to create a spiritual harvest that would reproduce and multiply.

Stop and think about how you reached maturity in your Christian walk. Who were the spiritual fathers and mothers in your life? Who were the leaders that took a chance on you as a young, insecure and inexperienced leader? Someone saw the potential in your life and was willing to take ministry risks with you.

## The elders set the pace as spiritual parents

The church is to function as a family. Ephesians 3:14-15 speaks of His whole family in heaven and earth. The church is not an institution; it is a family. In order for a family to be healthy, parental guidance is needed. Elders provide this parental guidance.

According to 1 Corinthians 4:15-17, there are "ten thousand instructors, but not many fathers." Because of the lack of spiritual fathers, many spiritual children today have fallen away. The church has often focused on meetings rather than on fathering! Timothy was "fathered" by Paul. Parenting takes time and effort, but the end result is definitely worth it! Stable spiritual families have spiritual parents. Elders are spiritual parents. Cell leaders should be trained to be spiritual parents. Elders are called by God to be spiritual midwives to prepare and help the church to have spiritual children.

## Three levels of spiritual maturity

According to the scriptures there are three levels of spiritual maturity...children, young men, and fathers. In the church and in every small group, it is important for elders to understand the spiritual maturity level of each person. It is the elders' passion to encourage everyone to grow toward maturity. They believe that eventually every believer will become a spiritual parent. But how do spiritual children become parents?

We go through life in stages, spiritually—as little children, young men and fathers. At each point in our journey, we function in a particular way and have distinct tasks to perform. John addresses all three spiritual stages in 1 John 2:12-14:

> I write to you, dear children, because your sins have been forgiven on account of his name. I write to you, fathers, because you have known him who is from the beginning. I write to you, young men, because you have overcome the evil one. I write to you, dear children, because you have known the Father. I write to you, fathers, because you have known him who is from the beginning. I write to you, young men, because you are strong, and the word of God lives in you, and you have overcome the evil one.

Seeing His people come to a place of fatherhood is the cry of God's heart. International speaker, teacher and spiritual father, Alan Vincent from San Antonio, Texas, has this to say about these verses in 1 John: "The cry of the apostle John was not only for strong men who knew the Word of God and could overcome the evil one, but for *fathers* who really knew God and who would come forth to father the church. If men as a whole became strong fathers according to the biblical pattern—in home, church and society—then most of our social problems would disappear and Satan's kingdom would be severely curtailed. Fatherhood is the foundation on which God has chosen to build the whole structure of society."

Since fatherhood is so crucial to God's divine order, He established a natural training ground consisting of "growth stages." We grow to fatherhood as we progress through each of these stages. Only then do we receive the heart and revelation of a father.

Our stages as babies in Christ, young men and women, and spiritual fathers and mothers have nothing to do with our chronological age but everything to do with how we eventually progress on to spiritual maturity. If we fail to take the steps required to become spiritual parents, we remain spiritual babies—spiritually immature and lacking parenting skills. It is sad, but this is often the case in the church. Many times there is no provision for believers to go on to maturity within our church systems.

Nevertheless, with the restoration of New Testament Christianity, with elders in place to lead the church, and with some type of small group ministry in the church, each person is given the opportunity to "do the work of ministry" and to connect in vital relationships with others. Through modeling and impartation, spiritual reproduction happens naturally. Let's look at these stages and use them as gauges to identify where we are in our spiritual maturity. Let's discover how we can all come to the place of becoming spiritual parents.

## Spiritual children

According to 1 John 2:12, spiritual children know their sins are forgiven, and they know the Father. They are alive to what they can receive from their Savior. They freely ask the Father when they have a need. It is exciting to see how the Lord answers children's prayers even when their prayers may not always be theologically correct, but that is okay because they are babies. Every church should have babies—brand new believers.

A new believer will often act like a natural child with the marks of immaturity, including instability and gullibility. They will need constant assurance and care. They often do the unexpected because they are still learning what it means to follow Jesus. They may be self-centered, selfish and irresponsible. Spiritual parents must help these children learn the early lessons of Christian faith and move on to new horizons so that they grow in maturity.

But what happens when spiritual babies do not grow up? Quite simply, they remain babies! The sad thing is, the church can be filled with children (some 50 years old) who have never grown up! They live self-centered life-styles, complaining and fussing and throwing temper tantrums when things do not go their way. Some do not accept the fact that God loves them for who they are. Others may wallow in self-pity when they fail. Still others may live under an immense cloud of guilt and condemnation.

We expect children to grow up. Elders cannot be expected to spoon-feed new believers in their congregation indefinitely. Spiritual babies are expected to learn to feed themselves and grow into spiritual young men and women who eventually become parents themselves.

## Spiritual young men and women

Fearless and strong, spiritual young men and women bring zeal to the body of Christ. They no longer have to be spoon-fed. According to 1 John 2:14, the Word of God abides in them and they have learned to feed on the Word to overcome the wicked one.

They do not need to run constantly to others in the church to care for them like babies do, because they have learned to apply the Word to their own lives. When the devil tempts them, they know what to do to overcome him. Herein is the church's crop of potential leaders. We need to do everything we can to encourage those who are young. We need to allow them to begin to develop their ministries while they are young. They are strong in the Word and Spirit. They have learned to use the strength of spiritual discipline, of prayer and the study of the Word.

Yet both natural and spiritual young men and women can often be arrogant and dogmatic and need to be "tempered" by parenting. The elders provide opportunities for the young people to use their spiritual energy in evangelism—and in the process, become parents themselves who will mature even more as they learn the joys and disciplines of training others in the Lord.

## Spiritual parents

How do spiritual young men and women grow up to become spiritual fathers and mothers? There is only one way—to have children! God's will is for everyone to become a spiritual parent. You become a spiritual parent either by adoption (fathering someone who is already a believer but needs to be mentored) or by natural birth (fathering someone you have personally led to Christ).

Onesimus was a "natural" spiritual son to Paul while Timothy was a spiritual son to Paul by adoption. Paul led Onesimus to Christ while in prison (Philemon 10). Paul met Timothy while in Lystra after Timothy had come to Christ due to the influence of his mother and grandmother (Acts 16:1-3). Paul treated both "adopted son Timothy" and "natural son Onesimus" like spiritual sons. He was committed to helping them mature spiritually.

Spiritual fathers and mothers are mature believers who have grown and become fruitful in their Christian walk; they are called *fathers* according to 1 John 2:13. They have a profound and thorough knowledge of Jesus through knowing His Word. They are deeply acquainted with God and have a strong passion for Jesus. They understand what it takes to be a spiritual parent and are willing to pay the price to become one.

## Elders encourage training from the ground up

Small group ministry[3] is an ideal structure for spiritual parenting. This is one reason why it is important for an elder to have successfully led and multiplied a small group before his appointment as an elder. The small group is a spiritual family. It is the perfect training ground for future elders. The small group leader and assistant leaders are spiritual parents. Parents take responsibility for their children and young men and women. They have a heart of compassion for them.

It is time for the church to take up the mantle of spiritual parenting. The church will only realize the potential of spiritual parenting if the elders set the pace. Jesus took 12 untrained men (Mark 3:14) and fathered them for three and one half years. His model worked, and is one to pattern ourselves after.

## Local church elders release their sons

Sometimes the team of elders in a local church is made up of individuals in a similar age group. That is why it is especially important for the elders on the team to continually mentor younger leaders. These younger Christians may look different and act differently than the elder team, but these are the very ones the team should be listening to. We must strive to raise up the next generation of leadership and take risks. Mature fathers will always release their children to step out and try new things. They protect them but also allow them to make mistakes.

Secure elders have the glory of seeing their sons and daughters develop as leaders and succeed. Elders are experienced, mature leaders who mentor, coach, train, support, correct, trust, and believe in young leaders. Their fathering gives the younger leaders a great sense of protection and confidence to go for it and pursue the call of God on their lives.

Remember the spiritual parents in your life? We encourage you to call them or send them a note of appreciation. Let them know where you are today because of their parenting hearts. We are sure they will be blessed and encouraged!

In the next chapter, we will discuss how elders are often challenged by the Lord to send out their best young leaders into church plants or other ministries. Let's discover how elders can joyously and freely release those they have trained.

## Questions for discussion

1. Explain the three levels of spiritual growth and maturity.
2. Why is mentoring of future leaders so important?
3. Describe the process of training and raising up leaders within your local church.

[1] "The Man Behind Michael," Charisma Magazine, April 2000.
[2] For more on Spiritual Fathering and Mothering, read Larry Kreider's book, *The Cry for Spiritual Fathers and Mothers,* (Ephrata, PA: House to House Publications, 2000).
[3] For more on small group ministry, read Larry Kreider's book, *House to House,* a manual for small group ministry.

# Elders and Church Planting

**14**

What happens when elders are faced with sending out their best spiritual sons and daughters? Since the heart of every healthy elder is to give a double "portion" to his children, elders should expect their sons and daughters to go far beyond them in the Lord!

Steve's son, Marc, is a born drummer. They have pictures of him at age two playing drums on pots and pans with wooden spoons. His first drum set was a cartoon character toy set from his grandparents. Marc beat those drums until they fell to pieces. As a young man, Steve was also a drummer, and he would have to be a blind and deaf father not to realize his son's potential as a drummer.

Steve recalls, "We started with a practice pad and finally a single snare drum. Marc learned the rudiments of drumming on those two instruments. He begged me for a 'real' drum set, but the time had not yet come." Sometimes as spiritual fathers, we want our children to go from pots and pans to the whole set almost instantly, but it is premature.

Eventually, when the rudiments became second nature to Marc, Steve passed on to Marc his vintage drum set. Marc was ready for lessons that took him beyond a single snare drum.

Today, as a senior in college, Marc has far surpassed Steve in drumming. If Steve had tried to hold him back to his own level, he would be a selfish, insecure parent. A secure parent releases his children, encouraging his sons or daughters to excel to greater heights than he ever did.

Talented young leaders in the church will want to pave their own way in the world. Elders should expect some of their best worship leaders, cell leaders and others to eventually leave in order to pioneer new things on their own.

## Will we release them?

Elders must regard their spiritual sons and daughters as the Lord's and be willing to release them into their calling as they come to maturity. Only a dysfunctional parent would try to keep his son or daughter at home to help him fulfill his own vision.

Brian played baseball in tenth grade in high school. But in the eleventh grade, he was cut from the team. Now that Brian has sons of his own, should he force them to play baseball and in this way fulfill his own unfulfilled dreams of being a great baseball player? Of course not! His sons might enjoy playing soccer or basketball instead. He will encourage them to fulfill whatever dreams they have in their hearts. Proverbs 22:6 states, "Train a child in the way he should go, and when he is old he will not turn from it."

The emphasis here is on the way *he* should go, not the way *his father thinks* he should go. Of course, children need training in areas of morality and character. But when it comes to personal vision and calling, a parent's job is to find out what God has put in their children's hearts. The same is true for elders who are parenting spiritual sons and daughters.

Healthy parents desire to send out their sons and daughters to start their own homes. This is why cells multiply and this is why churches need to multiply and plant new churches. Fathers desire to see their children grow up and have their own homes and families.

## Elders in church planting

Although in the Old Testament the term for *elder* translates "older in age," we do not see in the New Testament that old age was required for one to be an elder. Paul and others would plant a new church and then come back in a short time to take note of and install the elders in the church—those who had matured spiritually.

In Acts 14:23, Paul and Barnabas set out on their first missionary trip to Derbe. After having a revival at Derbe, they traveled back through Lystra, Iconium and Antioch on their return trip and appointed elders. Notice they had just preached the gospel in these cities on their way to Derbe so the elders were saved at the same time as the rest of the congregation. The elders appointed were those who had matured spiritually.

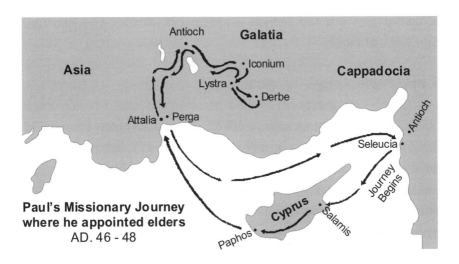

**Paul's Missionary Journey where he appointed elders** A.D. 46 - 48

Scriptures do not say whether they were old or young in natural age; however, the elders must have been relatively young believers, both Jews and Gentiles, who were placed in these leadership positions. They apparently did not fit the traditional Old Testament model of aged, gray-haired, Jewish elders.

Rick Joyner points out that it is not old, gray-haired men and women who have children. It is usually young men and women, perhaps in their twenties and thirties, that conceive and give birth to children in the natural. Rick spoke prophetically when he warned the church not to "sterilize" or "neuter" the young stallions, referring to the young leaders that God is anointing and giving to a body of believers. The local church must release them to serve as elders in the local churches. We cannot overlook them when considering who should be elders.

In Keswick, Canada, Jim Pesce is a great example of a senior leader who has made full use of younger leaders in the church. When elders were appointed in the church that he and his wife, Debbie, had planted, all of the elders who were commissioned were people that they had won to the Lord. They were their spiritual children who were mentored into maturity until they were ready spiritually to be trusted as local church elders. Jim and Debbie as spiritual parents are realizing their spiritual heritage.

## Church planting—the goal

The ultimate success of spiritual parenting for local church elders is for them to see the church come full circle and plant a new church. The long-term vision of every local church should be to multiply and plant new churches. We are commanded to be fruitful and multiply and replenish the earth. As we look at the world around us, everything with life will multiply. The examples of this in nature are endless...plants, animals and humans. Believers also multiply by leading others to Christ. Cell groups multiply. Churches multiply. Anything that is healthy and has life will reproduce and multiply.

## Church planting is the New Testament pattern

The New Testament church was a church planting movement. In Acts 2:37-47, the Jerusalem church was planted. In Acts 8:1-25, the Samaritan church was birthed. In Acts 9:20-22, the Damascus church came to life. Acts 9:31 reports churches throughout Judea, Galilee and Samaria. In Acts 19:9, we find out about a church planting school Paul ran in the lecture hall of Tyrannus. The churches the Apostle John wrote to in Revelation are believed to have been started by students from this school. The list goes on—Joppa, Caesarea, Antioch—the book of Acts reads like a church planting manual.

## Unity in diversity!

We should not be afraid to plant churches with different visions, missions and goals in mind. Churches led by biblical eldership come in many kinds, sizes and shapes. Before continuing, we need to briefly clarify what the different types of churches are. This will help us to realize that God uses multiple models to build, and He has a purpose for each one.

We could categorize, by size and structure, three main kinds of churches in the current landscape. We will call them "community churches," "mega-churches" and "house church (or micro church) networks." The *community church* (a church of approximately 50-900) and *mega-church* (generally a church of over 1,000) are probably the most familiar to us. The community church reaches out to its local community, while the mega-church reaches a wider area. The community church is like a community store in your neighborhood: the store serves the local area. The mega-church is like the "Wal-Mart superstore." People will travel for a longer distance to shop at a Wal-Mart (one of the world's leading discount retailers) because they love the low prices, the huge inventory of consumer products, and they can find everything they need to buy in that one store. A mega-church is large and offers an abundance of services to the churchgoer.

Thirty years ago, nearly every church in America was a community church. Then, American Christians and pastors started hearing reports about massive churches in places like Seoul, Korea. Dr. Yonggi Cho, pastor of the world's largest church in Seoul, taught American church leaders to obey the voice of the Holy Spirit to release more of the ministry of the church to trained and gifted lay leaders. Many churches, especially those in large metropolitan areas, experienced rapid multiplication and growth. This new approach to the meaning and application of what a church can be led to a wave of mega-churches growing across America. Many of these churches implemented small group ministry to facilitate this growth.

Both the community church and mega-churches meet in a church facility each Sunday morning. There are many styles and flavors of community and mega-churches. There is the Methodist flavor, the Baptist flavor, the Congregational flavor, the Episcopal flavor, the Presbyterian flavor, the Vineyard flavor, the Assembly of God flavor, and the list goes on. Although these churches are different in their styles, most meet in church buildings every Sunday morning and function within the traditional church structure of having a salaried pastor as the leader of the church.

The micro churches have a unique structure that requires us to think about church in a different way. Believers in micro churches do not focus on growing larger like the community church or the mega-church. They promote growth by starting new micro churches through multiplication. Micro churches are like the stores in a shopping mall. If the average store found in a shopping mall were taken out of the mall and left to stand on its own, it would most likely not still be in business a year later. The smaller store in a shopping mall needs the others to survive. Each specialized store flourishes within the cluster of the others. Yet, each store is fully a store in its own right, despite being in a mall. Micro churches function like these shopping mall stores. They are individual and specialized, yet they flourish as they network together with other micro churches.

Each micro church is a church in itself with its own leadership. Each meets in a home or another location that does not require constructing buildings that would be needed to accommodate a larger group. Many of these non-traditional churches are already utilizing the New Testament mode of church eldership, having elders who lead and protect the church. DAWN Ministries, a church planting movement, describes this kind of church and its leadership like this:

"[The micro church's] responsibility structure is very simple and effective: individual churches are fathered by elders, who in turn are equipped by itinerant servants like those in the five-fold ministry. They often relate to a regional spiritual father-figure, who, through his humble apostolic passion and vision, often becomes something like a "pillar of the church," an anchor-place for a regional movement that fills its cities and villages with the presence of Christ."[2]

Each kind of church—the community church, the mega church and the micro church—has its strengths and weaknesses as it empowers people for ministry. As we follow the path the Lord has laid out for our church, and honor what God is doing through others,  we can walk in unity with others in the body of Christ. Each kind of church should be about the business of multiplying people. A healthy church family will train its members, and expect their spiritual children to grow up and start new ventures of their own.

## Church planting develops new leadership

Church planting provides the opportunity for new and young leaders to stretch their wings and fly. As parents have children, each child may have a different room in the house to call their own bedroom. But there will come a time when just a room in their parent's house is not enough. They will want their own house.

Healthy elders are willing to release their leaders to move out on their own. It is a stretching, learning experience for the children, but church planting allows spiritual children to reach a new level of maturity which they would not reach if they continued to live in the house where they grew up. As leaders, we must be prepared to send out our best leaders. We must be kingdom-minded and make decisions based upon the advancement of the kingdom—not on the expansion of our own perceived empire.

## Church planting prevents church splits

Could it be that one of the reasons that churches split is because the next generation of leaders is not released and sent out to establish their own churches? Insecure spiritual leaders frustrate developing leaders by not releasing them. Insecure spiritual leaders wonder about what would happen if the new church plant grew to be larger than the sending church. Frustrated by a glass ceiling, sometimes young leaders eventually leave disgruntled and take people with them.

When the local church sends out a new small group leader, they cannot always be sure that leader is entirely ready. This will also be the case with church planters. That is why it is important for some kind of apostolic oversight to be in place. Apostolic spiritual oversight helps the young leader to make wise decisions and yet releases him to obey the Lord.

In fact, the new leader may not be ready, but the challenge of the church planting could be the very thing that will develop him to the next level of leadership. If you are an elder, remember: someone believed in you before you began serving as an elder.

## Church planting is efficient

C. Peter Wagner states, "There is no more practical or cost effective way of bringing unbelievers to Christ in a given geographic area than planting new churches." This profound statement is the result of Peter's extensive research and analysis of church growth around the world. Church planting provides the infrastructure to support and maintain the fruit that is coming forth.

Not all churches are supposed to be mega churches. A German church growth researcher, Christian Schwarz, reports that statistically small churches are 16 times more effective at winning new members than mega-churches. For example, two churches of 200 generally win twice as many people for Jesus as a single 400-member church.[3]

Planting new churches gives the opportunity for more people to come to faith in Christ. Fuller Theological Seminary reports similar findings in a study that reveals that if a church is ten or more years old, it takes 85 people to lead one person to Christ. If the church is four to seven years old, it takes seven people to lead one to Christ. If a church is less than three years old, it takes only three people to lead one to Christ (see table below):[4]

| Age of church | people/salvation ratio |
| --- | --- |
| 10 years + old | 85:1 |
| 4-7 years old | 7:1 |
| 3 years & under | 3:1 |

So let's not be mesmerized into thinking that every church needs to have thousands of people, or that larger churches are more effective than smaller ones. Maybe some churches are destined to grow to around two hundred people (addition) and then start planting new churches (multiplication).

## Church planting reaches Christians who are currently not in churches

In almost any community in the western world, there are many Christians who have not been growing in their spiritual lives. They are not contributing to the kingdom of God simply because they do not fit into the existing churches in their area. What they really need is a new church where they can feel at home. A new church can often provide an entry point for people not connected to a church. They don't have to break into an already established group so it is easier for them to join.

## Church planting provides more options for unchurched people

As long as there are unsaved people in our communities who are not being reached, there is a need for new churches. New churches provide more options for the unchurched. They are a key to outreach and statistically they generally grow faster than old ones. Simply stated, it is easier to have a baby than to raise the dead. This is not to say that existing churches are dead. It is just to point out that the maternity ward in the hospital represents more exciting potential for growth than the wards that merely heal the wounded.

## Cross-cultural mission for every local church

Every local church is called by the Lord to help fulfill the Great Commission. The senior leader of the church and the team of elders are responsible to be sure that the local church they oversee is involved in helping to reach the unreached in the nations of the world rather than focusing solely on themselves. Very few churches have the expertise or the resources to properly train and equip missionaries for cross-cultural missions without some "outside" help. This is why partnering with a mission agency that honors the local church is usually the best way to help missionaries from local churches find proper training and oversight. Some churches have a mission committee or mission awareness team within the local church. This team serves in a deacon type role and its members are in touch with the Lord's heart for cross-cultural missions. This team is given oversight by the elders.

In the DOVE Christian Fellowship International family of churches, clusters of churches from each area of the world are forming "Centers of Mission." These Centers of Mission are made up of mission specialists who can serve the local churches in their region by helping with recruiting, training, sending, overseeing, and caring for missionaries. They also are committed to helping missionaries re-enter into active church life after the Lord calls them home from the mission field.

The senior leader of the church and the elders are responsible to make sure money is budgeted each year from the local church to be sowed into missions. Church leadership also leads the way by encouraging faith promises for missionaries and mission ministries they are supporting as a local church. It is healthy to have missionaries, church leaders from other nations, or missionary leaders speak to the local church regularly to raise mission awareness among those we serve.

In Acts 15, the church in Jerusalem was encouraged by Paul and Barnabas when they gave a firsthand report of what the Lord was doing in the new mission churches that had sprung up among the Gentiles. Obviously, the senior elder and the elders are responsible to open the door to these missionaries to speak in the local church.

All churches will be healthier and more quickly grow when we look outside ourselves and serve others, be it in our community or the larger spectrum of cross-cultural missions.

## Questions for discussion
1. What happens if we do not release new leaders in our churches?
2. Discuss why church planting needs to be a goal for every church.
3. Why is missions involvement important for every local church?

[1] For a more thorough understanding of house church networks (micro churches), read Larry Kreider's book, *House Church Networks: A Church for a New Generation,* (Ephrata, PA: House to House Publications, 2001).
[2] DAWN Report, "The Church Comes Home," August 1999, p.1.
[3] Christian Schwarz, *Natural Church Development,* (Carol Stream, IL: ChurchSmart Resources, 1996).
[4] "Enlarging Our Borders," Report presented to the Executive Presbytery, January 1999.

**RESOURCE**
*Helping You Build Cell Churches* by Brian Sauder and Larry Kreider contains a helpful chapter on "church planting." *Helping You Build Cell Churches* is a training manual for church leaders and for small group ministry.

# Staying Healthy: The Secret to Longevity

15

How does an elder stay in the game without burning out after several years of ministry? Most elders that we meet want to remain faithful in ministry and not give up when things become difficult. However, the fact is that elders often face incredible difficulties in the church. They witness heartbreaking situations in people's lives. Misunderstandings and suspicions sometimes arise in leadership teams. Because of a deep commitment to their calling, elders put in many hours tending to the needs of their flock. They will visit the sick, counsel the distressed, comfort the bereaved and fulfill many other responsibilities related to church life.

## The team helps to carry the load

Senior elders need a strong team surrounding them to help bear the responsibilities of the flock in leading, feeding and protecting them.

In 1 Chronicles 12:16-17, some leaders who were defecting from Saul came to join up with David. One of David's first questions to them was *"Have you come peaceably?"* As a leader, he needed to know if there were things in their background or their previous experience that would hinder them. Were they bringing extra baggage to the team, or were they laying everything down at the door?

If elders come with past hurts from previous experiences, they are wounded and will not be able to stand the spiritual heat of leadership.

Wounds from the past need to be healed before these individuals can be placed in an authority role in the church. If they are not healed, before long they will bring hurt and frustration into the church.

Another question David asked was, *"Have you come to help me?"* An elder must lay down any previous vision or agenda of his own and embrace the vision of the church he is serving. If he is unwilling to do this, it will only be a matter of time until there is more than one vision operating in the church. And with more than one vision, you have "division." David wanted to know if they would support him and support the vision the Lord had given to him.

*"Will you betray me to my enemies?"* was another question David asked. The shortcomings of individuals may cause them to be disloyal when times get rough. We have worked with a lot of different people but all of us are alike in this one sense: none is perfect! David was asking these men what they would do when they saw his flaws. Similarly, will the elders stand and help make up for the weaknesses of their senior elder, or will they expose them? Will they use his weaknesses as weapons against him by pointing them out or exaggerating them to others?

When the men replied in affirmation and support of David's leadership, David finally replied, *"Then my heart will be knit with yours."* David then commissioned these men to serve on his team, making them leaders of his raiding bands.

In verse 18, the chief of the captains pledged his loyalty to David, "We are yours, O David! We are with you, O son of Jesse! Success, success to you, and success to those who help you, for your God will help you." When leaders are working together in unity bonded by commitment and free from hurts of the past, they will experience success in ministry.

## The prayer life of an elder

Ministry flows out of the abundance of our hearts when we are in relationship with the Lord. Elders cannot just depend on "the anointing" (God's supernatural empowerment) to see them through. Anointing is like adrenaline. It comes and manifests with power, but it does not nurture in spirit, soul and body. Elders need to cultivate a sense of nurture and maintain a life-style of prayer. Maintaining a posture of spiritual oversight for the church is a priority for an elder.

There are times when elders have to rely totally on the Lord's strength because circumstances may tempt them to become discouraged and desperate. In 1 Samuel 30, David and his army returned to Ziglag to be reunited with their families, only to find the city destroyed by fire and their wives and sons and daughters captured. Initially David and his men wept until they had no strength left to weep. Soon the mood changed to anger as the men become bitter at David for leaving their families unprotected and vulnerable to attack. They were so angry, they started to talk of stoning David. Verse 6 tells us that David was greatly distressed that his men (those on his team) were upset, but he "found strength in the Lord his God." As a leader, David knew he had to find his strength in the Lord to see him through this terrible time.

## Spend daily, quality time with God

An elder's first priority is ministering to the Lord. Spending time with the Father overshadows everything else in life and ministry. Call it what you want—quiet time, devotions, morning watch or individual worship. It is imperative for us to spend daily quality time with God. There are no substitutes for time alone with God.

Out of God's presence comes His anointing. When His anointing is present, there is power; when His power is released, there is deliverance; and when there is deliverance, there is freedom. As leaders, we must cultivate the presence of God in order to walk in His freedom.

## Life-style of prayer

If an elder is living a life-style of prayer and is maintaining a spiritual posture of covering the church, when he gets an "emergency call" late at night whereby someone is demanding immediate attention, he can simply and truthfully respond by saying, "I have already prayed for you today, let's set up a time to meet tomorrow." Of course, he must discern if it is a real emergency that actually requires immediate attention, but he will not be ruled by the "tyranny of the urgent."

## Meditate on God's Word

To maintain spiritual vitality, elders need to regularly hear a word from the Lord. They must meet with the Author by reading and meditating on the Bible. His Word is full of living power and meditating on it provides a spiritual washing and cleansing. As it says in Ephesians 5:26, we are washed by the Word, and each of us needs a daily spiritually refreshing bath.

## Train potential leaders to hear God's voice

Elders should be listening to God's voice but also teaching potential leaders to hear from Him. This will cause potential leaders to look to God for revelation and direction instead of depending on the elders in an unhealthy way. In short, it takes some of the spiritual pressure off the elders when other leaders are hearing from God for themselves.

Elijah trained others as he learned to hear God's voice. While Elijah was depressed and living in a cave, he found that God was not in the wind, the earthquake, or the fire, but spoke through a still, small voice. The Lord told him to anoint Elisha, a prophet, in his place (1 Kings 19:16). For the remainder of his life, Elijah trained Elisha and other young prophets. He was a spiritual father to them. The fathering grew out of his own walk with the Lord as he learned to hear God's voice. Like Elijah, God has granted us the priceless privilege of fellowship with Himself as we train others.

We can train young elders like we train our natural children. At eleven years of age, Brian's son tried out for a basketball team which required a big commitment on his part. Of course as an sports enthusiast, Brian greatly encouraged him in his endeavors. After awhile, Brain's son was praying about it, and he said, "Dad, I'm not sure God wants me to go ahead with the team." Brian was momentarily stunned but also greatly encouraged by his young son who was hearing from God about an important decision in his life. Brian backed his son in his decision.

## Become offense proof

God desires for leaders to stay full of joy and the Holy Spirit, remaining flexible and creative as they mature and grow. Too many Christian leaders become cynical and sour from the challenges of leadership. The obstacles they face as leaders make them bitter instead of better! The fresh oil of the Holy Spirit will counteract the poisons that would try to taint our leadership.

We should become aware of the poisons that can paralyze and eventually destroy an elder's faith and leadership. Some of these poisons are unbelief, discouragement, apathy and the taking of an offense. Spending quality time with the Lord each day will cause our spiritual resistance to be strong against these spiritual poisons.

Elders especially need to become "offense proof." For example, there may come a time when an elder is attempting to rescue a sheep (believer) that is in the grip of a lion (personal struggle). The sheep is kicking and struggling to get free, and in the struggle the elder gets kicked by the very sheep he is trying to rescue! This believer, blinded by his own issues, may lash out at the elder when confronted.

Matthew 13:57 tells us that the people in Jesus' home town were offended because of Him. Jesus said in Matthew 18:7 that offenses must come, but in Luke 7:23 He said, "Blessed is he who is not offended because of Me." In John 16:1 Jesus declared, "These things I have spoken to you that you should not be made to stumble (be offended)." One of the greatest struggles in leadership is in the area of offenses.

A biblical study relates the word "offense" to bait used to catch animals. Monkeys are trapped by bait that is placed in a cage. When the monkeys reach into the cage to take the bait, they can escape only by releasing the bait and running away. But they usually do not want to release the prize, so they end up being trapped. If they would only release the bait, they could go free. When we forgive and release those who have offended us, we also can go free. It is up to us!

At various times in the scriptures, prayer and forgiveness are coupled together (Matthew 6:9-15; Mark 11:24-26). Forgiving others is crucial to maintaining a healthy, intimate relationship with Jesus.

## Only do what the Father is doing!

The Lord calls us to acknowledge Him in all of our ways, and then promises to direct our steps (Proverbs 3:6). We are exhorted in 1 Thessalonians 5:17 to pray continually (without ceasing). As we learn to practice the presence of the Lord in our lives, we will hear God's voice.

In John 5:17, Jesus said, "My Father has been working until now, and I have been working," and two verses later, Jesus says He does only what the Father is doing. The scriptures describe elders as co-laborers with Christ. So if we apply this in the local church setting, we can say that because the Father is already working there, the elders' approach should be to find out through prayer and fasting what the Father is doing and then reinforce and encourage it.

Ministry as an elder is much easier and more fruitful if we can find out God's vision and His plan for the church. If we don't take the time to do this, we can actually oppose the work of God with our own well-intentioned ideas.

## Fasting keeps elders spiritually fresh

In Matthew chapter six, Jesus taught that there was more power available through "prayer and fasting" than through "prayer" alone. When Jesus was questioned about fasting in Matthew 9:17, He responded that we should not pour new wine into old wineskins. He was teaching that fasting changes the wineskin (you) to receive the new wine (what God is speaking).

Fasting is often misunderstood because we cannot always see or feel what fasting is doing while it is in progress. The spiritual success of fasting cannot always be measured while we are fasting, but many victories are gained that we see evidence of later. Fasting brings us face to face with doubts and unbelief that have to be removed before faith arises in our hearts. It produces results, because Jesus said it would bear fruit.

Fasting, many times, will give a leader the correct understanding of how the scriptures speak to a certain situation. It paves the way for true Holy Spirit, prophetic enlightenment of the Word of God. Fasting may very well prevent divisions and strife in the church because the elders will walk in unity when they have fasted and heard clearly from God.

Daniel spent three weeks fasting when God revealed, through a vision, that there would be a great war in the not-too-distant future. He wanted to have some answers from God concerning the vision. Finally, an angel came to comfort him saying, "Do not be afraid, Daniel. Since the first day that you set your mind to gain understanding and to humble yourself before your God, your words were heard, and I have come in response to them" (Daniel 10:12). From the very first day Daniel had "set his mind to gain understanding," God promised to reveal the answer. Often the key to answering questions we have comes during seasons of fasting. Fasting keeps us fresh—spiritually, mentally and emotionally.

Should an elder tell others or not tell others about his fast? Many people have assumed that fasting should always be done secretly due to Jesus' rebuke of the Pharisees when they fasted for public show. However, Jesus did tell His disciples about His forty-day fast. Moses told the children of Israel about his fast. Paul spoke of frequent fasts. It is almost impossible for someone in spiritual leadership to fast and not tell anyone about it.

Jesus' admonition to "not look sober as the hypocrites do," when fasting (Matthew 6:16-18) has to do with drawing attention to your fasting. He is referring to those who say they are fasting and put on a long face to appear like they are suffering for Christ. The Pharisees were famous for drawing attention to themselves by tearing their clothes and putting ashes on their heads. This kind of behavior really shows spiritual pride in the heart. It stems from insecurity and immaturity.

Usually, it is not wrong to communicate that you are fasting. In fact, there are many good reasons to tell others. If you are weak, you can ask others for prayer. When church members know you are fasting, you set an example and others can be encouraged to fast or even join in. It demonstrates to young believers that God honors prayer and fasting as they observe an elder's prayers being answered. It will open the door for an elder to ask advice from other more experienced "fasters" in the church. However, if the Lord is requesting that you maintain a silent fast, then certainly you must obey Him.

Occasionally there will be specific times when the Lord will direct the elders to proclaim a corporate fast. This will generally be for major issues affecting the whole church. Although there is room for general fasting, the most significant  moves of God in response to fasting have been when individuals have a specific request and focus.

## Allowing God to speak through the people

Elders should realize that they do not have the final word or a private advantage to hearing God. Many times God will speak through members of the congregation. We find a great example in Acts 6:1-7. "Deacons" were selected by the people and then appointed by the apostles. Wise leaders will listen to what God says through His people. As an elder, you should receive input from those whom you serve before making a decision that affects them.

Deuteronomy 1:21-23 seems to indicate that the idea to send the spies to the Promised Land came from the people. However, Moses still made the decision. As mentioned earlier, wise parents will not plan a family vacation without consulting their children. It just makes sense. Many times small group leaders or other ministry leaders will have a sense of the spiritual climate of the church or more knowledge about specific needs in the body. Their input should also be sought after and considered. Hearing God through the small group leaders and the people takes undue pressure off of the elders. It defrays potential frustration that people could feel when leaders appear not to understand them or listen to them.

## Personal intercessors for elders

Intercessors in the church are believers with a mature gift of intercession who will hear things from God on a regular basis concerning the local church. These committed Christian pray-ers sense they have a special assignment from the Lord to pray for their elder(s) and their church. Elders should prayerfully consider any prophetic input they receive from intercessors as they make decisions and give leadership.

Senior elders should build a team of personal prayer partners who intercede for them. This small band of prayer warriors from the local church (and perhaps some from other churches), need to be handpicked by the Holy Spirit and the elder. As they serve the elder in prayer, they must be trusted in confidential matters. An elder could meet with his intercessor(s) every two to three months and receive ministry from them for himself and his spouse. The elder could also send his intercessors a list of prayer requests regularly so that the intercessors' prayers are accurately focused.

Personally, as leaders we have been so blessed by a team of intercessors who have stood with us in prayer during the past few years. It has made a tremendous difference for us, our ministries, our marriages, and our families. We recommend C. Peter Wagner's book *Prayer Shield* for more information on this topic.

## The elder's identity and emotional life

Elders must have a healthy sense of who they are, where they came from and where they are going. In John 13: 1-5 we find that Jesus was clear with these issues:

> It was just before the Passover Feast. Jesus knew that the time had come for him to leave this world and go to the Father. Having loved his own who were in the world, he now showed them the full extent of his love. The evening meal was being

served, and the devil had already prompted Judas Iscariot, son of Simon, to betray Jesus. Jesus knew that the Father had put all things under his power, and that he had come from God and was returning to God; so he got up from the meal, took off his outer clothing, and wrapped a towel around his waist. After that, he poured water into a basin and began to wash his disciples' feet, drying them with the towel that was wrapped around him.

Jesus knew that He had come from God and was returning to God, and thus He was free to serve the disciples. Jesus was secure enough in His own identity to put Judas in the seat of "honored guest" at the Last Supper. He was motivated by love. (See also John 8:14.)

An elder with a healthy sense of identity in Christ can lead and influence others most effectively. This will help an elder stay spiritually and emotionally strong because his identity comes from God and not from the expectations or approval of others. The elder is at peace with delegating to others and letting others use their gifts. Since the elder's identity comes from God and not from a title or from the function of being an elder, he can truly be at rest when leading.

## Four areas of life that must be in balance

In his book, *The Rhythm of Life*, Richard Exley states that there are four areas of life that must be in rhythm or balance to have a healthy life: work, worship, play and rest.[1] An elder should balance these areas of life.

## Work

Our work is a good and godly thing. Adam and Eve were assigned a job in tending the garden. Leaders, however, often try to accomplish more than is humanly possible! The number one reason leaders have too much to do is that they only feel good about themselves if they are involved in a lot of activity.

If completing more work is somehow better, then we can justify taking shortcuts to get things done. This rationalization leads to ethical compromise and character flaws, and it is a trap. According to Matthew 11:29-30, we should not be striving. Jesus' yoke is easy and His burden is light. Life is supposed to be a joy. This should be true if we are preaching or fixing refrigerators.

## Worship

Regular disciplines of prayer, scripture study, fasting, meditation, solitude and corporate worship lead to an abundant spiritual life. Taking a walk on the beach with your spouse and watching the sun set also qualifies as worship! Live a life-style of lavish worship and appreciation to the Father.

## Play

If you feel guilty when you relax, then you have a problem. Proverbs 17:22 teaches us that "a cheerful heart is good medicine." In our culture today, we experience emotional tiredness; it comes from the "inside out." This is unlike our grandparents, who experienced physical tiredness. It came from the "outside in" because they were plowing fields and beating rugs all day long. Play gives us refreshment from emotional tiredness and a healthy, rejuvenating sense of detachment.

## Rest

In Exodus 34:21 we find the "Sabbath principle." It speaks of times of rest, reflection and seasons of emotional release. A senior elder who works most of the day on Sunday needs to have a Sabbath day off during the week.

In addition to the weekly Sabbath rest, elders also need extended periods for rest and refreshing. A sabbatical is an extended leave of absence from full-time or part-time ministry. The term *sabbatical* is from the Hebrew word *Sabbath* which means *to rest*. According to Exodus 16:23, the Sabbath was a day set aside for rest as holy to the Lord. A sabbatical is like an extended Sabbath. The central purpose of a sabbatical is for spiritual, physical and emotional rest, and for assessment and evaluation of past, present and future ministry. It is a time of reflection and a time of retooling for the future. Retooling can include reading, taking classes, or attending a conference or a training seminar.

Sabbaticals should be taken on a regular basis. The purpose is to renew the leader and his or her family spiritually, physically, and emotionally. It is a time of reflection on the past and present and a time to renew focus and vision for the future. It is a time to get off the "treadmill," slow down, and recharge spirit and soul. The sabbatical is a time that should be planned in advance. It is not to be taken out of crisis or because a leader is ready to "crash and burn."

By definition, a sabbatical is intended to be preventative. Every seventh year, God instructed the people to allow their fields to rest (Leviticus 25:3-4). This Sabbath provided a time of recovery for the land as well as the people. The sabbatical is not an extended vacation or a chance to move in to other ministry opportunities. It is not a sick leave or a time to pursue academic degrees. It is not a time to accomplish all other life tasks for which one does not normally have time to do. It would not be healthy to enter into areas or environments during a sabbatical that would distract from the purpose of personal and family renewal.

In Mark 2:28, Jesus declared that He was *Lord of the Sabbath,* and He also revealed that man should benefit from a time of rest. We know this from Mark 2:27 which states, "…the Sabbath was made for man, not man for the Sabbath."

If sabbaticals occur in a systematic pattern, they will not have to be crisis-oriented. We recommend two to three months of sabbatical every seven years for elders who are considered church staff. One of the strengths of living a Sabbath life-style is that it allows an individual to detach from ministry.

When our church started as a new fellowship, we had no thought of sabbaticals. They were not even in our vocabulary. We wanted to save the world before Jesus came back—and time was running out! But as the years progressed, we realized that leaders often came to a place of burnout if they did not have a season of rest. Leaders were experiencing personal crisis and needed a sabbatical due to this crisis. So, rather than waiting for crisis and burnout, we realized the need for a life-style of sabbath rest and planned sabbaticals; that is, planned periods of detachment from ministry. Sabbaticals have been a great blessing to us.

For some guidelines on taking sabbaticals, see Appendix, page 219. Keith Yoder of *Teaching The Word Ministries* also has an excellent sabbatical resource for churches. [2]

## The importance of detachment

When Ronald Reagan was president of the United States, he would chop wood when he had free time. Why? Did they need wood to burn in the White House? Of course, not! It was detachment for him. It helped him keep a good perspective on leadership and make better decisions. Others will play golf or read books or cut their grass for detachment.

In his book, *Healthy Leaders*, Keith Yoder clearly expresses the importance of detachment when he says that a leader "must learn to detach himself from the burdens, emotions, struggles, weights, conflicts, pressures, weariness, and the monotony of leading the group. Detachment is important because a leader needs to be able to back off from his responsibilities and take a fresh look at them. To detach is that capacity to remain above circumstances, entanglements and problems that are present in your field of ministry." [3]

Detachment means staying or getting a little removed to have an eagle's eye or overall perspective of our ministry field. Detachment gives a leader the big picture. Why can this be so essential to good leadership for elders? Because excessive busyness and emotional entanglement with leadership responsibility can be devastating. It can result in burnout, loss of perspective, and confusion of identity for the elder(s) and the congregation. Elders need to get their heads out of the game for a while, so that they can think more clearly and make better decisions when in the heat of battle!

## Avoiding burnout

When four members of our apostolic team attended our international advisory meeting in Europe, we found ourselves discussing the subject of burnout. We all began to share what we do to avoid crashing in ministry. The following twelve guidelines to avoiding burnout in ministry are the result of that discussion. We trust that these guidelines will be helpful to eldership teams and to those with whom they minister.

## 1. Spiritual parents

An elder needs those who can observe his ministry and then lovingly speak into his life. Spiritual parents are those who can give fatherly or motherly advice to an elder. Often these people are apostolic individuals who will not be afraid to ask an elder difficult questions about his spiritual life, family relationships, priorities, or any other areas of struggle. These are persons who are not afraid to confront and speak the truth in love.

## 2. Friends with whom to be accountable

An elder needs friends, who know his other friends, so that he cannot hide. These should be people he can be free with, have fun with, share his struggles with, and pray with. It would, as well, be wise to have a network of friends who are not part of the congregation that the elder is leading to help provide a free atmosphere for sharing and support.

## 3. Healthy self-identity

An elder needs to look inside himself to discern whether his identity is found fully and completely in Jesus. Discovering who he is means letting go of the person that he or others think he ought to be so he can be who Jesus wants him to be. An elder knows where he has come from and where he is going (John 8:14). He will examine his life to see whose approval he is ultimately seeking (Galatians1:10). Is he trying to win the approval of men or of God? If he is trying to please men, he will be distracted from a full focus on God's will for his life and the ministry.

## 4. Stress control: Exercise / Diet / Sleep / Fun

An elder must maintain a balance of exercise, diet and sleep. Taking care of his physical body is just as important as taking care of his spiritual needs. An elder should follow a sensible exercise program, and avoid either overeating or following fad diets. An elder needs to know how much sleep he needs to be able to function well, and then maintain it. Sleep is a good and godly activity! "...he [God] grants sleep to those he loves" (Psalm 127:2). An elder should also find time for activities or hobbies he enjoys that provide an enjoyable release from constant work.

## 5. Sabbath rest

An elder can be tricked into thinking that no one else can possibly replace him. He can be made to believe that if he is not there, things will fall apart. But on the contrary, he should take mini sabbaticals and prayer retreats to refresh himself, including weekends away with his spouse and/or family. When he takes vacation time, he should actually be vacating! In addition, we recommend taking a sabbatical every seven years in the form of two to three months off, away from all ministry responsibilities.

## 6. Maintain emotional health

An elder should not allow himself to be depleted emotionally, but rather should stay emotionally healthy so that the ministry of Jesus can effectively flow through him. He would be wise to ask himself the following questions. Are there emotional wounds in my life that I have not dealt with? Am I harboring any bitterness or unforgiveness? Am I taking time to look inward and listen to Jesus honestly? Do I have time for prayer and study of the Word? Am I staying so busy that the Lord cannot speak to me about my inner self—my soul?

## 7. Carry out evaluations

It is advisable to do an annual evaluation that identifies needs in an elder's life, needs in his ministry and needs in his family. This recommended evaluation includes both self-evaluation and evaluation from others on the elders team. Even spiritual parents can be involved in this evaluation, depending on their relationship to the ministry. An elder needs the honest feedback of others who will encourage him and speak the truth about areas where growth is needed. The key question would be, "Is this elder responsibly carrying out his personal values and the values of the ministry?"

## 8. Have a clear ministry description

An elder must ask himself, "What is it that I am doing in ministry?" Clear descriptions, written by the elder in consultation with the elders team, keep him from feeling as though he *needs* to do everything. An elder needs to have boundaries or limits of ministry, because no single individual *can* do everything. When Jesus left this earth, not everybody was saved, healed and delivered.

## 9. Engage in ongoing study

Studying to grow both within and outside his ministry description is healthy for eldership individuals. For example, studying management principles might not directly be part of his job, but every leader must learn how to administer effectively. He should read and study for personal growth and personal education. Studying Christian and non-Christian books can challenge and expand the leader's thinking process.

## 10. Schedule regular medical exams

An elder needs regular medical checkups including, cholesterol, sugar level, and blood pressure checks. He should be advised if he finds his body susceptible to illnesses or has reoccurring physical problems.

## 11. Practice delegation

An elder must learn to train and release others. He must be proactive in giving away his responsibilities to others whom he is raising up in ministry. This involves having a "go and do likewise" mentality. Jesus sent out the twelve and then the seventy to eventually replace Him after He left the earth.

## 12. Prayer cover

Even when an elder takes all necessary precautions against burnout, he might still fall prey to its symptoms. We must remember that we are in a spiritual battle, and the enemy will try to attack us—especially those of us in leadership—in any way possible. To help shield an elder from spiritual attack, it is crucial to have prayer cover—people who are praying for him and hearing from God about him. These intercessors help fight the spiritual battles in the elder's life.

## Questions for discussion

1. Discuss ways in which fasting can bring about change in your life.
2. Describe ways in which you maintain balance as a leader.
3. Becoming "offense proof" as an elder is extremely important. Why?
4. Look over numbers 1-12 on pages 193-196. Which areas are you strong in and which areas do you need to grow in?

---

[1] Richard Exley, *The Rhythm of Life, (Tulsa*, OK: Honor Books, 1987).
[2] Keith Yoder, *Sabbatical Resource*, (One Mayfield Drive, Leola, PA 17540), Web site: www.ttwn.org or Email: mail@ttwm.org
[3] Keith Yoder, *Healthy Leaders,* (Ephrata, PA: House to House Publications, 1998), p.45.

# Passing the Eldership Tests

16

Roy Riegals was an All-American center for the University of California football team. He has gone down in history for making a humiliating mistake in the grand final game of the 1929 season.

Excitement and tension ran high as the California Golden Bears and the Yellowjackets from Georgia Tech battled for victory. Roy played both offense and defense. Close to the end of the first half, a Tech player fumbled the ball. Roy saw his chance, scooped up the loose ball and bolted towards the goal 65 yards away.

There was one problem however. Roy was running toward the wrong goal! Fortunately, one of his teammates went after him in hot pursuit and managed to tackle him just before he crossed the opposition's goal line!

It's hard to even imagine the embarrassment and shame that Roy must have felt there on the field with thousands of startled eyes focused on him, then walking off the field with head hanging low, and sitting in the locker room with his teammates and coach during the halftime break. No doubt the thousands of spectators wondered what Coach Nibbs Price would do with him.

In the locker room the dead silence was broken only by the sobs of the All-American star. Then Coach Price announced, "Men, the same team that started the first half will start the second half."

Roy, with red face and swollen eyes blurted out, "Coach, I can't do it. I've ruined you. I've ruined the University of California. I've ruined myself. I couldn't face that crowd in the stadium to save my life."

"Get up, Roy," the coach said. "Go back on. The game is only half over." Riegals was given a second chance, accepted it, returned to the game and gave one of the most inspiring individual efforts in Rose Bowl history![1]

Can you relate to Riegals "going the wrong way mistake"? From Moses to Deborah to Paul to Esther to Joshua—these leaders made mistakes and had to fight their battles to make it through to the end. They were tested, but they continued on in perseverance to the end. "I have fought the good fight, I have finished the race, I have kept the faith" (2 Timothy 4:7). Notice the progression in this verse. When God calls us to start, He will see us through to the finish, but there is always a fight until the end!

God will provide elders the grace to fight until the end, but let it be known that not everyone receives this grace and actually finishes the race. Absolom, the handsome and promising son of King David, was called of God. But he used unholy tactics to try to steal the throne from his father and died an untimely death without accomplishing what he could have in life.

Judas, one of the twelve disciples, because of greed and demonic influences on his life was another leader who did not finish the race or keep the faith. Today we have witnessed many national and international Christian leaders not finishing the race well because of falling into sin.

We all go through seasons in life. Church elders will be sure to go through at least three seasons of church life—the honeymoon season, the problem season and the perseverance-to-victory season.

The honeymoon season is the send off, the initial start when all is new and exciting. Then the reality of the struggles involved in ministry hits. You could call this the problem stage because this period can bring

*The Biblical Role of Elders for Today's Church*

confusion and conflict. The future is uncertain, and an elder may feel like he has entered a danger zone. Problems he never thought possible arise and sap his energy. It is during this season that he has to make a decision to deal with these problems effectively by confronting one problem at a time. It helps to separate them, so they are manageable. Often during this season an elder feels like quitting. He can quit and abort the plan of God, or he can continue on in perseverance.

A key posture to maintain in the perseverance stage is to "not look back." When you are driving, you keep your eyes on the road ahead, that is if you want to reach your destination intact. If you focus on what is happening behind you, you could very well end up wrapped around a telephone pole or plowed into the traffic in front of you. Focusing on our past failures and problems is mostly counterproductive. It will prevent us from moving forward. We can all look back at our lives and make the comment, "If only I had done such and such in that particular situation, maybe things would be different now." If we can see that the Lord wants to use our mistakes, trials and tribulations for His glory, we will be able to move on; otherwise, we get discouraged and give up.

Like Riegals, we must determine to regain what we have lost and stay in the game. We cannot give up.

## The tests in the wilderness

The Israelites spent forty years in the wilderness waiting to get into the promised land. They had to learn to survive in less than ideal conditions. It was a time of testing to see if they would remain faithful and persevere.

An elder will have a renewed vigor to obey God after going through a time of "testing in the wilderness," along with surviving and persevering. Here's what the Lord said to His people who persevered in the wilderness. "The people who survived the sword found grace in the wilderness—Israel, when I went to give him rest" (Jeremiah 31:2). After years of captivity, God promises that His people would again live together under His blessing. He promises rest for the weary after surviving the attacks of the enemy. Problems only provide the opportunity to grow and become more mature for leadership. Surviving the tests makes us humble, because we have been tested and remained faithful. In his book, *Spiritual Warfare for Every Christian,* Dean Sherman says leaders are tested in the wilderness to see if they will stand up in the heat of the battle:

God is looking for leaders. If the body of Christ lacks anything, it lacks secure, mature and consistent leaders. We don't need more positions filled. We need leaders who lead in humility and strength. Satan has launched an awesome attack on leaders in every level of society. From pastors to politicians to parents, they are falling every day. When a leader falls, the consequences are horrendous. But fallen leaders were not necessarily the wrong ones to lead. Perhaps they were never properly tested in the wilderness. Perhaps fame and fortune or their own theology kept them from tests that would have strengthened and established them, or exposed them as unprepared for leadership.

Thousands of individuals are not surviving because they believe they have a God-given right to escape the wilderness. They wake up one morning to find themselves in the midst of a most unexpected wilderness, and they fall apart. God wants leaders who will willingly stand and be tested by the wilderness. The greater a person's potential for leadership, the greater the tests he or she will face.

As you read this, I can unreservedly promise you leadership. I cannot promise you a title, but I can promise you leadership. If you give yourself to developing Christian character, if you go through the tests and prove yourself, the world will beat a path to your door, regardless of your gifts, background or personality. They will want what you have. You will lead them to Christ by your example. The church needs those who will allow God to develop them so that they will stand up in the heat of the battle and not betray nor disappoint those who look to them for strength and stability.

We all go through wilderness experiences to see whether or not we will keep God's commandments. It is almost always in the wilderness that we blow it: that's where we fall. The wilderness is where we have a tendency toward certain sins, where it is easier to move in the wrong direction. If we are prone to lust, we will lust in the wilderness. It will be a time when we are tempted to quit, to fall, to sin, and to step out of the will of God.

God sends us through these times not to fail, but to prevail. If we can remain faithful and obedient, keeping His commandments in the wilderness, we will excel in every situation. This is God's desire for each of us. If we continue to obey Him in difficult times, we are truly committed. However, if we cannot keep His commandments in the wilderness, we are not really committed.

The wilderness is one of the best places for us to grow. When we go through the wilderness, resisting sin, obeying God, and withstanding every temptation, then we truly have character and are growing spiritually. But even if we blow it, we shouldn't give up. We should repent, humble ourselves and determine again to overcome by God's grace. We should never let the enemy force us out of the wilderness school.[2]

## Twelve "wilderness tests" you may face as an elder
## 1. The test of your calling

An elder is called by God. He is called to service and is one who serves by leading. Elders have heard God's call and have an inner conviction and desire to lead the family of God in the local church. This desire has to be Spirit-generated or an elder will want to give up when the task becomes difficult and demanding.

Paul knew he was called by God to be an apostle and said so in his letter to the Corinthian church. "Paul, called to be an apostle of Christ Jesus by the will of God...." [3] This is why he did not seek to win the approval of men. He was secure in his calling. He knew who had called him and he had his priorities in order. "Am I now trying to win the approval of men, or of God? Or am I trying to please men? If I were still trying to please men, I would not be a servant of Christ."[4]

Paul knew there was a cost to his calling because Christ said, "Come after me, take up your cross and follow me." Though tremendously fulfilling, the leadership role of an elder can be marked with pain, sacrifice, and conflict. There will always be those who disagree with the elder's style of leadership. Some will think he makes decisions too fast, and some will think he makes decisions too slowly. Others may question whether you should even be an elder. Remember, God calls us— not man.

Daniel, Joseph and Esther are just a few of the many biblical examples of godly people who were severely tested in their callings. They were placed in situations that were out of their control, but they allowed God to take over. They knew they were called for "such a time as this," and they hung in there during the tests.

Elders grow when they are in situations that are out of their control. In these situations, they have to depend totally on the Lord or they will fail. Elders that have been tested in their calling are secure and mature.

## 2. The test of humility

Humility is an attitude of total dependence on Jesus. Why should we be humble? 1 Peter 5:5 tells us, "All of you, clothe yourselves with humility toward one another, because, 'God opposes the proud but gives grace to the humble.'"

Humility is an absence of pride in our lives. It is a total dependence on God. It is being conscious of your weaknesses and willing to give God all the credit for things you have achieved and accomplished.

The word "clothe" in the Greek means to attach a piece of clothing to oneself. In the New Testament times, slaves attached a white piece of cloth on their clothing so that others would know that they were slaves. Peter exhorts us to tie the cloth of humility on ourselves in order to be identified as believers in Christ as we act humbly toward others. In this way we will receive God's grace and help.[5]

Jesus contrasted Himself with the proud religious leaders in Matthew 11:29 by saying, "Take my yoke upon you and learn of me, for I am gentle and humble in heart, and you will find rest for your souls."

A test of an elder is to ask, "Who am I as a person? Am I gentle and humble, or dominating and proud?" Pride gives an elder an exaggerated sense of his own importance. An elder who walks in genuine humility understands his deficiencies as well as his capabilities. He is willing to share his authority with others so they can be empowered for ministry.

Elders do not seek honor or titles or special treatment. They serve because they are called by God and see the need for godly leadership in His body.

Separating ourselves or exalting ourselves above others is sectarianism. God hates sectarianism. This spirit that says "We are right and you are wrong" divides the family of God. If we believe our church has the only right doctrine or has a better model of doing church than others, we can easily fall into pride. There is nothing wrong with being unique and finding what works best for us and our church. But be advised that not everything that works for us will work for everyone. Yes, even if we promote our interpretation of "elders in the church" as the only leadership model that is valid in today's church, it is wrong. God loves diversity and will use many people and methods to build His kingdom.

## 3. The test of teamwork and relationship

Teamwork is demonstrated for us in the way the Father, Son and Holy Spirit work together as one, yet each has his own role: God uses teamwork. The early church appointed elders to work together "in every town" (Titus 1:5).

Sometimes a senior elder may think, "If only I had a more experienced, mature team, we could move full-steam ahead." At the same time, the team may be thinking, "If only our senior elder were a better leader, we could really go somewhere!" Teamwork means that each elder on the team is convinced without a shadow of a doubt that every other elder is vital to the team's success.

In George Barna's book *Leaders on Leadership*, "teamwork" is described as "working together toward the fulfillment of a desired outcome without the loss of one's individuality."[6] Senior elders should find others to work with who have the strengths they lack. Each person on the team has something unique to offer, and their differing gifts round out the mix. Allow each person to use their gifts to get specific jobs done. God will put others on a team who can do things much better than the senior elder. That is exactly what a senior elder should look for—he wants to find those who, through relationship rather than competition, can resource his weaknesses.

A senior elder was heard saying, "Every act of courage I take is usually sparked by the team around me." Teamwork encourages the senior elder to listen to his team, be inspired by them and remain steadfast so as not to let his loyal armor-bearers down.

If the team is not focused and in unity about the direction of the church, the team will be tested. Good communication and respect for each other through committed relationships will result in successful teamwork.

## 4. The test of idolatry

The elders of Israel were guilty of idolatry in their hearts. God refused to answer their prayers anymore because they desired an ungodly way of life (Ezekiel 14:3). If we want the Lord to speak to us and guide us, our hearts cannot be filled with desires that rise above our love for Jesus.

If something means more to us than Jesus, it is idolatry. Idols in our lives may be our churches, ministries or even our families. If an elder's church takes first priority in his life, it is an idol in his life. God wants our first love. He wants to be the first in our desires before our ministries. If we are in love with a method, philosophy of ministry, or church structure, it is an idol. Only Jesus is worthy of our true worship and full devotion.

In the early 1980's, our new cell-based church started with much excitement about small group ministry and its potential in church life. Pouring all our energies into it, we discussed, thought and dreamed about "cell vision." Eventually, it dawned on us that we were exalting a cell vision above Jesus. In *Helping You Build Cell Churches,* we recall our mistake:

> 1 John 5:21 tells us to keep ourselves from idols. Jesus shares His glory with none other, not even a good cell vision. This was the biggest mistake we ever made as a church! We repented for exalting the cell vision above Jesus.[7]

Although we continue to believe a small group vision is a successful strategy for church growth, we also recognize that we need many kinds of churches to fulfill the Great Commission. Promoting one particular way of "doing church" can be an idol if it becomes more important to us than Jesus.

## 5. The test of spiritual fathering and mothering

There is such great potential for elders to spiritually parent potential leaders in the church and help them find their identity and purpose in life. When elders model spiritual parenting, they are willing to raise children who may go way beyond them in ministry with double-anointings that surpass their own. True fathers and mothers will joyously release their children to start their own homes.

It can be tempting to keep our best and promising leaders "in house" to help us fulfill our vision. We pass the test when we can release them to step out on their own and encourage and support them in the process. Churches that do not send out people to plant new churches risk eventual stagnation.

## 6. The test of timing and change

In Acts 6:1-7 we read of the early church in a time of change. The apostles realized they were spending far too much time attending to the mundane affairs of the church and did not have enough time for prayer and the preaching of the Word. This situation required that the leaders take a new look at what they could do to alleviate this burden. Consequently they appointed deacons to help them. The change worked well for the church and allowed its leaders to be more fruitful.

Usually change is not easy. When it occurs in a church, people often feel lost or even go through a grieving process as they give up the old and accept the new. Some people feel hostility in times of transition.

Elders realize the importance of teaching the church values from the Word of God. Vision will change, but the values stay the same. If people see it in the Bible, they will have faith to endure the change.

Stability in the local church and healthy leadership decisions allows people to place trust in their leaders. If too many changes happen too quickly, the trust can disappear. It is like keeping money in a bank account—too many withdrawals will lower the balance. Elders must be aware of the balance in their trust accounts. They must maintain credit in their "trust accounts." We discourage elders from making major changes in the church when the "trust account" is low.

Elders should not move too fast. They must give people time to go through changes. Larry grew up on a farm and recalls driving a truckload of potatoes in from the fields. If he traveled too fast or turned too sharply, the potatoes went bouncing off the truck. People will "bounce off the truck" if we make abrupt decisions during transitional times in the church.

In 1996, our church went through some radical change. We transitioned from one mega-church into eight smaller churches. Releasing the people and the elders took up to three years, but it was worth the effort and time.

Steve and his wife Mary were conducting a couples' seminar with a church and discovered that several years earlier this church had transitioned from a program-based church to a cell-based church. Intrigued, they asked the leaders how they accomplished such a radical change and how much time it took.

*The Biblical Role of Elders for Today's Church*

The senior leader replied, "We, as an eldership team took the necessary time to make the transition ourselves. We placed ourselves within a leadership cell and developed the needed material that our congregation could utilize for themselves."

The next phase of his explanation was really impressive. "We knew people change slowly, and they must be convinced of the need for change. Consequently, we divided the church into thirds and over the period of one year, took each third away on a retreat."

During that weekend, the leaders shared the vision, trained cell leaders and placed participants into cell groups. It was costly, but it worked. It gave the leaders the platform to speak about the values of small groups and to build trust. These wise leaders took the necessary time and transitioned a very large congregation successfully.

## 7. The test of false accusations

In the Old Testament, if a man had suspicions that his wife was adulterous, he could bring her before the Lord to determine her guilt or innocence. She had to drink holy water with the dust from the tabernacle floor mixed in. If she were guilty, she would become ill and never bear children (Numbers 5:11-28). Whether she was innocent or guilty, she had to drink the bitter cup, because God was her only vindicator. This is how it is for us when we are misunderstood. God will vindicate us.

Tom was a senior elder of a successful church who had to face the horrible test of false accusations. God spoke to Tom during this test that He Himself was Tom's vindicator and if he tried to defend himself, he would not prosper. Here is Tom's story.

Tom was well-respected in his community and church and around the world as an international speaker. One day, after returning home from an overseas trip, his team of five elders informed him that they were taking over the church. One of the outspoken and stronger elders had seduced the others into believing lies about Tom, convincing them that he was unfit for leadership. The elder convinced the others that his actions were for the best and that he would implement discipline to preserve Tom and his ministry. Although the accusing elder never really defined exactly what it was that Tom had done, wild rumors circulated and ran rampant. Tom's reputation was destroyed by innuendo. Since the Lord told him not to defend himself by seeking legal action for this false allegation, Tom chose to resign and walk away. Tom was devastated but chose not to strike back.

Finally, months later at a meeting of the church elders and other outside leaders, the accusing elder was discovered to be lying about the accusations. But it was too late. The people in the church were confused and distraught. After several months, the thriving church of 350 soon dwindled to 40, then 10, and then disappeared. Twenty years of ministry, including all the resources of ministry—church building, video equipment, tapes, books—was lost.

In all this drama, Tom did not try to defend himself. He drank the bitter cup without fighting back. Today, God has given Tom a ministry far beyond the scope of what he had before. Tom feels that the most valuable thing he learned was that his value is not in substance—how many people are in his ministry or how successful he appears as a leader. He learned that it is only in the presence of the Lord that he could find forgiveness for those who wronged him. Today, he preaches a message that "mercy triumphs over judgment."

"If you do not forgive," he says, "you are the one who pays the price. Don't bad-mouth other churches or ministries or believe the worst."

There are two types of ministry before the throne of God: Jesus' ministry of intercession and Satan's ministry of accusation. These same two "ministries" can be found in the church. Let's be leaders who extend Jesus' ministry of intercession to others. If we are falsely accused, we must become offense proof and extend forgiveness. Truth will triumph. We do not have to defend ourselves. Instead, we must focus on the Lord and His presence in our lives. He will vindicate.

## 8.The test of dependency on the Lord

Paul told the Corinthian believers, "But by the grace of God I am what I am, and his grace to me was not without effect. No, I worked harder than all of them—yet not I, but the grace of God that was with me" (1 Corinthians 15:10). We must love with the realization that we are completely dependent on the grace of God. If our church is growing and healthy, it is because of the grace of God, not because of our leadership abilities. If our church is in a season of struggle, it could be much worse, except for the grace of God.

In Philippians 3:10 Paul tells us, "I want to know Christ and the power of His resurrection and the fellowship of sharing in his sufferings, becoming like him in his death." Paul had passed the test. After all that he accomplished as a leader in the New Testament church, he was convinced that knowing Christ better was to be his main focus and ultimate desire.

It is our ministry in the church to help each other stay close to Jesus and dependent on Him. Christ is the head of the body, the church, so "that in every respect He might have first place" (Colossians 1:18). Jesus wants first place in our lives. We must be desperate for the Lord. When we stay close to the Lord, we become more and more like Him. Are we desperate to know more of God? Desperate leaders produce desperate people.

## 9. The test of vision

Vision will be tested, so we should constantly watch to see what God is doing and what He is saying. Things change on an eldership team—the leaders, the opportunities, the demographics, etc. Certain parts of the vision may need to be refined, although the core of the vision remains the same.

Every church needs a compelling vision. Vision articulated clearly and carefully will build trust among the people as it is something they can believe in. People will follow if they choose to embrace the spoken and written vision as their own.

Habakkuk 2:2-3 not only tells us to write the vision down but also says the vision may be tested. This verse mentions that God's purposes in the vision are moving ahead toward fulfillment, but there may seem to be unnecessary delays. Every eldership team must seek the Lord and have faith to see the vision fulfilled as they move forward. Proverbs 29:18 says, "Where there is no vision, the people perish" (KJV). Unless your local church has a sense of direction and purpose, the people will struggle with a relational connection to the church and its leaders.

Relationship connection is important at all levels. Leaders can project vision, but if relationships of trust are not evidenced between the senior elder and the elders, as well as the congregation with the elders, vision will remain unfulfilled. If leaders are only interested in their vision being fulfilled by those within the congregation, it will not be long until people feel used or taken advantage of. Wise leaders recognize that the process of sharing vision, building trust, and taking enough time for God's people to own the vision is as important as the vision itself.

## 10. The test *of agape* love

*Agape* love is giving without the expectancy of return. It is the straight arrow of love that flies free in one direction to give to others unselfishly. John 3:16 speaks of this love, "For God so loved..." We can be sure that an elder's love will be tested to see if it is unconditional.

Beware of showing partiality in the church. Everyone, great and small, is precious in God's sight. Elders may be tested when they have the opportunity to spend extra time with wealthy members of their church and become infatuated with their "creature comforts." One church leader repented after he realized he was favoring a wealthy church member who owned a yacht, and his underlying motivation was to spend time on the yacht.

Our Savior was compassionate about people and their needs. When Jesus saw the crowds, He had compassion (Matthew 9:36). Compassion compels us to give and not be upset if something is not given back to us. Colossians 3:12 tells us to clothe ourselves with compassion. Compassion, unlike pity, gives people a path out of their pain. We must, however, pass the test if our compassion is rejected.

## 11. The test of purity

Elders will be tested in purity. Every Christian believer is well-aware of the dreadful realities of human depravity and the deceitfulness of sin. This should cause us to desire accountability in our lives. Everyone needs practical accountability, including church leaders. Church elders need to be accountable to others for the way they live their Christian lives and for the way they are directing the church.

Since elders are those chosen and appointed from within the church, their lives are known to the church. Their qualifications speak to their temperaments, their values, how they treat their spouses and children, and their personal character. Because they live their lives in full view of others, they are well known by the church. This is extremely healthy. With these close relationships, they have a built-in accountability surrounding them.

Athletes who train together push each other to greater heights. The same is true in eldership teams as elders sharpen and encourage each other in every area of life. A team of elders working together in close relationship provides a structure for genuine accountability. It is hard to hide sins of pride, greed or the love of power when the surrounding team of elders provides built-in accountability. The peer relationships of elders serve to help each other in weaknesses and nudge each one to accomplish his responsibilities before the Lord.

An elder walking in accountability with other elders also walks in close proximity with Jesus so that sin will have no hold on his life, "...for the prince of this world is coming. He has no hold on me, but the world must learn that I love the Father and that I do exactly what my Father has commanded me" (John 14:30-31). This kind of church leader, who welcomes accountability, chooses to walk in purity and accountability in full view of his congregation.

Elders, as visible leaders of the church, are examples to the rest of the church, but they are not immune to temptations. Adam and Eve, David and Bethsheba—the failures of Bible greats are on public display to attest to the fact that leaders are as susceptible as anyone. Satan is out to steal, kill and destroy and he will target leaders because he knows "the bigger they are, the harder they fall." In other words, the ministry of an elder touches a great number of people, so if he is tempted and succumbs to sin, the repercussions are often more heartbreaking and far-reaching.

With leadership and its responsibilities and potential stressors, there are three major temptations that can lurk, waiting to derail an elder's ministry and integrity before God. 1 John 2:16 lists these three temptations as sexual temptation (the cravings of sinful man), the love of money (the lust of the eyes), and pride (the boasting of what he has and does).

Notice that these three are twisted versions of legitimate and wonderful gifts God wants to give us. Sex, within its perimeters of marriage, is a wonderful gift. But the emphasis of sex outside of marriage in today's sex-saturated society makes it a challenge to stay morally pure, bringing great devastation to those who succumb. Billy Graham set a standard in this area. He would not spend time alone with a woman other than his wife or daughters. He has been committed to "abstaining from every appearance of evil," and Billy is finishing well. He passed the test!

God blesses us with money to advance His kingdom here on earth and provide for our needs. On the other hand, *the love of money* turns some away from serving the Lord faithfully. If Jesus is not Lord of an elder's money, He will not be Lord of his life.

If we trust in our accomplishments, it leads to pride. An elder is often a self-motivated person and willing to step in where others are hesitant. This drive, which may lead the elder to great success, can negatively lead him to pride. A senior elder with a thriving church needs to guard his heart to avoid the temptation of becoming puffed up with pride. God-esteem is knowing who we are in Christ and is needed to live a healthy spiritual life.

## 12.The test of security

Jesus was secure in His Father's love. As stated earlier, He knew where He had come from, why He was here on earth, and where He was going (John 8:14). That's how He could kneel down and wash His disciples' feet in the upper room, even when He knew what would soon happen. His healthy relationship with His heavenly Father enabled Jesus to pass on to His disciples a spiritual inheritance and example of servanthood (John 8:28). Elders who are secure in their heavenly Father's love are free to serve their spiritual sons and daughters in the local church, expecting nothing in return. They do not need their egos stroked in order to function in their role as leaders. They are happy to serve. They know they are deeply loved by God.

## Overcoming the tests

God will take us through tests to build our character. Abraham Lincoln was a man who overcame incredible setbacks and disappointments in his life before he became president of the United States. His mother died when he was nine years old, and he grew up poverty-stricken. Abe had less than one year of formal education. As a young man, he lost his job as a store clerk. He later became a partner in a business that failed and left him with a large debt. After courting a young lady for years and asking for her hand in marriage, he was rejected. Later he met a young women he had an interest in, but she died.

In his early thirties, he decided to run for state office and lost. He ran again and lost. Finally after several years, he was elected, but when reelection time came two years later, he lost again. At age 40, he was rejected for another political appointment and suffered a nervous breakdown. He also had a son who died during this time. In his mid-forties, he ran for the Senate and was defeated. A few years later, when he ran for the vice-president of the United States, he lost. Finally, at age 51, he was elected president of the United States!

Abe Lincoln refused to quit. He was a godly man who persevered and went on to become one of the greatest presidents of the United

States. During the Civil War, he led the nation with wisdom and patience, and is known as the Great Emancipator for helping to abolish slavery in the United States. If this great man had quit in the wilderness, who knows what would have happened to the course of history in the United States? Lincoln faced the tests and persevered to victory.

Hebrews 12:2 gives us great advice for moving ahead when faced with tests in the wilderness. "Let us fix our eyes on Jesus...who endured the cross...." Jesus endured the cross, the most horrible pain and suffering imaginable, and yet He persevered.

Elders must keep their eyes on Jesus, only then can they persevere and enter the "perseverance to victory" season. When elders enter this season, they have decided to finish the plan God has given them. This is the kind of biblical elder God is giving the church today. They refuse to give up as they continue to trust Jesus who is their source of strength and help.

## Questions for discussion

1. Which season is your church currently going through? Is it the honeymoon season, the problem season or the perseverance-to-victory season?

2. How have problems provided you with an opportunity to grow and become more mature in your leadership?

3. Name and describe a wilderness test you have faced.

4. Are you going through a wilderness test at this time in your life? Are you willing to share it so we can pray for you?

[1]  Dick Innes, "Thank God for Second Chances," Lifehelp Ministries, Living Message Fellowship, 1999.
[2]  Dean Sherman, *Spiritual Warfare for Every Christian*, (Seattle, WA: YWAM Publishing), p. 148-149.
[3]  1 Corinthians 1:1
[4]  Galatians 1:1,10
[5]  *Full Life Study Bible*, (Grand Rapids, Michigan: Zondervan Publishing Company, 1992), p. 1962.
[6]  George Barna, *Leaders On Leadership*, "Building a Team to Get the Job Done" by Tom Phillips, (Ventura, California: Regal, 1997), p.214.
[7]  *Helping You Build Cell Churches*, by Brian Sauder and Larry Kreider, (Ephrata, PA: House to House Publications, 2000), p.71

## Epilogue

Throughout this book, we, the authors, have endeavored to present to you a concise, fair and experiential view of God's plan for eldership. We truly have enjoyed the opportunity to write about our experiences and our discoveries in this area of New Testament church leadership.

Whether you are praying about building an eldership team, considering eldership, or have been an elder, we pray that what we have attempted to communicate is helpful, inspiring and perhaps even life-changing for you and the segment of the body of Christ that you represent.

Certainly this has not been an exhaustive volume, but it is presented to you and to our Lord in a spirit of love and humility. We feel honored that you have chosen to take the time to read this book. We would like to close with a prayer for you to be able to practically apply what the Lord has taught you and spoken to you specifically.

*Dear Heavenly Father, we come to You on behalf of the precious men and women of God who are called to oversee Your church. We confess that within ourselves we do not possess these abilities, but like Paul, we know that when we are weak, You are strong within us. Lord Jesus, we ask for the gift of Your government to come upon elders to care for, oversee, teach, and direct the flock. We pray that this is not just a position, but embraced as a life call. May we each remember who it is we serve and remain humble in Your sight. We love you, Jesus, and we love your family. In your Holy Name, Amen.*

# Church Leadership
# Evaluation Tools

On the next 3 pages are some sample questionnaires for teams of elders

**The complete set includes 17 evaluations: Eldership Evaluations, Senior Elder Evaluations, Apostolic Evaluations, Staff Evaluations, Interim Evaluations, Team and Cell Group Evaluations**
*Purchase the complete, reproducible set of Church Leadership and Staff Evaluation Tools, by Steve Prokopchak, in a three ring binder at House to House Publications. Call 800.848.5892 or order online at www.dcfi.org/House2House*

## Personal Evaluation for Team Members

Name _____

Date _____

*Instructions: As an elder, prayerfully respond to the following questions about your role and function on the eldership team. Be sure to include your spouse's input as you reflect upon these questions.*

1.  Comment on the joys, disappointments and growth in your personal experience as a leader in the past year.
2.  Analyze the balance of priorities within your life-style (work, play, rest, Sabbath, relationships, health, etc.)
3.  How have your eldership responsibilities affected your marriage/family life (both positively and negatively)?
4.  Describe your specific areas of responsibility as you see them.
5.  What have you learned in the past 6-12 months that has significantly changed or helped your ministry?
6.  Report on two or three major goals that you have achieved in the past year.
7.  List several areas of strength in your ministry.
8.  List several areas that need improvement in your ministry.
9.  How have you grown in your leadership responsibilities in the past year?
10. How would you describe your own working relationship with the eldership team?
    Are you satisfied with the quality and quantity of relationship with elders and with the senior elder?
11. What recommendations for improvement do you have for the way the eldership team functions together? Do you feel comfortable to make suggestions and give input?
12. Comment on your level of satisfaction concerning prayer and worship together as a team.
13. Are there any adjustments in your responsibilities of leadership that you sense the Lord wants you to make in the coming year?

# Questions for Senior Elder to Consider in Evaluating Team Members

Elder being evaluated _____

Your name _____ Date _____

*Instructions: As a senior elder, review the following questions in light of the elder you are evaluating. On the next page, make note of responses you desire to expound upon in order to provide helpful and accurate feedback.*

| Yes | No | Usually | Don't know | |
|-----|----|---------|-----------|---|
| ☐ | ☐ | ☐ | ☐ | Does this elder honor and value you as a senior elder? |
| ☐ | ☐ | ☐ | ☐ | Is this elder open in his walk with the Lord including his struggles? |
| ☐ | ☐ | ☐ | ☐ | Is the elder open with you and the other elders on the team about his family? |
| ☐ | ☐ | ☐ | ☐ | Does the elder give healthy affirmation to you as a senior elder? |
| ☐ | ☐ | ☐ | ☐ | Do you feel the elder releases you in a healthy way to obey God? |
| ☐ | ☐ | ☐ | ☐ | Does the elder clearly communicate to you the vision he has within his heart for the church? |
| ☐ | ☐ | ☐ | ☐ | Does the elder clearly communicate the vision the Lord has given to this church? |
| ☐ | ☐ | ☐ | ☐ | Do you feel valued by the elder as a person? |
| ☐ | ☐ | ☐ | ☐ | Does the elder make decisions too quickly without receiving enough input? |
| ☐ | ☐ | ☐ | ☐ | Does the elder take too long in making decisions and drag things out? |
| ☐ | ☐ | ☐ | ☐ | Does the elder value input from cell leaders and other people in the church? |
| ☐ | ☐ | ☐ | ☐ | Does the elder place enough value and emphasis on training and equipping of cell leaders/small group leaders? |
| ☐ | ☐ | ☐ | ☐ | Are the elder's teachings inspiring and do they minister grace and conviction? |
| ☐ | ☐ | ☐ | ☐ | Does the elder take a clear stand on sin? |

| Yes | No | Usually | Don't know | |
|---|---|---|---|---|
| ☐ | ☐ | ☐ | ☐ | Do you see the Lord working in the elder's life in a way that others would desire to imitate? |
| ☐ | ☐ | ☐ | ☐ | Is the elder viewed as a trusted leader by others in the church? |
| ☐ | ☐ | ☐ | ☐ | Does the elder encourage decision-making in a way that builds trust? |
| ☐ | ☐ | ☐ | ☐ | Does the elder honor and encourage other leaders for their service in the Lord? |
| ☐ | ☐ | ☐ | ☐ | Does the elder provide you with sufficient and clear communication? |
| ☐ | ☐ | ☐ | ☐ | Does the elder think in terms of empowering God's people when making decisions? |
| ☐ | ☐ | ☐ | ☐ | Does the elder fulfill the responsibilities that you give him? |
| ☐ | ☐ | ☐ | ☐ | Are you able to freely confront this elder in regards to any area of needed correction? |

List the elder's strengths.

1.

2.

3.

List some areas in which the elder can grow.

1.

2.

3.

# Sabbaticals for Church Leaders
## Guidelines for a Meaningful Sabbatical

### Definition

The term sabbatical is from the Hebrew word *Sabbath* which means *to rest*. According to Exodus 16:23, it was a day set aside for rest as holy and unto the Lord. A sabbatical is an extended leave of absence from full-time or part-time ministry. The purpose is to renew the leader and his or her family spiritually, physically, and emotionally. It is a time of reflection on the past and present and a time to renew focus and vision for the future. It is a time to get off the "treadmill," slow down, and recharge your spirit and soul.

The sabbatical is not an extended vacation. It is not a sick leave or to be used for pursuing other ministry opportunities. It is not a time to pursue academic degrees. It is not a time to accomplish all other life tasks that one does not normally have time for. It would not be healthy to enter into areas or environments during a sabbatical that would distract from the purpose of personal and family renewal.

### Purpose

The central purpose of a sabbatical is for spiritual, physical and emotional rest, assessment, and reevaluation of past, present, and future ministry. It is a time of reflection and a time of retooling for the future. Retooling can include reading, taking a class or classes, attending a conference or training seminar.

### Prevention

This time is to be planned for. It is not to be taken out of need or "burnout." By definition, a sabbatical is to be preventative. Every seventh year God instructed the people to allow their fields to rest (Leviticus 25:3,4). This Sabbath provided a time of recovery for the land as well as the people. Sabbaticals would be recommended at seven year intervals.

In Mark 2:28, Jesus declared that He was Lord of the Sabbath and He also revealed that man should benefit from a time of rest. We know this from Mark 2:27 which states, "...the Sabbath was made for man, not man for the Sabbath."

### Length/Support

The length of a sabbatical can be determined by the need and the leaders of the local church. Generally, a sabbatical would not exceed three months and not less than two months. The staff member receives his or her full salary and benefits during the sabbatical. Compensation for counseling, travel, training, etc. should be considered by the overseers.

## Preparation

Because sabbaticals are meant to be preventative and because budgets are set approximately one year in advance, it is best to request a sabbatical 12 months ahead of time or before the budgeting process. This will allow preparation for interim persons to serve and cover ministry descriptions when the staff person is on his sabbatical.

## Qualifications

Sabbaticals are for those persons serving in a full-time or part-time "pastoral" ministry description.

## Supervision

Supervision throughout the sabbatical time is important. This person provides the necessary accountability factor for the one on sabbatical and the personal touch needed from "home base."

It is the responsibility of the one providing supervision to call the staff person at least once every three weeks to be sure there is follow through with the purpose and goals of the sabbatical for the staff member and his/her family.

## Evaluation

Evaluation is made before the sabbatical begins to determine needs: for example, educational/training needs, family needs, counseling needs, and financial needs. At this time, an outline can be designed for the purpose, goals, and needs of the staff member. It is to be determined who will oversee this person while on sabbatical and provide regular accountability checkups.

An evaluation overview is also to be performed two weeks before the predetermined end of the sabbatical to assess further needs of the staff member and whether or not there is need to extend the sabbatical time.

Lastly, a final evaluation at the close of the sabbatical can help process the predetermined goals of this time and provide for feedback. This evaluation meeting should also serve to transition the staff member back into their ministry function/role.

## Guidelines for Discipline and Restoration
### for DCFI Partner Church Members

This policy is a guideline only. DCFI partner churches will apply discipline (and if appropriate) restoration, as deemed appropriate in any particular situation.

As we look at the subject of "Church Discipline, Reconciliation, and Restoration," let us do so with the understanding that the Lord God we serve is a God who disciplines, reconciles, and restores. Hebrews 12:11 tells us, *No discipline seems pleasant at the time, but painful. Later on, however, it produces a harvest of righteousness and peace for those who have been trained by it.*

Discipline in all that it is, is an essential element of healthy and vibrant growth. This is true in the natural as well as in the spiritual. We only need to look around at our culture to see the fruit of undisciplined lives. With this lack of discipline has come a lack of personal integrity and responsibility. Rather than accepting responsibility for our actions, there is a projecting of blame and responsibility. This abdication of personal responsibility and trust, has led to an avoidance of issues through a deep need for personal self preservation.

True discipline flows out of our need for relationships and accountability. Mankind was designed by the Lord to have limits and for correction to occur when those limits are breached. We can easily see this in the Garden of Eden. Limits were both in the Garden itself and in the command not to eat of the tree of the knowledge of good and evil. When the limits of the command were broken, discipline occurred. Even as Christians, we have been given freedom and limits. These freedoms within their corresponding limits are there to serve us in the discipline of our lives.

The Father has the right to discipline our lives because we are His. The fact that He disciplines us at all, is a proof that we are His children (Hebrews 12:1-13). Since we are His children, we need to recognize, be thankful for and submit to His disciplining (shaping) process.

There are various types of discipline, but they all have the same purpose: to so shape our hearts and lives, that we are brought into conformity with the image and likeness of Jesus Christ. The Bible says, *Him we preach, warning every man and teaching every man in all wisdom, that we may present every man perfect in Christ Jesus. To this end I also labor, striving according to His working which works in me mightily* (Colossians 1:28-29).

When we look at types of discipline mentioned in the scriptures, we see two general distinctions: Discipline that teaches, instructs and equips us through a *positive* form of discipline and discipline that teaches, instructs and equips us through a *punitive* form of discipline.

### Positive Discipline

The shaping of our hearts and lives to ever increasingly reflect the person and glory of Christ Jesus our Lord, through correction, warning, reproof, rebuking, teaching, training in righteousness, prayer, personal ministry, deliverance, relational accountability, friendship and discipleship.

## Punitive Discipline

Punitive discipline is the shaping of our lives through direct application of governmental authority and consequence. This often results in punitive measures being taken to assert the authority of Christ Jesus within the hearts and lives of the people of God, his church. This may result in public rebuke, direct actions of a corporate accountability, loss of position, loss of fellowship with the church, etc.

## Seek Positive Discipline

The Lord does not want us to dread His positive discipline. In fact, we're to desire it, be grateful for it, and to seek it. The positive discipline of the Lord is highly valued in the scriptures. It's the punitive discipline of the Lord that we're warned against incurring. This warning is not a devaluing of it. This warning is simply to say that we do not have to walk the road of punitive discipline if we'll heed the clear Word of the Lord's positive discipline.

The simple truth is, if we continually do not heed the positive discipline of the Lord, we will come under the punitive discipline of the Lord at some point in time. In fact, the punitive discipline of the Lord comes because of unbelief, rebellion, stubbornness, pride and hard-heartedness, without repentance. It comes simply because the positive discipline of the Lord hasn't been heeded, time and time again (Proverbs 5:12;15:10).

## Authority for Discipline

The church has been given authority, in cooperation with the Lord Jesus Christ, to see that His discipline happens within the life of the church.

As Christians, we all have been given power and authority in and through Christ Jesus (John 1:12). Church leadership has also been assigned power for the building up of the kingdom of God, and to provide protection, direction, and correction for the saints within their sphere of responsibility. This power comes with an entrusted right of use, called authority. Leadership within the church of Christ Jesus, has been vested with the power and authority of Christ Jesus. It is a trust. It's a trust that church leadership will be and are indeed, held accountable for.

When we speak of the authority of Christ in church leadership, there are generally two types of authority that we need to look at: relational and governmental.

## Relational Authority

Relational authority speaks first of that authority and power that is given in the midst of our relationship with Christ Jesus. Secondly, it speaks of that authority and power that is given in the midst of our relationship with others. It is not authority or power that we should ever presume upon. It is an authority of relationship and therefore of influence. It is an authority of permission; an authority of the heart; and its power lies in the influence that we bring to bear in our relationship with others through Christ Jesus. That influence flows out of the genuine heart of Jesus being revealed in, to, and through church leadership, for the benefit of others.

## Governmental Authority

Governmental authority builds upon relational authority. Then and only then, should it speak of the authority and power of position (i.e. of eldership or cell leadership). This authority is direct, legal and deeply trustworthy. It's the kind of authority that has the power to enforce the will, Word and ways of the Lord Jesus. It's the right to command, judge and expect obedience to the Lord and His Word. Governmental authority comes with the role, office, call and appointment. It isn't inherent in the person; rather it lies in the position itself. This authority doesn't exist by permission of man but of the Lord God and His living and alive Word.

## Regarding Church Discipline and Restoration

- It is important to see discipline as an opportunity to reassess what's going on in your family, cell, partner church, etc. As is true of parenting, that children will most often reflect the parents, so it is true of ministries and churches. Proper church discipline should cause us all to seek the face of the Lord for insight into what He is saying to us in and through this circumstance.
- Some discipline issues should result in policy changes. It also may give an opportunity to discover weaknesses within your teaching, training or organizational dynamics. In other words, don't be so consumed with the discipline issues and so narrow in your focus that you miss the gift of growth and change the Lord has presented you through this or any other discipline circumstance.
- In some cases of church discipline, (leadership and / or members) there can become opportunities for discerning issues that need ministry or prayer. An example would be territorial issues, or family issues, historical issues, open wounds of the past becoming evident in the present; thinking that reflects a cultural dimension rather than a kingdom of God dimension.

No Christian leader rejoices over the need for corrective discipline. It is a duty which must be performed when other more positive methods to cause growth and maturity have failed. Most leaders would prefer not needing to discipline any church member. Wherever the fault may lie, the need for corrective discipline is an indication of failure, not of success. The wise leader enters into a corrective discipline situation with compassion, understanding and an abundant supply of grace.

A wise leader also enters into corrective discipline with firm resolve. While the need for such discipline may be tragic, the outcome is at the heart of every leader's purpose. What leader does not want to see individuals cleansed and restored into a protected, united, healthy church? Especially at times of spiritual disease in the church, God's leaders can be grateful that this important tool is available, thus sparing the flock and keeping the "disease" from spreading. The Bible clearly develops this tool for the use of the wise shepherd leader.

## Reasons for Discipline

Church members may need corrective discipline for any number of reasons. When a member enters into sin in a way that threatens his own spiritual life and those around him, he and the church must be protected. The church needs wise and decisive action of its leaders in such a case. In addition, other church members must understand their own role in the process of corrective discipline and restoration. Areas that may require decisive discipline of church members:

| | |
|---|---|
| Unresolved offenses between members | Racism |
| Moral impurity | Unbiblical divorce |
| Covetousness | Rebellion |
| Extortion | Idolatry |
| Any form of disobedience in the Bible | Railing |
| Active, aggressive divisiveness | Drunkenness |
| Ongoing refusal to receive input from leadership | |

## Failure to Discipline

A church's leadership may fail to discipline a sinning member for any of several reasons. It is good to explore them briefly, to know and understand them in advance. When discipline situations occur, a foreknowledge of the difficulties involved can support the resolve and effectiveness of church leadership. Fear and ignorance are the two primary reasons, expressed in several ways:

### FEAR

Fear of the congregation's distaste for the process
Fear of the people developing an emotional identification with the problem
Fear of the church receiving a reputation in the community of being legalistic
Fear of angry, bitter or destructive reactions from those under discipline
Fear of wounding the tender spirits of children and young people
Fear of embarrassment and damaged ministry or reputation to the ones under discipline

### IGNORANCE

Ignorance of the necessity for discipline
Ignorance of the biblical principles of discipline
Ignorance of the process of discipline

## Benefits of Church Discipline

1. It has the potential for bringing about change and growth in the individual's life when nothing else will.
2. It evidences a standard of biblical conviction for living that the Christian is commanded to uphold.
3. It prohibits the leavening influence of sin from gaining a foothold in other members of the congregation.
4. It counteracts the spirit of lawlessness of our age.
5. It underscores the value of righteousness as the basis for all relationships in the body of Christ.
6. It is part of the responsibility of the oversight of the local church.
7. It may save some other pastor or Christian leader the task of disciplining an even worse case later.

8. It helps the individual member deal with sin that by himself he has been unable to eliminate.
9. It can potentially save a congregation from a church split in some cases.
10. Without church discipline, there is no clear standard of right and wrong among the congregation.
11. Without church discipline, sinning members go on sinning, destroying their own potential fruitfulness in God.
12. Without church discipline, others may do outwardly what they have only been tempted to do inwardly, because the lack of discipline implies approval of an activity.
13. Without church discipline, the spiritual life of the body as a whole becomes greatly weakened. Spiritual vitality and life seep out and a progressive spiritual stagnation sets in.
14. Without discipline, confidence and respect for church leadership is lost.

## Process of Church Discipline

The New Testament contains very clear injunctions about the need for discipline, and its place in church life. We will now look at important verses describing the process of church discipline.

### • Confrontation

We begin with the words of Christ in Matthew 18:15-17:

*If your brother sins against you, go and show him his fault, just between the two of you. If he listens to you, you have won your brother over. But if he will not listen, take one or two others along, so that 'every matter may be established by the testimony of two or three witnesses.' If he refuses to listen to them, tell it to the church; and if he refuses to listen even to the church, treat him as you would a pagan or a tax collector (Matthew 18:15-17).*

### • Exclusion From Fellowship

Discipline, then, may reach a stage of putting a person out of fellowship with the church. This reached a very strong expression in a case at the church at Corinth which the apostle Paul addressed:

*Even though I am not physically present, I am with you in spirit. And I have already passed judgment on the one who did this, just as if I were present. When you are assembled in the name of our Lord Jesus and I am with you in spirit, and the power of our Lord Jesus is present, hand this man over to Satan, so that the sinful nature may be destroyed and his spirit saved on the day of the Lord.*
*What business is it of mine to judge those outside the church? Are you not to judge those inside? God will judge those outside. "Expel the wicked man from among you" (1 Corinthians 5:3-5,12-13).*

Discipline involves clear judgment, to pronounce an opinion of right or wrong, and to separate the unrepentant. It is exercised as an internal function of the church, and does not function in regard to non-Christians or people who are not part of a church fellowship.

*And if any man obey not our word by this epistle, note that man, and have no company with him, that he may be ashamed. Yet count him not as an enemy, but admonish him as a brother (2 Thessalonians 3:14-15).*

The Greek word for "note" in this passage involves a process where the church uses an act or circumstance which has a clear meaning and message to the person under discipline.

God protects the church from the spiritual attacks of the enemy. In some cases, an unrepentant sinner may take harbor under the protective covering of the church, and will not fully reap what he has sown. That is why Paul states in 1 Timothy 1:20, *Among them are Hymenaeus and Alexander, whom I have handed over to Satan to be taught not to blaspheme.* The vicious attacks of Satan without the protective covering of the church may be the only thing that break through a spiritually hardened condition to reactivate a person's conscience.

### • Sin Beyond Repentance

It is possible for a Christian to fall beyond repentance. The church cannot recover those who have consigned themselves to hell. *Warn a divisive person once, and then warn him a second time. After that, have nothing to do with him,* Paul commands in Titus 3:10. A heretic is a sectarian, one who follows his own preferences in a self-willed way, to undermine the church. In the last days, also, blasphemers would do harm to the work of God, and must be cast out of fellowship irretrievably (2 Timothy 3:2).

### • Protecting the Church

In very severe cases, then, discipline in the church ceases to be a matter of restoring an individual's soul, and becomes a function of the church defending itself against the attacks of the enemy. As in all areas of church discipline, but especially in this one, church leadership must act in a decisive and timely manner. Discipline may benefit not only the ones disciplined, but the rest of the church as well: *Those who sin are to be rebuked publicly, so that the others may take warning (1 Timothy 5:20).*

But when a person refuses to recover from sin, the church must protect itself:

*I urge you, brothers, to watch out for those who cause divisions and put obstacles in your way that are contrary to the teaching you have learned. Keep away from them. For such people are not serving our Lord Christ, but their own appetites. By smooth talk and flattery they deceive the minds of naive people (Romans 16:17-18).*

### • Confession and Cleansing

The Bible gives us clear guidance on the next step of effective discipline that leads to recovery. In this state, the guilty party is responsible to confess, and God is faithful to cleanse.

*When anyone is guilty in any of these ways, he must confess in what way he has sinned (Leviticus 5:5).*

Acknowledge and confess (Psalm 35:1-5).

*Therefore confess your sins to each other...(James 5:16).*

*If we confess our sins, he is faithful and just and will forgive us our sins and purify us from all unrighteousness (1 John 1:9).*

*But if we walk in the light...the blood of Jesus, his Son, purifies us from all sin (1 John 1:7).*

*He who conceals his sins does not prosper, but whoever confesses and renounces them finds mercy (Proverbs 28:13).*

Confession must be directed toward two parties: to God, and to the people who have been injured by a sin (Romans 14:7).

## • Restoration and Reception

In this stage, the church has a responsibility to its fallen and cleansed member. In 2 Corinthians 2:1-11, the apostle Paul is speaking to the church about restoring a previously disciplined person to the fellowship of the body. The goal of discipline has been achieved: this individual has repented of his sin. To receive this individual back into fellowship, the church is told to:

**Forgive** (2 Corinthians 2:7). To forgive someone is to remove all condemnation and critical attitudes toward a person, to release from your spirit all wrong feelings.

**Console** (2 Corinthians 2:7). Speak encouraging words; lift up the hands that hang down.

**Love** (2 Corinthians 2:8). The church is to assure the repentant one of their love, to reaffirm their love for him, to restore him to his full place in their affections. This step is critically important! Especially when someone has just been separated, the devil will try to turn that into a permanent division. The church must aggressively step forward to re-incorporate the person into the body.

**Give Satan No Advantage** (2 Corinthians 2:11). It's time for a cautious double-checking now. The church must make certain that it has definitely and effectively performed the first three steps above, and that no wrong spirits have crept into the process anywhere along the line, among any of the people involved in the process. "We don't want Satan to win any victory here!" is the J.B. Philips translation of part of this verse. The church is forewarned to not be overcome by evil, but to overcome evil with good.

## GUIDELINES FOR THE PROCESS OF DISCIPLINE

Cell and partner church levels:

## Step One: Discovery

- You become aware of the issue(s) potentially needing disciplinary attention.
- Begin to seek the face of the Lord for His wisdom and His discernment, praying also for a full disclosure of the truth concerning all that is going on.
- You also begin written documentation of all that has and continues to occur throughout this process, from beginning to end. Be sure to keep thorough and accurate notes of each meeting, discussions, agreements and disagreements. This will help you to remember and provide a timeline of events if needed for future reference. Be sure to date each meeting and note attendees.

- Keep lines of communication open with all parties concerned at all times. On the cell level, there must be a commitment to openness, honesty, transparency, and genuine vulnerability by the oversight team (partner church eldership) leading this process. On the partner church eldership level, there should be a commitment to openness, honesty, transparency, and genuine vulnerability by the oversight team (Apostolic Council or designates) leading this process.

## Step Two:  Assessment
- You now engage the process discovering the truth concerning these issue(s).
- Remember: you are not only looking at the truth of specific actions and behavior, but a clear discernment of the heart conditions of those involved. This will be important to your judgment process.
- This is the information and fact-finding process. Look for truthful and accurate facts, not senses or suspicions, or emotions and accusations, etc.
- This is where you speak to all those involved in the process, if need be.

## Step Three:  Judgment
- It is here that you will make a judgment based upon all that has been weighed and assessed. This includes the heart issues as well as the specific nature of the events involved.
- If need be, you will seek outside counsel concerning these issues as to your legal options.
- You will also consider resources available to you to deal with these issues redemptively as you prepare for the discipline process.
- It is at this point that you will render a clear decision. If your decision is such that discipline must essentially follow, then move to the next step.

## Step Four:  Consequence
- Lay out the strategy of discipline.
- The oversight of the discipline process is clearly set in place. Specific person(s) are assigned as a team to walk through the disciplinary process with those being disciplined.
- Schedule a periodic assessment of the discipline effectiveness.
- A follow-through to a godly conclusion is committed to by all those involved in this process.
- Remember: church discipline is a lot of work and all of that work must flow out of a heart that is submitted to our Lord Jesus Christ. There must be a commitment to seeing God's redemptive purposes fulfilled in each other.
- The implementation of discipline actually begins.

## Step Five:  Reconciliation with Full Restoration
After following through with the disciplinary process successfully, there needs to be as much heart-felt commitment and prayer to the restoration process as there

APPENDIX C

was to the disciplinary process. Closure does not happen without restoration and healing having taken place.

## DISCIPLINARY ACTIONS THAT COULD BE TAKEN

Here are some possible steps of action:

- Increased commitment to building relationships with steps of follow-through
- Specific prayer and fasting for a brief season
- Personal ministry, inner healing and deliverance
- Teaching and personal study of the Word as specifically relates to issues
- Counseling (personal, marriage, family)
- Conflict mediation
- Bringing in outside specialist(s) to aid in this healing process
- Confrontation and rebuke (personal and private)
- Confrontation and rebuke (cell level or corporately)
- Removing from areas of responsibility for a set season of time
- Removal from fellowship in one cell or partner church and placement in another
- Cutting off from all cell activities for set season of time
- Cutting off from all celebration activities for a set season of time
- Involvement of and cooperation with public authorities
- Outside medical help
- Withdrawal of membership (from cell and or celebration)

**Warning:** If at any time in the process of church discipline, a member resigns and leaves the church, all church disciplinary action must be considered ended. {Right to Privacy Law}

When considering how to handle a given issue, be sure that you are soaking this process with prayer, and receiving outside godly counsel from wise men and women of God. Accurate discernment of the heart conditions of those you are working with is critical to a godly and just strategy of church discipline and restoration. All church discipline strategies must be truly redemptive in focus and objective with a strong biblical foundation and with a New Testament focus upon Christ Jesus and not of the law. There also must be absolute agreement to the discipline process by all the leadership involved.

As we seriously look at the discipline process, let's review a few recommendations for church leadership desiring to operate in biblical discipline.

1. Consult an attorney
2. Be consistent
3. The bylaws of the church and its doctrines should be clear and understandable to the average member.
4. Signed documents: All documents that reflect the government of the church, including disciplinary procedures, bylaws, doctrinal statements, etc. should be given to the people in writing. Some partner churches require all membership, especially new members, to sign off on having read them, submit to them, and that they understand them.

5.  Have membership classes that teach the basic biblical doctrines from the scriptures. The Biblical Foundation Series books by Larry Kreider could be used. Teach clearly from the scriptures about biblical church discipline. Then have all persons completing the course sign a document stating they understood and submit to these scriptural guidelines.
6.  The scriptural principles and doctrines as expressed by the church should be practiced by the church.
7.  1 Corinthians 6 should be understood and practiced by the church
8.  Be up front and honest; if a mistake is made, admit it, correct it and move forward.

Always remember: the purpose of all discipline is reconciliation and restoration through the grace and mercy of our Lord Jesus Christ. May we always remember the scriptural admonition in Galatians 6:1-2: *Brothers, if someone is caught in a sin, you who are spiritual should restore him gently. But watch yourself, or you also may be tempted. Carry each other's burdens, and in this way you will fulfill the law of Christ.*

## Guidelines for Discipline and Restoration of Fallen Leaders

This policy is a guideline which is not binding and DCFI will apply discipline, and if appropriate, restoration, as deemed appropriate in any particular situation.

The scriptures make it clear that God expects purity of heart and holy living in all His people, and emphasize that those in church leadership are expected to live blameless lives, above reproach. Due to their high visibility and responsibility, apostolic council members, elders, fivefold ministers, ordained and licensed ministers, and stewardship team members, must be Christ-like in their life-styles and conduct. When ministers of the gospel fall into sin, the integrity of the church is called into public question. There are four basic areas of sin that a leader may commit that may require a process of discipline and restoration: moral failure, irreconcilable disputes, disorderly conduct, and apostasy.

One of the most important areas in which corrective discipline protects and heals the church is when a moral breakdown occurs in church leadership. The following outline of scripture policy concerning discipline of church leaders is derived from 1 Timothy 3:1-7 and 5:17-25, and Titus 1:5-9. We are not addressing divorce or remarriage, but dealing specifically with immorality which defiles the sanctity of the marriage bed. This is probably the most serious failure which destroys ministries in the church today. When handled properly, however, redemptive restoration can be achieved, ministries can be resurrected, and the church can move forward in health.

## Effects of Moral Breakdown in a Leader's Life and Ministry

Marital infidelity affects a person, and especially the ministry, in the following areas of life:

**Morally** A minister disqualifies himself from ministry through a moral breakdown. A wife can also disqualify her husband from ministry by immoral conduct.

**Domestically** If an elder or a minister does not have his own house in order, he cannot rule the house of God. This order and rule involves all family relationships. The husband-wife relationship, especially, must be rebuilt and restored for family healing to take place.

**Mentally and Emotionally** Damage to relationships and the torment of guilt involve deep mental and emotional wounds that can be healed only through God's working. Cooperating with God's healing requires genuine repentance, confession, and reception of cleansing and renewal. Rationalizations for sin cannot be justified or tolerated. They make healing impossible, and open the leader to even greater deception and sin.

**Ethically** Any leader who fails morally should step down from public ministry for a period of time. This is an important visible return to scriptural ethics which aids in the healing process. The time period of this removal from ministry should allow fulfillment of discipline, including healing to all parties involved.

**Spiritually** Moral breakdowns especially wreak damage and devastation on a public ministry where the leader is in public view and is held up as an example of godly life-style. Spiritual restoration must be sought for the good of all individuals concerned.

**Ecclesiastically** Proper and scriptural discipline must be upheld because the ministry, which functions before the "ecclesia" (God's called-out people), has a very great area of influence. None of us live to ourselves, we all affect others, and this is most true of Christian leaders. If we fail to uphold scriptural discipline, we set precedents for many other moral breakdowns, and the suffering of the church is magnified. The leader who sins, whether elder or governmental minister, should be openly rebuked before all so that others may fear. Such failings generally become church (or public) knowledge, and must be dealt with scripturally and decisively. This will cause gossiping and imaginations to cease.

## Guidelines for Corrective Discipline of Leaders

Because every circumstance and individual involved is different from case to case, we do not propose detailed disciplinary measures, nor does the Bible. Scripture does present some practical, general guidelines. Note that the process below must not be pursued in a legalistic or pharisaical, "holier-than-thou" spirit or attitude. When God forgives, He truly forgives. When God restores, He restores. The goal of the church throughout this process is to restore the fallen leaders...*gently. But watch yourself, or you also may be tempted (Galatians 6:1).*

**Confession and Repentance** The guilty party must genuinely repent and confess. He or she must make this confession to all appropriate parties, based on whom the sin affected, and the level of private or public knowledge of the sin.

**Forgiveness** After true repentance, all parties involved must offer forgiveness. This will involve all people directly affected by the sin, but may also involve people who suffer reproach as a result of the sin—the Lord Himself, family, other church leadership, and the church at large.

**Probation** The forgiven party should step down from public ministry. A period of probation should be instituted, for 6-12 months, allowing time for "rebuilding the walls" broken down through immorality in the areas mentioned above. This is a time to clear away the damage; truly rebuilding the marriage relationship takes more time than this. God's order of healing is forgiveness, probation and restoration.

**Counseling** The leader on probation should have an effective, ongoing counseling relationship with a counselor who can minister redemption in a restorative manner.

**Restoration** The ministry shall be restored to leadership after a suitable period of probation has given evidence of a sound restoration process. Church leaders must understand, however, that there are times when a sinning leader cannot be restored to a ministry office. Causes for this may be the number of failures, or the depth of deception involved. Wherever genuine repentance occurs, restoration of the individual is always biblical—but this does not always mean restoration of the individual's ministry. This is an area which requires great sensitivity and discernment of a church leader.

Integrity, both ethically and morally, is the issue that church leaders must address if we would come to some understanding of the problem of pastoral sexual misconduct and the related question of restoration to spiritual leadership.

Although much of the church and society in general seem to be operating in a mind-set opposed to restrictions and discipline, God expects the church to exercise discipline over its members. In so doing, it must guard against harshness and condemnation toward the one being disciplined. The general attitude on all sides must be aimed at restoration of the fallen, purification of the church, and in the end, glorifying and honoring God.

There have been three common approaches to handle the problem of fallen leaders.

1. Immediate restoration to leadership position. "Immediate" is defined as fewer than twelve months after the sexual failure.
2. Future restoration to the position of spiritual leadership after a period of time for counsel, as well as family and personal recovery. The procedure varies from church to church, but generally one to three years elapses before the fallen pastor is restored to spiritual leadership.
3. Personal restoration of the fallen leader but no possibility for restoration to spiritual leadership.

Biblical church government and a proper policy of church discipline and restoration protects the leadership from rebellious members, and protects the members from tyrannical leaders.

Scriptural guidelines from 1 Timothy 5 regarding the accusation against elders need to be heeded. Leaders who are accused should have the opportunity to respond face to face to their accusers. To avoid slander, an accusation against an elder should be taken to the elder by the individual. The accusation needs to be based on reality of actual events and facts (not "prophetic insight").

Matthew 18 should be followed with accusations brought. If Matthew 18 is violated and information is made public prematurely, 1 Corinthians 6 should be used. According to 1 Corinthians 6, a council of judges should hear the issues, evidence, testimony and render a decision. This should be done swiftly. Clear records should be kept of dates, times, evidence, discipline carried out, and specific sins confronted.

If an elder of a partner church has fallen, the senior elder and a member(s) of the Apostolic Council or designates should be involved in this process of discipline and restoration along with the other elders. If the senior elder has fallen, two Apostolic Council members or designates should lead this process with the involvement of the others in eldership. If a fivefold minister has fallen, his senior elder, eldership, and a representative from the Apostolic Council should be involved in the discipline and restoration process. If a member of the Apostolic Council has fallen, the international director, other Apostolic Council members and a recognized spiritual advisor should be involved in the process. If the international director has fallen, two or more of the recognized spiritual advisors should lead the process of discipline and restoration along with the other Apostolic Council members.

If sin is substantiated, it must be made public to the congregation or realm of influence. The details of the sin should not be made public. The facts and the process of restoration also need to be made public, so the sin cannot be brought up "down the road." True repentance and restitution includes a clear acknowledgment of the sin. "I was wrong, there was no excuse." There needs to be a willingness to submit to the process of discipline and restoration. Those responsible for administering the process of discipline and restoration should set clear goals for the fruit of repentance. The size of the church or ministry the offender is responsible for, his gifting or human charisma should not change the standards. A leader cannot opt out of discipline. Time does not change rebellion in a person's heart. "Gross" sin is evidence of major character weaknesses. The character qualifications of 1 Timothy 3 for spiritual leaders must be fulfilled. This takes time and accountability.

If someone leaves a church, denomination, or movement because of not responding appropriately to discipline, the bad report should go with him. This person should not be protected through privacy. There should be communication with other churches in the area that the church relates to.

There needs to be a public disclosure of facts and the restoration process so all can see if the process is complete. This gives the opportunity for future ministry to resume. The spiritual leader who has fallen should be removed from leadership for a period of time. Here are some guidelines:

If there has been a tryst—minimum of one year
If there has been a full affair—minimum of two years
If there has been financial misconduct—same as above
If there has been a very negative family situation—minimum of six months

There can be no set amount of time for a complete restoration. Leave it open-ended. Have the fallen leader submit to the "eldership" the Lord has placed over him. Restoration to ministry should not be assumed as the end result. There needs to be a genuine heart change and new habit patterns built into the life of the leader who is going through the discipline and restoration process.

Restoration should be first a personal restoration of the individual to God. Then there should be a restoration to his family (spouse). Then there needs to be a restoration to the local church. Next there needs to be a restoration to other churches. Then there is the possibility of restoration to a ministry position of spiritual leadership.

There may also be a need for counsel for the family to be healed. There needs to be weekly (or regular) counsel for the restoration of the leader. There should also be six months severance pay for transition if the person is in full-time supported ministry. This, however, should only apply if they are submitted to the discipline process.

The following are areas of sin and concern that may warrant the process of discipline and restoration:

1. Immorality; e.g., adultery
2. Sexual abuse
3. Sexual harassment
4. Physical abuse
5. Abuse of power (excess control, manipulation, intimidation)
6. Misuse and abuse of finances
7. Abuse of privileges
8. Divisiveness within celebration, DCFI, etc.
9. Advocating heretical teaching within cell(s), partner church(s), DCFI, etc.
10. Participation with an effort to subvert other leadership.
11. Slander, especially of cell, celebration, or DCFI leadership, etc.
12. Marital discord/divorce
13. Intense family conflict; e.g., teenagers out of control
14. Irreconcilable disputes
15. Disorderly conduct
16. Apostasy

### What does the process of discipline of a leaders look like?

At the cell, partner church and DCFI levels:

### Step One: Discovery

- You become aware of the issue(s) potentially needing disciplinary attention.
- Begin to seek the face of the Lord for His wisdom and His discernment, praying also for a full disclosure of the truth concerning all that is going on.
- You also begin written documentation of all that has and continues to occur throughout this whole process, from beginning to end.
- Keep lines of communication open with all parties concerned at all times.

There must be a commitment to openness, honesty, transparency, and genuine vulnerability by the oversight team leading this process.

## Step Two:  Assessment
• You now engage the process discovering the truth concerning these issue(s).
• Remember: you are not only looking for the truth of specific actions and behavior but a clear discernment of the heart conditions of those involved. This will be important to your judgment process.
• This is the information and fact finding process. Look for the truth and accurate facts, not senses or suspicions, or emotions and accusations, etc.
• This is where you speak to all those involved in the process, if need be.

## Step Three:  Judgment
• It is here that you will make a judgment based upon all that has been weighed and assessed. This includes the heart issues as well as the specific nature of the events involved.
• If need be, you will seek outside counsel concerning these issues as to your legal options.
• You will also consider available resources to assist you in dealing with these issues redemptively as you prepare for the discipline process.
• It is at this point that you will render a clear decision. If your decision is such that discipline must essentially follow, then move to the next step.

## Step Four:  Consequence
• Lay out the strategy of discipline.
• The oversight of the discipline process is clearly set in place. Specific person(s) are assigned as a team to walk through the disciplinary process with those being disciplined.
• Schedule a periodic assessment of the discipline effectiveness.
• A follow-through to a godly conclusion is committed to by all those involved in this process.
• Remember: church discipline is a lot of work and all of that work must flow out of a heart that is submitted to our Lord Jesus Christ. There must be a commitment to seeing God's redemptive purposes fulfilled in each other.
• The implementation of discipline actually begins.

## Step Five:  Reconciliation with Full Restoration
After following through with the disciplinary process successfully, there needs to be as much heartfelt commitment and prayer to the restoration process as there was to the disciplinary process. Closure does not happen without restoration and healing.

There needs to be genuine repentance before the restoration process can begin. The scriptures tell us in 2 Corinthians 7:10-11: *Godly sorrow brings repentance that leads to salvation and leaves no regret, but worldly sorrow brings death. See what this godly sorrow has produced in you: what earnestness, what eagerness to clear yourselves, what indignation, what alarm, what longing, what concern, what readiness to see justice done. At every point you have proved your-selves to be innocent in this matter.*

Repentance, according to the scriptures, speaks of a genuine change of heart that has been touched by the Lord Jesus. When this occurs, there will be plenty of evidence that will stand the test of righteousness and godliness.

Due to the intensity and severity of the actions of a Christian leader, the process in going from step one to step four may only take a few hours. It is important to note however, that having come to a point of judgment concerning the sin of a fallen leader and having taken a proper course of action, you are not through with your responsibilities. There will need to be a clear assessment of the damages to God's people, the cells, and the congregation.

There will need to be an assessment where we may have missed something along the way that could have prevented this from going this far. Were there warning signs, procedures, structures in place that helped this occur? If so, how and what do we need to change? What preventative steps can we take that will diminish the risk of this occurring again?

**Warning:** don't fall into the trap of assuming that once the fallen leader has been taken care of, there's no longer any concern. In reality, you may be only beginning the real work.

## Here are some possible additional steps that could be taken:
- Specific prayer and fasting for a brief season
- Personal ministry, inner healing and deliverance
- Teaching and personal study of the Word as it specifically relates to issues you are dealing with.
- Outside training (specialized to specific disciplinary issues)
- Counseling (personal, marriage, family)
- Conflict mediation and reconciliation
- Bringing in outside specialist(s) to aid in this healing process
- Confrontation and rebuke (personal and private)
- Confrontation and rebuke (cell and/or corporately)
- Removing from areas of responsibility for a set season of time
- Suspension with pay and or removal of license to minister within the DCFI field of ministry
- Removal from fellowship in one cell or celebration and placement in another
- Cutting off from all cell activities for set season of time
- Cutting off from all celebration activities for a set season of time
- Involvement of and cooperation with public authorities
- Outside medical help
- Restitution
- Withdrawal of membership (from cell and/or celebration)

## Extra Guidelines on Disciplinary Action Concerning Sexual Sin(s)
### Step One:  Discovery
•   Once discovered, assessment must be quickly entered into.

### Step Two:  Assessment
•   Leader must be confronted at once.
•   If he/she admits to this event (sin), then move on, determining the proper course of action.
•   If there is denial, then continue the assessment process.
•   Once assessment has taken place, and all that is needed for a judgment is in place, move on to it prudently.

### Step Three:  Judgment
•   If all seems to be truthful in terms of discovery and assessment, a decision must be made as to guilt and or innocence.
•   If guilty, move on to consequences.

### Step Four:  Consequence
•   There needs to be an immediate removal of that leadership person from any and all responsibilities.
•   All primary leadership persons are to be immediately informed.
•   The cell, celebration, and partner churches must then be informed.
•   Information to be limited to the specific kind of sin, and of the plan of discipline set in motion, but no personal information
•   Depending upon the individual situation, financial compensation should continue for at least three months. This could certainly be re-evaluated at a later date.

### Step Five:  Reconciliation and Restoration
•   Time: How long should the suspension and removal last? At the least, a year. If the leader's heart has grown hard or rebellious, it could be much longer. If there is no godly sorrow, but only contrition (of regret, embarrassment, humiliation and the natural effects of simply having gotten caught), then it could take a long time, as well. There should be given only approximate time tables because there is no way of knowing how long it is going to take to see the heart issues genuinely change within an individual's life. Change must occur in their hearts before any kind of restoration can be honestly considered. Remember: you can change your mind, but keep your heart intact. We need to believe for and hold out for new hearts and new spirits in the lives of those being disciplined and restored.
•   Ministry and consequence for all who are or were involved in this sexual action, should be seriously considered. This especially applies to areas of complicity.
•   If the leader is willing to submit to the discipline process, then put into place everything reasonably possible to help him recover personally,  in his marriage, in his family.

The area of discipline, reconciliation and restoration needs to be thoroughly understood at a revelation level by all those in leadership. Teaching, training and even some sort of practical application training in these three areas would be of great benefit for all concerned.

Leadership persons need to develop their skill level in the areas of crisis management, conflict resolution, entry level counseling, and personal ministry. Those in leadership need to have their awareness level raised of the vital necessity of their walking out both positive and preventative discipline as a ministry life-style. Specialists in these areas need to be developed.

## Conclusion

God's leaders must use discipline wisely and firmly to help the church grow "in the midst of a crooked and perverse generation." Otherwise, the church will lose her ability to act as salt and light for a fallen world. We can all thank God that He has given us clear instruction in the Bible on how to deal with sinning church members and leaders.

As God restores New Testament leadership, which the church so desperately needs, we must keep our hearts open and changeable. God will have to change our thinking as well as our hearts as he brings His people back to scriptural patterns and priorities. Today, God is telling His leaders to allow His Spirit to prepare their inner attitudes and motivations and thoughts for a great moving of His Spirit in the future. Through His own tests and trials, God will prepare the vessels that He desires to use in specific functions. He will require His leaders to obey the Word, and be living examples of it, rather than just studying or hearing it.

Remember that the issue in preparing church leadership is not the ability of the leaders but the ability of the One who prepares them. If you are called by God to a governmental ministry, you can have confidence in the outcome of the process. Avoid digressions. Cooperate with the dealings of God and the anointing of the Holy Spirit.

The goal of anointed servanthood, of preparing the Bride for her wedding day, lies before us. Let all of God's people cooperate with him as he continues the making of a leader in each one of us.

*Written by Larry Kreider. Thanks to Philip McAlmond Jr. for his input with these Guidelines.*

### Additional resources on discipline and restoration of church members and leaders
*Due Process,* by Dan Juster, (Destiny Image Publishing).
*The Making of a Leader* by Frank Damazio (Bible Temple Publishing).
*The Church in the New Testament* by Kevin Conner (Bible Temple Publishing).

### Additional sources for church leaders
*Healing the Wounded* by John White and Ken Blue (Intervarsity Press).
*Can Fallen Leaders be Restored?* by John H. Armstrong (Moody Press).

### DOVE Christian Fellowship International
# Our History of Training Elders

**D**OVE Christian Fellowship International (DCFI), started with a group of young Christian believers who had a burden to reach the unchurched youth in their community in northern Lancaster County, Pennsylvania.

It was the early 1970's and the time of a nationwide awakening among young people in the United States. The nation had been through tumultuous times in the 1960's with rapid changes tearing at the fabric of our society, including the sexual revolution and the Vietnam War. They were now turning to God in great numbers after a decade of dabbling in the occult and drug culture seeking answers for life but being disillusioned.

It was in these times that we started an organization called "The Lost But Found." Through friendship evangelism, we saw many young people come to know Jesus as their Lord. A Bible study under the direction of Larry Kreider called "Rhema Youth Ministries" nurtured many of these young Christians.

Although we tried to get the new believers involved in the established churches in our community, they simply didn't fit. It seemed clear there was a need for new church structures flexible enough to relate to new converts from a variety of backgrounds. That's why Jesus said we need to put new wine into new wineskins (Matthew 9:16-17).

Increasingly, there became a need for a flexible New Testament-style church (new wineskin) that could relate to and assist these new believers (new wine) in their spiritual growth. In 1978, God spoke to Larry about being "willing to be involved with the underground church."

## Our adventure into cell groups

So began our church's adventure into cell groups. A cell group was started in Larry and LaVerne Kreider's home and when their living room was filled to capacity, they turned over the responsibility to leaders they had trained and started a second cell in another home. The roots began to grow for this "underground church" where believers were nourished in these "underground" cell groups as they gathered together to pray, evangelize and build relationships with each other.

By the time our church, DOVE Christian Fellowship, officially began in October, 1980, there were approximately 25 of us meeting in a large living room on Sunday mornings and in three cell groups during the week. We discovered cell groups to be places where people have the opportunity to experience and demonstrate a Christianity built on relationships, not simply on meetings. In the cell groups, people could readily share their lives with each other and reach out to a broken world. We desired to follow the pattern in the New Testament church as modeled in the book of Acts, as the believers met from house to house.

Twelve years later, as these cell groups continued to grow and to multiply, more than 2,300 believers were meeting in over 125 cell groups throughout south-central Pennsylvania. Churches were planted in Scotland, Brazil, Kenya, and New Zealand. Believers met in cell groups in homes during the week and in clusters of cells in geographical areas for celebration meetings each Sunday morning. Here believers received teaching, worshiped together and celebrated what the Lord was doing during the week through the cell groups.

## We made our share of mistakes

Although the church had grown rapidly in a relatively short span, we made our share of mistakes. The Lord began to deal with pride and unhealthy control in our lives. We found the Lord's purpose for cell groups was to release and empower His people, not to control them. We repented before the Lord and before His church.

Our cell-based church had reached a crossroads. We were experiencing the pain of gridlock among some of our leadership. There was an exodus of some good leaders from our ranks. It was painful, and Larry Kreider, who was serving as the senior elder, almost quit.

In retrospect, we feel the mistakes we made were partly due to our immaturity as leaders and partly due to our not having an outside accountability team to help us when we ran into conflicts in decision-making. And perhaps the Lord in His providence was repositioning some of His players elsewhere in the body of Christ.

But the Lord kept taking us back to the original vision He had given, calling us to be involved with the "underground church." Today we walk with a spiritual limp, but we are so grateful to the Lord for what He taught us during those days.

## Transition to several churches, all having elders

It became clear that in order for DOVE (an acronym for "Declaring Our Victory Emmanuel") to accomplish what we were originally called to accomplish, we needed to adjust our church government and "give the church away." The vision the Lord had given us, "to build a relationship with Jesus, with one another, and reach the world from house to house, city to city and nation to nation," could not be fulfilled under our current church structure. We recognized the Lord had called us to be an apostolic movement, but we did not know how it should be structured.

It took more than two years to prepare for this transition. On January 1, 1996, our church became eight individual churches, each with their own eldership team. We formed an Apostolic Council to give spiritual oversight to DCFI, and Larry Kreider was asked to serve as its International Director. The Apostolic Council gave each church eldership team the option of becoming a part of the DCFI family of churches and ministries or connecting to another part of the body of Christ. Each of these eight churches expressed a desire to work together to plant churches throughout the world and became a part of the DCFI family. The majority of the overseas church plants also desired to become a part of the DCFI family of churches.

We have found apostolic ministry provides a safe environment for each congregation and ministry partnering with DCFI to grow and reproduce themselves.

This new model emphasizes leading by relationship and influence rather than hands-on-management. A senior elder and team has a leadership gift to equip believers to do the work of ministry in cell groups within a congregation. The Apostolic Council members are responsible to spend time in prayer and the ministry of the Word and give training, oversight and mentoring to local church leadership. They also are called to give clear vision and direction to the entire movement.

## Becoming an apostolic movement

Unlike an "association of churches," which gives ordination and general accountability to church leaders, we see an "apostolic movement" as a family of churches with a common focus—a mandate from God to labor together to plant and establish churches throughout the world.

As a cell-based and house church planting movement, we are intent on training a new generation of church planters and leaders just waiting for a chance to spread their wings and fly! We are called to mobilize and empower God's people (individuals, families, cells and congregations) at the grass roots level to fulfill His purposes. Every cell group should have a vision to plant new cells. Every church with its team of elders should have a God-given vision to plant new churches.

In addition to church planting and multiplication, the Lord has given us a process of adopting churches who are called to partner with us. After going through a one-year engagement process of discernment, churches with similar values and vision are becoming partner churches with the DCFI family.

Our desire is to see congregations of cell groups clustered together in the same area so leaders can easily meet as regional presbyteries for prayer and mutual encouragement, and to find ways to be more effective in building His kingdom together. Senior elders of DCFI churches in Pennsylvania have the blessing of meeting together each month for prayer and mutual encouragement. An Apostolic Council member also meets each month individually with each senior elder. Each DCFI partner church is governed by a team of elders and consists of believers committed to one another in cell groups. Each cell and each local church has its own identity while being interdependent with the rest of the DCFI family.

## Networking with the body of Christ

We believe another important aspect to kingdom building is networking with other churches and ministries outside of the DCFI family. In this way, we can resource one other.

God has given us a wonderful support team at DCFI consisting of the Apostolic Council, a team of Fivefold Translocal Ministers, a Stewardship Team which handles the administration of financial details and legalities, and various ministries who are committed to resource the leadership and believers in DCFI partner churches and serve the greater body of Christ.

These various ministries offer leadership training and ministry development on many levels. An essential twenty-four-hour Prayer Ministry includes a team of "prayer generals" who recruit, train and encourage a team of "prayer warriors" responsible to cover segments of time each week while praying for the entire DCFI family twenty-four hours a day. Nelson Martin oversees this vital prayer ministry.

The Apostolic Council and leadership from DCFI partner churches throughout the world meet together each March for our annual DCFI International Leadership Conference for the purpose of mutual encouragement, leadership training, relationship building, and to receive a common vision from the Lord. We believe the Lord has called us to work as a team together—*with a shared vision, shared values, a shared procedure, and to build together by relationship.*

In order for the DCFI family of churches and ministries to be effective in laboring together, we wrote our procedure in a DCFI Handbook. This handbook is available by contacting the DCFI Office.

## Training and releasing God's people

An important philosophy of ministry at DCFI is to release each believer and local leadership in order to provide a delegation of authority and responsibility to all believers. Unless elders can release responsibility and authority to the cell leaders at a cell group level, this principle will not work. In this way, the Lord releases every believer to be a minister.

Every church elder is encouraged to maintain his security in the Lord and take the risk of empowering and releasing cell leaders to minister to others by performing water baptisms, serving communion, praying for the sick, giving premarital counseling, and discipling new believers. A major aspect of cell ministry is preparing and training future spiritual fathers and mothers. And many of these cell leaders will be future elders and church planters. They are experiencing "on the job training."

The *House to House Church Planting and Leadership School* is now being used to train cell leaders, pastors and elders in cell-based churches throughout the body of Christ. It is both a live school and a video correspondence school used as a satellite school in churches throughout the world. We expect the believers in our cell groups and churches to soon have their own families—new cell groups and new churches that they plant.

## Fivefold translocal ministry

According to Ephesians 4:11-12, the five ministry gifts of the apostle, prophet, evangelist, pastor and teacher are called by the Lord to equip the saints to minister and encourage the body of Christ. Within the DCFI family, fivefold ministers, who have proven ministries and are recommended by their elders as having a larger sphere of ministry than their own cell and congregation, are recognized and affirmed by the Apostolic Council to serve translocally. These translocal ministers are often invited by other cell groups and congregations for ministry.

## DCFI missions outreaches

During the past 20 years, DOVE has sent hundreds of short and long term missionaries to the nations. Each long term missionary is "embraced" by a cell group, a congregation, and by individuals from DCFI partner churches. A team of people join a missionary's support team by giving financially and praying for the missionary. Cells who "embrace" a missionary or missionary family pray for them, write to them, and serve practically while on furlough or during times of crisis.

The DOVE Mission International team endeavors to serve all DCFI missionaries who are sent out from DCFI partner churches regardless of which "field" they serve on. Some missionaries are directly involved in the DCFI church planting "field," while others may serve instead with the YWAM "field" or with some other missions agency. We are called to build the kingdom, not just our own network of churches. Yet, as a network of churches, we are called by the Lord to plant new cell-based churches together in the unreached areas of the world.

## Looking unto Jesus, the Lord of the harvest

We believe as we continue to commune with the Lord and obey His voice, build together as a family of churches, and reach the lost in our generation, there is going to be a need for thousands of new houses (new churches) and new rooms (new cell groups). Every generation is different and has different needs and preferences. We are committed to empowering, releasing, and supporting the next generation among us as they fulfill their call in God. As Elisha received a double portion of Elijah's anointing, we want to see our spiritual children far exceeding us in their depth of spiritual experience and church leadership. Believers will be called to various areas of leadership: some are called to cell group leadership, others to local church leadership, others to fivefold ministry, and others will serve in apostolic leadership.

Our long term goal is to establish many apostolic councils in various regions of the world. There are already apostolic leadership teams who are responsible for oversight of DCFI churches in seven regions of the world. Eventually, we believe the leadership for the DCFI movement will be a true DCFI International Apostolic Council, whose members will include apostolic leaders from many nations. This International Apostolic Council will be responsible for the spiritual oversight and mentoring of apostolic leaders and councils located around the world.

## The vision continues

The Bible tells us without a vision the people perish. The DCFI family is called to keep actively involved in what the Lord is doing in the world and participate in the present expressions of His anointing. We desire to empower, train, and release God's people at the grass roots level to fulfill His purposes. Jesus values people. He has called us to look at people and see the Father working in those whom the Lord has placed in our lives.

Simply put, these are our "roots," and our continued focus today. You could say that the very DNA of who we are as an international family of believers in Jesus Christ today includes our specific calling as an "underground church" to reach our world from house to house, city to city and nation to nation. May Jesus Christ be honored and glorified!

# DCFI Vision

To build a relationship with Jesus, with one another, and to reach the world from house to house, city to city, nation to nation.

# DCFI Mission

To exalt Jesus Christ as Lord, obey His Word, and encourage and equip each believer for the work of ministry. We are called to build the church from house to house, city to city, and nation to nation through cell groups. This "underground church" is built through prayer, reaching the lost, and making disciples. Our mission includes reaching adults, youth and children for Christ. We are also called to church planting, proclaiming the gospel through media, and building unity in the body of Christ. As a spiritual army, we will cooperate with the church that Jesus is building throughout the world in fulfilling the Great Commission.

# DCFI Plan

By the grace of God we will accomplish our mission by:

1. **Strengthening** our faith through the daily meditation of the Word of God and **developing** an intimate relationship with Jesus.

2. **Committing** ourselves to other believers in a cell group.

3. **Praying** to the Lord of the harvest to send out laborers into the harvest fields: locally, nationally and internationally.

4. **Encouraging** every believer to be involved in prayer, reaching the lost, and making disciples.

5. **Helping** each believer to learn to serve and discover the gifts and callings within his life.

6. **Teaching** the Word of God with power and authority in a way that is practical and applicable to everyday life.

7. **Releasing** apostles, prophets, evangelists, pastors and teachers to equip the saints for the work of ministry and to build up the body of Christ.

8. **Training** and **equipping** leadership in home cell groups and congregations to minister to others and to plant new churches.

9. **Planting** and **multiplying** home cell groups and congregations locally, nationally and internationally.

10. **Sending** laborers to identified harvest fields.

11. **Caring** for, **loving, healing,** and **restoring** those who are wounded and need deliverance, healing, and restoration.

12. **Promoting** unity by **supporting, networking** together and **laboring** with other churches and ministries locally, nationally and internationally.

13. **Mobilizing** and **challenging** adults, youth, and children to be radically committed laborers for the harvest.

14. **Utilizing** all forms of media to proclaim the gospel.

15. **Resourcing** each believer through the ministry of helps, administration and communication.

16. **Ministering** to the poor and needy.

17. **Encouraging** each child, young person and adult to be a worshiper.

18. **Giving** of tithes, offerings, material possessions and our time to the building of the kingdom.

19. **Exemplifying** a life-style of accountability, integrity, and purity in every level of leadership and throughout every area of church life.

20. **Supporting** and **encouraging** the spiritual leaders that the Lord raises up among us.

21. **Edifying** one another daily through encouragement and speaking the truth in love.

22. **Celebrating** Jesus as we come together in various locations to worship together, pray together, and receive the Word of God together.

23. **Partnering** with believers within the DOVE Christian Fellowship International family of churches and ministries who are meeting from house to house and city to city to reach the world together.

24. **Receiving** the filling of the Holy Spirit to minister Jesus to our generation through the demonstration of His supernatural power and gifts.

25. **Recruiting** disciples to carry the gospel to new regions of the earth.

26. **Training** mission personnel in cross-cultural communication of the gospel.

27. **Placing** seeds of mission into the hearts of each new church plant.

28. **Encouraging** youth revival and awakening, and training teenagers and young adults to go into the harvest fields of the world.

29. **Worshiping** our God and Father through our Lord Jesus Christ.

30. **Spiritually fathering and mothering** within every sphere of kingdom life as the Lord turns the hearts of the fathers to the children and the hearts of the children to their fathers in our day.

# DCFI Values

## 1. Knowing God the Father through His Son Jesus Christ and living by His Word is the foundation of life.

We believe that the basis of the Christian faith is to know God through repentance for sin, receiving Jesus Christ as Lord, building an intimate relationship with Him, and being conformed into His image. God has declared us righteous through faith in Jesus Christ (John 1:12, John 17:3, Rom. 8:29, II Cor. 5:21).

All values and guiding principles for the DOVE Christian Fellowship International family must be rooted in the scriptures (II Tim. 3:16-17, II Tim. 2:15). DOVE is an acronym: Declaring Our Victory Emmanuel (God with us).

## 2. It is essential for every believer to be baptized with the Holy Spirit and be completely dependent on Him.

We recognize that we desperately need the person and power of the Holy Spirit to minister effectively to our generation. Changed lives are not the product of men's wisdom, but in the demonstration of the power of the Holy Spirit as modeled in the New Testament church (I Cor. 2:2-5, John 15:5). We believe it is essential for every believer to be baptized with the Holy Spirit and to pursue spiritual gifts (II Cor. 13:14, John 4:23-24).

All decisions need to be made by listening to the Holy Spirit as we make prayer a priority and learn to be worshipers. Worship helps us focus on the Lord and allows us to more clearly hear His voice.

We recognize that we do not wrestle against flesh and blood, but against demonic forces. Jesus Christ is our Lord, our Savior, our Healer and our Deliverer (Eph. 6:12, I John 3:8).

## 3. The Great Commission will be completed through prayer, evangelism, discipleship, and church planting.

We are committed to helping fulfill the Great Commission through prayer and fasting, evangelism, discipleship, and church planting locally, nationally, and internationally reaching both Jew and Gentile (Matt. 28:19-20, Matt. 6:5-18, Acts 1:8).

We are called to support others who are called as co-laborers, as churches are planted throughout the world. The Great Commission is fulfilled through tearing down spiritual strongholds of darkness and church planting (I Cor. 3:6-9, Matt. 11:12, II Cor. 10:3-4, Acts 14:21-23).

We are also called to proclaim the gospel through the arts, publications, and the media and will continue to believe God to raise up other resources and ministries to assist us in building the church (I Cor. 9:19-22).

## 4. We deeply value the sacred covenant of marriage and the importance of training our children to know Christ.

It is our belief that marriage and family are instituted by God, and healthy, stable families are essential for the church to be effective in fulfilling its mission. Parents are called by God to walk in the character of Christ and to train their children in the nurture and loving discipline of the Lord Christ (Mark 10:6-8, Eph. 5:22-6:4).

The Lord is calling His people to walk in the fear of the Lord and in a biblical standard of holiness and purity. Marriage covenants are ordained by God and need to be honored and kept (Prov. 16:6, Mark 10:9, I Thess. 4:3-8, I Cor. 6:18-20).

## 5. We are committed to spiritual families, spiritual parenting and intergenerational connections.

Believing that our God is turning the hearts of the fathers and mothers to the sons and daughters in our day, we are committed to spiritual parenting on every level of church and ministry life (Mal. 4:5-6, I Cor. 4:15-17).

Participation in a cell group is a fundamental commitment to the DCFI family. The cell group is a small group of believers and/or families who are committed to one another and to reaching others for Christ. We believe the Lord desires to raise up spiritual families in many levels including cells, congregations, apostolic movements and the kingdom of God  (I Cor. 12:18, Eph. 4:16).

We believe each spiritual family needs to share common values, vision, goals, and a commitment to build together, with the need to receive ongoing training in these areas (Ps. 133, II Pet. 1:12,13, II Tim. 2:2).

We are committed to reaching, training and releasing young people as co-laborers for the harvest, as the young and the old labor together (Acts 2:17, Jer. 31:13).

## 6. Spiritual multiplication and reproduction must extend to every sphere of kingdom life and ministry.

Multiplication is expected and encouraged in every sphere of church life. Cell groups should multiply into new cells and churches should multiply into new churches. Church planting must be a long term goal of every congregation (Acts 9:31, Mark 4:20).

The DCFI family of churches will be made up of many new regional families of churches as apostolic fathers and mothers are released in the nations of the world (Acts 11:19-30, Acts 13-15).

## 7. Relationships are essential in building God's kingdom.

Serving others and building trust and relationships is a desired experience in every area of church life. We believe the best place to begin to serve and experience trust and relationship is in the cell group (Acts 2:42-47, Eph. 4:16, Gal. 5:13).

We are joined together primarily by God-given family relationships, not by organization, hierarchy, or bureaucracy (I Peter 2:5).

## 8. Every Christian is both a priest and a minister.

According to the scriptures, every Christian is a priest who needs to hear from the Lord personally (Rev. 1:5-6).

Every believer is called of God to minister to others and needs to be equipped for this work with the home as a center for ministry. Fivefold ministers are the Lord's gifts to His church. He uses fivefold persons to help equip each believer to become an effective minister in order to build up the body of Christ (I Pet. 4:9, Eph. 4:11-12).

We need to be constantly handing the work of ministry over to those we are serving so they can fulfill their call from the Lord (Titus 1:5, I Tim 4:12-14).

## 9. A servant's heart is necessary for every leader to empower others.

We believe every sphere of leadership needs to include a clear servant-leader called by God and a team who is called to walk with him. The leader has the anointing and responsibility to discern the mind of the Lord that is expressed through the leadership team ( II Cor. 10:13-16, Num. 27:16, I Peter 5:1-4).

Leaders are called to listen to what the Lord is saying through those whom they serve as they model servant-leadership. They are called to walk in humility, integrity, in the fruit of the Spirit, and in the fear of the Lord  (Acts 6:2-6, Acts 15, Matt. 20:26, Gal. 5:22-23).

We believe God raises up both apostolic overseers and partner church elders to direct, protect, correct and discipline the church. These leaders must model the biblical qualifications for leadership (Acts 15, Acts 6:1-4, I Tim. 3, Titus 1).

Those with other spiritual gifts including administrative gifts (ministry of helps) need to be released to fulfill the Lord's vision on each level of church life (I Cor. 12).

In every area of church life we believe we need to submit to those who rule over us in the Lord and esteem them highly in love for their work's sake (Heb. 13:17, I Thess. 5:12-13).

## 10. Biblical prosperity, generosity and integrity are essential to kingdom expansion.

Biblical prosperity is God's plan to help fulfill the Great Commission. The principle of the tithe is part of God's plan to honor and provide substance for those He has placed over us in spiritual authority. Those who are over us in the Lord are responsible for the proper distribution of the tithe and offerings (III John 2, Matt. 23:23, Heb. 7:4-7, Mal. 3:8-11, Acts 11:29-30).

We believe in generously giving offerings to support ministries, churches, and individuals both inside and outside of the DCFI family, and emphasize giving to people as a priority. We encourage individuals, cells, congregations, and ministries to support fivefold ministers and missionaries in both prayer and finances (II Cor. 8:1-7, Gal. 6:6, Phil. 4:15-17).

We believe that every area of ministry and church life needs to be responsible financially and accountable to those giving them oversight in order to maintain a high standard of integrity. Spiritual leaders receiving a salary from the church are discouraged from setting their own salary level (Gal. 6:5, Rom. 15:14, I Thess. 5:22, II Cor. 8:20-21).

## 11. The gospel compels us to send missionaries to the unreached and help those least able to meet their own needs.

Jesus instructs us to take the gospel to the ends of the earth to those who have never heard. Our mission is to reach the unreached areas of the world with the gospel of Jesus Christ by sending trained missionaries and through church planting. Together we can join with the body of Christ to reach the unreached (Matt. 24:14, Acts 1:8, Acts 13:1-4, II Cor. 10:15-16).

We are also called to help the poor and needy, those in prison, orphans and widows. This includes our reaching out to the poor locally, nationally and internationally. When we help the poor, both materially and spiritually, we are lending to the Lord (Deut. 14:28, 29; Deut. 26: 10-12, Matt. 25:31-46, James 1:27, Prov. 19:17).

## 12. We are called to build the kingdom together with the entire body of Christ.

Our focus is on the kingdom of God, recognizing our cell group, our local church, and DCFI is just one small part of God's kingdom. We are called to link together with other groups in the body of Christ and pursue unity in His church as we reach the world together (Matt. 6:33, Eph. 4:1-6, John 17, Ps. 133).

We believe in utilizing and sharing the resources of people and materials the Lord has blessed us with. This includes the fivefold ministry, missions, leadership training, and other resources the Lord has entrusted to us (I Cor. 12, Acts 2:44-45).

Our unifying focus is on Christ, His Word and the Great Commission, and we believe we should not be distracted by minor differences (Romans 14:5).

We subscribe to the Lausanne Covenant as our basic statement of faith and Christian values. The scriptures serve as a light to guide us and the Lausanne Covenant along with these values and guiding principles unite us as partner churches as we walk together in the grace of God (Matt. 28:19-20, Amos 3:3, I Cor. 1:10, I Cor. 15:10).

# Developing a Vision/Values Statement

What kind of church do you want to plant? Why would someone be interested in coming to this church? What are the things you value? What is the purpose of this church? What is the mission of this church? To answer the above questions, it is sometimes helpful to start from the desired end product and work backwards (Isaiah 46:10). Picture what the church will look like in five years. Make a list of 30 reasons why someone would want to be involved in this church. Keep trying until you can list 30.

*Note: You should complete your demographic research before you develop your vision statement.*

## Values

Core values in our lives determine what we really believe. Unless these values are based in the scriptures, we are just trying another good idea. Read DCFI's scriptural values on pages 246-248, then list 10-15 scriptural values for your own church plant.

## Mission statement

What is the divine purpose of this church? Who is it going to reach? What is going to be done to reach them? How is it going to be done? The mission statement answers all of the previous questions. Go ahead and write a first draft of your mission statement. Remember it must answer the three questions...who? what? how? Have a few peers read it and give their input.

Compare it with other mission statements. Read the DCFI mission statement on page 244. Review the 30 reasons why someone would want to be involved in your church. Is your mission statement compatible with the 30 reasons you gave?

**Modify your mission statement to fit in one paragraph.** Be sure this mission statement is what is on your heart. It will be challenged. People may question it. The enemy will oppose it. You have to be committed to it.

## Vision statement

Now you want to condense that mission statement to just one sentence that is concise, easy to say and motivational. Your vision statement should be able to fit on a banner but yet make sense on a bulletin cover. This is the toughest step of the process and may take the longest time to complete.

**Pray, pray, and fast and pray**...this is very important. Complete the vision statement, get some input from peers or team members, and revise if needed. Be sure this statement communicates what is in your heart.

# Sample Cell-Based Church Bylaws

## ARTICLE I: NAME

The name of the organization shall be _____ (herein after spoken of as the church) a partner church of DOVE Christian Fellowship, International. Its duration is to be perpetual.

## ARTICLE II : PURPOSE

The purpose of the church shall be to provide spiritual oversight for the membership and to meet spiritual, emotional and physical needs of people through faith in Jesus Christ and by resourcing and networking with the Body of Christ in fulfilling the Great Commission.

## ARTICLE III : OFFICES

The business office of the church shall be located at _____

## ARTICLE IV: GOVERNMENT PRIVILEGES

The church shall have self-governing privileges in harmony with the authority and vision of the Apostolic Council of DOVE Christian Fellowship International (DCFI). Local authority in vision, direction and doctrine shall be vested in the Eldership Team. The Eldership Team may appoint others under them as required to assist in spiritual oversight of geographic areas or ministries. This church is a Partner Church with DCFI as evidenced by a Partnership Agreement entered into between the church and DCFI. Within the Partnership Agreement, the Eldership Team members acknowledge that they have read DCFI's Constitution, Bylaws and Handbook and that they are in agreement with the statements therein and agreed to be bound by the statements contained in these documents.

## GOVERNING DOCUMENTS

4-2A. The governing documents of (the church) are the Articles of Incorporation and Bylaws. The Articles of Incorporation take precedence over the Bylaws.

4-2B. No amendments or repeal shall be made to the Articles of Incorporation as adopted except by a 2/3 majority vote of the Eldership Team and affirmation by the Senior Elder. Amendments shall be within the guiding principles set forth in the DCFI handbook, Constitution and Bylaws.

4-2C. The Bylaws of (the church) or any portions thereof, may be amended or repealed by a 2/3 majority of the Eldership Team and affirmation by the Senior Elder. Amendments shall be within the guiding principles set forth in the DCFI handbook, Constitution and Bylaws.

## ARTICLE V:
## DOCTRINE STATEMENT OF FAITH

WE BELIEVE the Bible to be the inspired, infallible, and authoritative Word of God. The Holy Spirit moved upon the writers of the Old and New Testament and inspired them as they wrote the Words of God. God's revelation in Christ and in scripture is unchangeable. Through it the Holy Spirit still speaks today. (II Tim. 3:13-17; Heb. 4:12; Psalm 119:89, 105; I Pet. 1:23-25; Gal. 1:8, 9; Matt. 5:18; Isa. 40:8)

WE BELIEVE that there is One God, eternally existent in three personalities: Father, Son, and Holy Spirit. God the Father—Creator of all things. By His Word all things were created and through the power of His Word all things are held together. He sent His Son Jesus to redeem mankind unto Himself. A relationship with God only comes through Jesus Christ. Jesus Christ—is the only begotten Son of God, conceived by the Holy Spirit, and born of a virgin. He lived a sin-less life, and performed many miracles. He redeemed us by His atoning death through His shed blood, He ascended to the right hand of the Father, and He will personally return in power and glory. There is no other name given under heaven by which man must be saved. Holy Spirit—inspired the writers of the Bible, convicts the world of sin, teaches us all things, and brings to our remembrance the Word of God. (Deut. 6:4; Isa. 44:6-8; Isa. 43:10; Matt. 3:16, 17; Matt. 28:19; I Cor. 12:4-6; John 14:23, 25; I Tim. 6:15, 16; I John 5:7)

WE BELIEVE that mankind is perishing because of sin, which separates him from God. But God loves all mankind, not wishing that any should perish, but that all should repent. Mankind can only be saved through a complete commitment to Jesus Christ as Lord and Savior, being regenerated by the Holy Spirit. (Gen. 1:26, 31; Psalm 8:4-8; Gen. 3:1-7; Rom. 5:1, 12-21; Eph. 2:8, 9; Acts 3:19-21; I Cor. 15:21, 22; Gal. 6:14, 15; II Cor. 5:17)

WE BELIEVE in the present infilling of the Holy Spirit to all believers who desire it. The Holy Spirit's ministry to the body of Jesus Christ gives power to live, witness, proclaim the gospel and to make disciples. The Holy Spirit gives us power to cultivate a Christ-like character through the Fruit of the Spirit and to build up and mature the church through the miraculous gifts and ministries in this present day. (John 15:8-10; I Cor. 12:13; John 3:5, 6; Acts 1:4-8; Acts 2:1-4; Acts 2:38, 39; Luke 11:9-13; Joel 2:28, 29; I Cor. 12-14; Heb. 2:4)

WE BELIEVE that the local church is a body of believers brought together by the Holy Spirit as a visible part of the body of Christ and His church universal. The church is responsible to faithfully proclaim the whole Word of God in fulfilling the Great Commission, properly administer the sacraments, and humbly submit themselves to discipline, all for the glory of God. (Matt. 28:19, 20; Rom. 12:4, 5; I Cor. 12:27; Eph. 2:22; I Pet. 2:5, 9, 10; Titus 2:14)

WE BELIEVE that all mankind shall give an account of their deeds in this earthly life before the judgment seat of Christ. Those with their names written in the Lamb's Book of Life will be eternally with God in His glory, those without their names written will be eternally separated from God and tormented. (I Thess. 5:13-17; Rev. 1:7; Acts 1:11; Rev. 20:10-15; II Cor. 5:10; II Thess. 1:7-10; Rev. 21:1-4)

## ARTICLE VI: BOARD OF DIRECTORS
## FUNCTIONS AND MEETINGS

6-1A. The Eldership Team shall serve as the board of directors. They shall be responsible for the overall vision, direction, focus and shall fully control, govern and operate the business affairs of the church. As a Partner Church of DCFI, we submit to the vision, mission, basic values, and guiding principles of DCFI's Apostolic Council.

6-1B. The Eldership Team shall be given leadership to by the Senior Elder. The Senior Elder shall be the president of the board of directors.

6-1C. The Eldership Team shall meet annually for an official meeting in the month of January. The Eldership Team shall record the minutes of the annual meeting including the election of officers (vice-chairman, secretary, treasurer). The Eldership Team will meet regularly as determined by the Senior Elder.

## APPOINTMENT

6-2A. The Senior Elder shall be called by God, qualified (I Tim. 3:1-7 and Titus 1:5-9) and willing to fulfill this leadership responsibility. The Senior Elder shall be recognized and recommended by both the Eldership Team and DCFI's Apostolic Council. The

Senior Elder shall be appointed by a member of the Apostolic Council or an appointed designate. The Senior Elder shall not be appointed unless there is unanimous agreement with the Eldership Team, recommendation by DCFI's Apostolic Council and general affirmation of the Partner Church's cell group leaders.

6-2B. The Eldership Team members shall be called by God, qualified by scripture (I Timothy 3:1-7 and Titus 1:5-9) and willing to fulfill this leadership responsibility.

6-2C. The Eldership Team members are discerned through fasting and prayer, then nominated by the Senior Elder and the existing Eldership Team. General affirmation of the cell group leaders of the Church and the recommendation of DCFI's Apostolic Council is required for an individual to serve on the Eldership Team.

6-2D. An Apostolic Council member (or an appointed designate) and the Senior Elder shall install new members as set forth in 6-2B and 6-2C at the annual meeting or as deemed necessary by the Eldership Team.

6-2E. The Eldership Team shall consist of at least two members which includes the Senior Elder.

6-2F. The Senior Elder and each member of the Eldership Team shall be active members of a cell group and involved in the life of the church.

## SPECIFIC DUTIES

6-3A. Appoint and commission Deacons and cell leaders.

6-3B. Appoint persons to serve on an Administrative Committee if the Eldership deems an Administrative Committee is needed.

6-3C. Appoint and oversee specific committees or directors, e.g. Missions Council Representative, Worship, Children, Youth, Singles, as required to resource the spiritual needs of the Partner Church.

6-3D. Recognize, appoint, oversee, protect spiritually and provide accountability to the Fivefold Ministers who serve within the local Partner Church.

6-3E. Train and nurture leaders.

6-3F. Provide oversight and spiritual protection to members.

6-3G. Provide assistance during times of crisis for members in cell group or committees.

6-3H. Approve annual and all modified Partner Church Budgets.

6-3I. Recommend a representative to serve on the DCFI Stewardship Group to be appointed by the DCFI Apostolic Council.

## TERMS - VACANCIES

6-4A. Eldership Team members, including the Senior Elder, shall be willing to serve long term with an annual evaluation.

6-4B. This annual evaluation will first have the Senior Elder and each Eldership Team member mutually discern the call of God on their own life to serve another year.

6-4C. Annual evaluations shall be conducted by the Senior Elder in cooperation with the Apostolic Council, an evaluation team or a combination of both. A written report shall be given to the Senior Elder and the person being evaluated.

6-4D. Evaluations are for the purpose of growth. In the event of a report that one's service is unsatisfactory or that one is no longer suited for the position, the Eldership Team and Senior Elder shall review the specified deficiencies with the member. The Eldership Team and the Senior Elder shall determine whether it would be best for the member to relinquish their position or continue as a member and work to improve the specified deficiencies.

6-4E. In addition to the evaluations, at any time the Senior Elder and other Eldership Team members may vote to suspend or remove the member if deemed to be in the best interests of the organization. DCFI's Apostolic Council shall be included in the process of suspension or removal. Discipline shall be invoked in accordance with the written Policy of Discipline and Restoration outlined in the DCFI Handbook.

6-4F. The Senior Elder shall be evaluated by members of the Apostolic Council or appointed designates, an evaluation team or a combination of both. A full report shall be given to the Senior Elder and the Apostolic Council and a summary report given to the Eldership Team.

6-4G. In the event of the necessity of termination of the responsibility of the Senior Elder due to failure morally, irreconcilable conflicts, disorderly conduct or apostasy, the Apostolic Council shall give leadership to this process along with the Eldership members. The Apostolic Council, with counsel from the Eldership Team, shall suspend the Senior Elder pending a thorough review and application of the written policy for discipline and restoration. The DCFI Apostolic Council, with counsel from the Eldership Team will appoint an Acting Elder immediately, who will serve until restoration or a replacement is discerned.

6-4H. In the event that the number of persons on the Eldership Team drops below the required two for ninety days, then the longest serving cell group leader of the Partner Church shall immediately begin serving. If more than one replacement is required, then the next longest serving cell leader shall be selected until all vacancies are filled. This is a temporary position with full authority until either the person is confirmed or another person is appointed.

**Officers**

6-5A. At the annual meeting, the Eldership Team shall appoint a vice-chairman, secretary and a treasurer as officers of the Eldership Team. The Senior Elder as the president of the Eldership Team shall oversee the appointment process. Members of the Eldership Team may hold up to two offices. The president shall not serve in the capacity of secretary or treasurer.

6-5B. The designation of officers, except president, shall be by unanimous decision of the Eldership Team. Such appointed officers shall serve in their capacities until such time as the Eldership Team should appoint otherwise.

6-5C. It shall be the duty of the Secretary to keep an accurate record of the proceedings of the meetings of the Board and of Congregational meetings of business, and all such other duties as pertain to this office as may be prescribed by the Board.

6-5D. The Treasurer shall have the care and custody of all funds and securities of the Church and shall deposit the same in the name of the Church in such Bank or Banks as the Board of Directors may select.

## ARTICLE VII: COMMITTEES

The eldership team may appoint such additional committees to assist it in the discharge of its duties as it may deem advisable.

## ARTICLE VIII: MEMBERSHIP VOTING

The church has a no voting membership. Spiritual decisions affecting the life of the local body of the church are under the care of its Elders.

## QUALIFICATIONS

The membership of the church shall consist of those persons who meet the following qualifications:

1. They are in agreement with the statements as set forth in Article V.
2. They shall be a member in good standing of a cell group.

3. They shall be involved in the life of the church.
4. They shall recognize and submit to the elders leadership of the church.
5. They shall express commitment to the church with the understanding that biblical church discipline will be used if necessary.

## ACTIVE CELL GROUP LISTING
The Eldership Team will semiannually update the active cell group listing in accordance with its qualifications for members.

## ARTICLE IX: DISSOLUTION
## SECTION 1 - DISSOLUTION BY ELDERSHIP TEAM
9-1A. In the event that this organization shall be dissolved and liquidated, after paying or making provision for the payment of all liabilities of this organization, the Eldership Team shall distribute or dispose of any remaining property and assets to such organization or organizations established and operated exclusively for religious purposes as, in its judgement, have purposes which are most closely allied to those of this organization; it being provided, however, that each transferee organization, at the time of such transfer, shall:

1. be a tax-exempt, religious Christian organization within the meaning and intent of Section 501 (C) (3) and Section 170 (b) (1) (A) of the Internal Revenue Code of 1954 or the corresponding sections of any successor Internal Revenue Law of the United States of America;
2. have been in existence for a continuous period of at least sixty (60) months;
3. be an organization to which contributions are deductible under Section 170, Section 2055 and Section 2522 of the Internal Revenue Code of 1954 or the corresponding sections of any successor Internal Revenue Law of the United States of America.

9-1B. DOVE Christian Fellowship International (DCFI) shall be given first consideration in this dissolution of assets.

## SECTION 2 - DISSOLUTION BY COURT
Any of this organization's property and assets not disposed of in accordance with ARTICLE IX, Section 1, shall be disposed of by the court having jurisdiction of the dissolution and liquidation of a nonprofit corporation organized and existing under and in accordance with the laws of the Commonwealth of Pennsylvania and having jurisdiction in the county of this organization's registered office exclusively to such religious organization or organizations, each of which is established and operated exclusively for such purposes as are most closely allied to those of this organization and each of which, at the time of such disposal, is a qualified, tax-exempt organization as aforesaid, as said court shall determine.

## ARTICLE X: LIABILITY
10-1A. No member of the Eldership Team and/or committee shall be personally liable, as such, for monetary damages for any action taken unless:

1. the member has breached or failed to perform the duties of office in good faith, in a manner reasonably believed to be in the best interest of the corporation, and with such care, including reasonable inquiry, skill and diligence, as a person of ordinary prudence would use under similar circumstances; and
2. the breach or failure to perform constitutes self-dealing, willful misconduct or recklessness.

10-1B. This provision cannot by law release a member from liability under criminal laws or for proper payment of taxes.

# Releasing Fivefold Ministry

**How elders can facilitate
fivefold ministry and other guest ministry
leaders who serve their congregations**

by Ron Myer

**T**he Lord is restoring the fivefold ministry to the church today. With the increasing emphasis on the fivefold ministry, the Lord is doing a tremendous work in releasing these ministers into the body of Christ. Let's learn how proven fivefold ministers function, along with practical ways church leadership can relate to them as they minister in our churches and cell groups. It's time to take what we have learned and put it into practice!

I use the masculine gender when speaking of the fivefold minister in order to make the text easier to read. For the record, I believe fivefold ministry is not gender-specific, and women can serve in the fivefold ministry in the body of Christ. Some examples are Junia in Romans 16:7 and Priscilla in Acts 18:26.

Since the form and function of fivefold ministry is often misunderstood in the modern-day church, there have been false starts and mistakes made by both fivefold ministers and other leaders relating to them. Nevertheless, the Lord is helping us to learn from our mistakes. He is giving us wisdom to empower these ministers and ministries so that they may work with the local church as the Lord intended.

It is the Lord's plan for His people to be equipped to do the work of ministry. The Lord has given the gifts of apostle, prophet, evangelist, pastor and teacher to equip His people to minister and to build up and encourage the body of Christ. These five gifts to the body of Christ are often referred to as the *fivefold ministry*. Effective fivefold ministers "equip the saints for the work of ministry" and bring the body of Christ to maturity, according to Ephesians 4:11-12.

This is accomplished by fivefold ministers who have been recognized as having a discernible and functioning anointing—the power and presence of Jesus. They have been affirmed by their church leadership and are called by the Lord and commissioned to work alongside the local church to identify, acknowledge and stir up the diverse gifts within the body of Christ. Although many people have one or more of the fivefold gifts in seed form, they may not yet be considered fivefold ministers.

When a fivefold minister is fully developed, he will have the ability to train and release others of like gifts and calling. He will be affirmed by his local church leadership and be recognized and affirmed by other fivefold ministers and apostolic church leaders. These proven fivefold ministers, representing one of the ministry gifts of Jesus Christ, function similarly to the "circuit riders" in early Methodism, ministering translocally from church to church and cell group to cell group.

The translocal fivefold ministry is desperately needed in the body of Christ today. Jesus Christ Himself gave these gifts for the equipping of the saints for the work of ministry and for the edifying of the body of Christ. Because their gifts are so critically needed, it is important that church leaders learn how to assist these fivefold ministers.

## Fivefold ministers build alongside local church elders

For too long, the translocal fivefold ministers have been looked upon as a threat to the local elder/pastor (I will use the term "elder" throughout this booklet to identify the leader(s) who gives oversight to a local church). The fivefold ministers have been accused of trying to build their own ministries rather than working with the local church. They have not been seen as supporting the local senior elder to build locally in the way they should.

I believe the fivefold ministers shy away from the local church and look after themselves because they have not been properly taken care of by the local church. Subsequently, they have become more independent in nature and are sometimes viewed by others as being aloof, hard to work with, and not willing to make an investment in the local church.

Consequently, they have been held at arm's length by many local church leaders, often viewed as ministers to be utilized for a short time and then sent on their way. I believe this stems from the fact that many elders have a false understanding of the fivefold ministry. As elders, they feel that it is their sole responsibility to feed the flock, so they utilize fivefold translocal ministers for special occasions only. They are unaware that the fivefold ministers have been given by the Lord to assist them in building the church. God's plan is for fivefold ministers to walk alongside elders to help build the local church—not be used as "flash-in-the-pan" ministries and then leave again.

The Lord wants to change our former way of thinking. He gave the fivefold ministers for the building of the church—not apart from the local leadership, but alongside the local leadership. The Lord intends for both to work together so they may see the church come to maturity and strength. To this end, the church will be filled with the power of God with the saints doing the work of ministry as Jesus intended!

The worst mistake we can make at this point is to give up on the fivefold ministers because of problems of the past. If we ignore these ministers, we lose their valuable contribution and impartation to the body of Christ. Jesus never intended the local elder(s) to work alone. He provided the fivefold ministry so that the elder does not need to be "everything" the flock needs. Instead, he can draw from the anointing of the *evangelist* to see people saved. He can receive the help of the *prophet* to keep the work on track and "up to speed." The elder can draw on the *teacher* to impart the deeper things of the Word into people's hearts which is able to save their souls and bring about change. He can receive the help of the *apostle* to keep things on track, making sure they hold fast to the vision the Lord gave them and ensuring a continuous outward and forward thrust of ministry. Not only can the elder draw on these fivefold gifts, but these ministers would impart into the lives of the people to bring them to a greater level of spiritual maturity.

It should be the goal of local church leaders to identify, train, equip and release fivefold ministers from within. However, a local fellowship should not only desire to raise up fivefold ministers from within, they should invite fivefold ministers from outside of their local body to come in and minister. Someone from outside is often able to give a fresh perspective on things that could be overlooked by someone who is there among the people all the time.

One of the abilities of fivefold ministers from outside the local body is their capacity to identify others of like gifts within a fellowship. These newly identified individuals and their developing gifts have the wonderful opportunity to learn from the "outside" fivefold ministers as they function together within that local fellowship. When fivefold ministers spend time with those who have a developing gift, they can impart so much to them. The developing ministers can ask questions, talk about how their gift should function and experience the anointing of an established minister. (For more teaching on the different levels of fivefold ministry, consult DCFI's *Helping You Build Cell Churches* manual, or order the audio tape set entitled "Releasing the Fivefold Ministry.")

## Build lasting relationships with fivefold ministers

We need to be more aware of the needs of the fivefold ministers and how elders should respond to these needs. Most of the problems in dealing with fivefold translocal ministers center around unmet expectations. What is an elder expecting when he invites a fivefold minister to his church, and what is a fivefold minister expecting when an elder invites him in? A fivefold minister should know that his needs are going to be taken care of. The local elder should know how to communicate his expectations to the fivefold minister. The result of this understanding is fruitful ministry with long-lasting results!

The fivefold minister will minister with a sense that he has fulfilled the purposes of God in that congregation, while at the same time, feel honored and valued by the local elder. They know the Lord was in the experience and will remain open to what He has in the future as they continue to build a relationship.

Building through an ongoing relationship is an effective building process. Yet, far too many fivefold ministers are under-utilized, ministering on a one-time basis rather than building a lasting relationship with a congregation. There may be a wonderful anointing, but often, the fruit is not lasting. When the fivefold minister is deprived of an ongoing relationship with the local church body, he is deprived of an opportunity to build long-lasting fruit—fruit that will not only remain but also bear more fruit.

Countless times, I have heard elders remark about a visiting fivefold minister, "I will not have him back again." After ministering at his church, one elder invited me again to minister but admitted, "You are only the second person that we have ever invited back for the second time." He had a bad experience with previous fivefold ministers which made him understandably cautious. I believe the Lord

> Because their gifts are so critically needed, it is important that church leaders learn how to assist these fivefold ministers.

wants to bring some adjustment and correction so that lasting fruit is evident and there is more effective ministry occurring.

I have been a local elder, a senior elder, and a fivefold minister. I have experienced times when the relationship between the fivefold ministry and local church flowed really well. Other times, some minor adjustments would have made things flow more smoothly in order to facilitate more effective long-term ministry.

I received a call one day from a fivefold minister who had just served at one of the local churches I oversee. He stressed that he was not offended in any way, but just wanted to encourage me to do some training in the church on how to handle visiting ministers! I immediately knew what he was talking about because I recalled seeing him leave the church building that Sunday morning after speaking. He was crawling into the back seat of a tiny compact car, and because he was a fairly large man, I remembered thinking that using a larger car to take him to the airport would have been much more comfortable.

He went on to tell me the rest of the story. As they were driving out of the parking lot, the minister even mentioned to the driver that it would be nice if they had a larger car to go to the airport. The driver cheerfully responded, "When in Rome, do as the Romans do." However, they were following a large sport utility vehicle that was being driven by one of the elders of the church. Apparently, not every "Roman" drove a compact car! They could have easily found someone with a larger vehicle for the long drive to the airport.

To make matters worse, on the way to the airport, they experienced car trouble. The air conditioner failed and the car began to overheat. Although they made it, there was a question as to whether they would get there on time. While we have all had car trouble at one time or another, a quick decision to take a better car to the airport would have resulted in a much less stressful experience for the minister.

In addition, no one at the church had communicated whether the minister would receive an offering for his service or whether a check would be forthcoming in the mail. Or, was he donating his time and receiving nothing more that a "thank you" and "bless you for ministering to us this morning" from the church?

While all of us have ministered at times as a labor of love, and we may need to do that when there is a legitimate need, the fivefold translocal ministers also have bills to pay. Their cars get old, their children grow out of clothes and they even stop fasting at times to eat! God does not supernaturally grow finances on a tree in their back yard. They work and earn their financial support through their ministry.

Let's learn together how to relate to the fivefold ministers when we invite them to our cell group or church. Some of the following items may seem elementary, but sometimes it is the elementary things that are forgotten.

## 1. The worker deserves his wages

When you are inviting a minister to speak at your church or cell group, find out if there is a fee he is expecting to receive. Some ministers have a set fee they normally charge. Others receive love offerings or honorariums. If they have a set fee, you can decide right away whether you wish to have them come and minister. Fivefold ministers should be paid for their services. The Bible is very clear that you should "...not muzzle the ox while it is treading out the grain," and "the worker deserves his wages" (1 Timothy 5:18).

If the fivefold minister does not have a set fee, then payment for his services can be handled one of the following ways: honorarium, love offering, or love offering plus an honorarium. Since the beginning of our church, we have given an honorarium of $300 each time a fivefold minister spoke to our congregation.

I recommend that you give the minister a love offering plus an honorarium, especially if they are supporting a ministry. That gives the Lord the opportunity to bless the individual according to current needs and those needs for which he is believing God. It also gives the congregation the freedom to respond to the Holy Spirit without putting pressure on the finances of the local church. Notice, I said *love offering plus honorarium*. I believe a local church has the responsibility to "pay for services rendered." I am more than willing to pay for any other service that I receive, so I should be so much more willing to pay for services in the kingdom. I am blessing another one of God's children.

Do not be afraid to give too much in the way of financial blessing. This individual is a minister of the Lord to whom you have just entrusted the preaching of the Word and the ministry of the Holy Spirit to your cell or congregation. Certainly, you should be able to trust that if he receives "too much" he will pass it on to others in need. I know of individuals who, under the direction of the Holy Spirit, gave their entire honorarium away as soon as they received it because they saw a need right there within the body in which they were ministering. We must trust these workers with finances if we are going to trust them to deliver to us true riches.

An important principle to remember is this: be generous. God's kingdom is not one of stinginess. It is a kingdom of blessing. If the speaker has really blessed the people in your church, receive a love offering and allow the Holy Spirit to bless the individual as He wants to. If you are afraid to do that, check your heart. Are you concerned that it would take money away from other offerings? If so, you are communicating to your people that God will not supply your needs. It is thinking that once God provides, we should hold on to it because He may not provide again. That spirit will hinder the release of finances in your congregation.

Bob Mumford once stated, "Teach your children to be generous." I would add to that and say, "Once you have lost your ability to give, you have lost a major part of the kingdom. God's kingdom is centered around a heart of giving."

I have heard people say that Paul is talking about *respect* when he said, "The elders who direct the affairs of the church well are worthy of double honor, especially those whose work is preaching and teaching" (1 Timothy 5:17). While it is true that we need to respect those who minister the Word, my perception of this scripture is that Paul is referring here to *finances*. Verse 18 goes on to say that a "worker deserves his wages."

When you go to the garage to pick up your repaired car, you do not tell the mechanic, "I respect you, in fact I double respect you." His response is sure to be, "That's great that you respect me. Here is your bill. Please pay it immediately."

To bring things into perspective, imagine this scenario. If we give $150 to a minister, and he spent 10 hours in prayer and preparation for ministry, he is receiving $15 an hour. In the United States, we pay mechanics at a garage $55-75 an hour to repair our cars! This seems a little out of balance to me. Anytime we invest into a kingdom individual, we are investing into the kingdom. The kingdom of God pays dividends that are comparable to none. As we invest into God's people, the Lord invests in us.

**An important principle to remember is this: be generous. God's kingdom is not one of stinginess. It is a kingdom of blessing.**

An exception to this principle might be that I do not pay for training someone in the early stages of development in the local church. If I am giving someone the opportunity to learn by exercising his gift, I usually do not give him an honorarium. There may come a time, sometime during the training, that I begin to bless him financially for ministering. Again, the key here is expectation. I clearly tell him that I am training him and giving him an opportunity, but it is part of his training. He will not be paid for it other than being blessed by this opportunity to serve.

However you decide to handle it, either by honorarium, love offering, or a combination of the two, communicate to the individual what he should expect. Feel free to ask him if he has a preference. Don't be afraid to talk to him about money. There is nothing sacred or unholy about finances. They are a reality of life. Ask him, "To whom should the check be made out?" or in the case of a love offering, "Do you want cash"? In the USA, remember that if the check is over $600 and is made out to the individual rather than a ministry, you will need to send him an IRS 1099 form at the end of the year for income tax purposes. For accounting purposes, it is always better to write the check out to the ministry he represents.

While ministering, I have been in small churches and received $500 and in large churches and received $100. I have been in medium-size churches where I have received much more. Size is not the indicator of blessing.

Some of the aspects that influence our thinking about giving come from our backgrounds. Certain denominations may consistently give more or less than others. Some of that is the value that is placed on the mantle a minister carries. It often involves their understanding of finances and how ministers should be supported. We are all products of what we have been exposed to, and our values reflect that. We should ask ourselves, "Do our values reflect God's values of giving or do they reflect a certain denomination's values?"

A true kingdom-building fivefold translocal minister is not in it for the money. He ministers because he has sensed that the Lord asked him to. He is not looking at the money; he is looking to obey the Lord. A fivefold minister sees a much larger picture. There are places that the Lord asks him to go where, due to the economics of the church or the area, he needs to provide for his own expenses. I have done this while traveling both nationally and internationally. A minister does this willingly because he knows he is a servant of the Lord and desires to see God's kingdom advanced. A fivefold minister is looking to the Lord to supply his needs. He expects that the Lord will meet those needs from those who have abundance to help supply for him to go to those who have a great need (2 Corinthians 8:13-15).

## 2. Travel expenses

Whether the minister is flying or driving, there are travel expenses that need to be covered. Ask the individual how he wants it to be handled. Does he want a separate check? Or, can the amount be included on the honorarium check? Who should the check(s) be made out to? Do they need the travel expenses before they arrive to cover the costs of airline tickets? Or, can they wait until after the engagement to receive reimbursement? Do they wish to purchase the tickets and then get reimbursed, or would they prefer you to buy the ticket and send it to them? For those who are frequent flyers, there is usually an airline that they favor for a variety of reasons. Try to honor special requests when possible. By asking these kinds of questions, you are letting them know that you value them and that their needs are important to you.

Again, the key question is, "What does he expect?" Either provide transportation costs or give a large enough honorarium or love offering to offset the transportation expenses, even if there is a relatively short travel distance.

Just to help keep things in the proper perspective, think about this: If I travel 40 miles to the place of ministry and 40 miles home, that is a 80 mile round-trip. If I charge the current amount allowed by the U.S. government of 36.5 cents per mile, the total is $29.20 for mileage reimbursement. If I receive an honorarium of $100, that leaves $70.80 for my preparation and ministry time. If I've taken 10 hours to pray and prepare, that equates to $7.08 per hour. My son makes more than that sweeping floors in a cabinet shop!

We must make the distinction about what it costs for travel and how much we're paying for ministry. Sometimes it is easier to do this if we give two checks, one for expenses and one for ministering.

## 3. Lodging Arrangements

Ask in advance if the minister has a preference for lodging. Does he want to stay in a motel or would he prefer to stay in the home of someone from the fellowship? There is not a right or wrong to this; it is purely a preference. Some ministers desire to stay in the home of someone from the fellowship or perhaps even with the local senior elder. Others dislike the inconvenience of sharing bathrooms with family members and are very uncomfortable with this type of arrangement.

Some homes are laid out in such a way that it is almost like being in a motel—the minister has his own bathroom and does not feel like he is intruding on the hosting family. Ask him what his values are. One of my personal values is that I will not be alone with another woman other than my wife. I personally do not want to stay at a house without a man present. I do not want to be left alone in the house with just the wife if her husband needs to go to work or to a meeting in the morning.

If I'm staying in a home, I like to know what the sleeping arrangements are. I've slept in many different places. I've slept in the son's bedroom on the top bunk with "glow in the dark stars" just above my head. I've slept in the daughter's bedroom with the dolls and a mound of stuffed animals I had to move off the bed so I could crawl in. There is nothing wrong with any of these arrangements. In fact, I believe there is a blessing in store for the young child who is willing to give up his or her room for the visiting minister. Usually it depends upon how close a relationship I have with the family. If I have no relationship, or I'm just beginning to build a relationship, it feels as if I'm intruding on the family to sleep in one of the children's bedrooms, and it can feel quite uncomfortable. If I already have an established relationship with the family, then I am very comfortable with this style arrangement. In fact, I look forward to this relationship-building time.

Some time ago, I was going to speak at a church where they informed me of arrangements for me to stay with two single women. I responded that I preferred a motel even if I had to personally pay for it. They quickly assured me that the women in whose home I would be staying were "older women." To me, that didn't matter. A story like that repeated through the "grapevine" can easily develop into a rumor that places me in a house alone with two women, and it will not include the fact that they are grandmothers! They were very gracious and found another place for me to stay.

Here are some things to be mindful of when considering the minister's lodging:

- Is there a place to pray freely?
- Does he have his own bathroom?
- Is there a desk and chair for study?
- Many ministers travel with laptop computers.
  Can he connect to email?
- Can he charge calls to his room?
- Can he charge meals to the room?

Be careful of "Bed and Breakfast" establishments since most are geared toward vacationers. Think of creating a work environment for the speaker. I stayed in a Bed and Breakfast one time and shared the bathroom with a young couple in the adjacent room who were celebrating their one year wedding anniversary. This was an old house where all the floors creaked and doors screeched when opened.

The whole environment was a bit uncomfortable, especially as I needed more privacy to study and pray.

We really must take into consideration the different dynamics to which we subject ministers. Sometimes it is just because we do not put enough thought into where we are placing them. In my opinion, another lodging location to avoid is a cabin in the woods. I have had some interesting experiences in rustic cabins in the woods, and while they are funny now, they were not while I was experiencing them!

Many speakers work with laptops and maintain contact with their personal intercessors. Try to make sure they have the opportunity to do that. They need places where they can pray and study. This is not a vacation for them. It is work. Provide a place where they can work properly. They need an environment where they can study, get alone with God, receive from Him and be refreshed.

## 4. Meal Plans

The fourth area to consider is food. If the minister is only there for a Sunday morning, take him to lunch. Mealtime is an excellent time to discuss issues relating to leadership, the Word that was spoken, and other things happening in the body of Christ. The translocal minister is usually someone who is traveling quite a bit so he is exposed to things that local leadership would not normally be exposed to. This is a great time to get outside input and fresh perspective on what is happening in the body of Christ at large.

If you, as an elder, cannot take the guest minister to lunch, have another key leader do it, especially one with a like ministry gift. For example, if the fivefold minister is an evangelist, send an evangelist-leader from your church. This indicates to your leader that he is of value and worth by allowing him to get some quality one-on-one time with the equipping minister.

As a fivefold minister, I have personally had the opportunity to communicate valuable principles to key leaders in a restaurant over lunch. Sometimes a visiting minister can impart things into leaders that the senior elder has not been able to. I can encourage teamwork, help them see things from a different perspective, and encourage them to walk through difficult situations. It is often helpful to have someone from the outside speak into existing situations or difficulties.

If the fivefold minister is ministering for more than one meeting, here are some different food options to consider:

- If he is there in the morning, does he want breakfast?

- If he is there in evening, would he rather eat before or after ministering?

- Be sensitive to how late you keep him up as he may want to pray and get a fresh sense of what the Lord is saying for the next service.

- Does he have food preferences, likes or dislikes? Some people love Chinese food, and others don't. Ask if there is a specific kind of food he would like.

- Does he like fresh fruit? Would he like some fruit in his room? It is always nice to have some bottled water and a few snacks in the room for when he returns from ministry.

- If he is staying in a hotel or motel and is arriving without you being there, make sure the room is reserved in his name, but billed to you.

- After he is checked in, call and ask if everything is satisfactory in the room. Let him know whether he can make long distance phone calls from the room. Inform him of a restaurant on the premises and whether he can charge food to the room.

All these things may seem basic, but they are important since they communicate that you care. Clear communication will help the fivefold minister to be more effective in ministering to your congregation or cell group.

## 5. Ministry Needs

You should take into consideration if the fivefold minister has any special needs for ministry. Does he need a white board, an overhead, or transparencies for his teaching? Does he use PowerPoint, and does he need a projector? Does he need copies of handouts printed for distribution? Does he have a microphone preference? Would he rather use a hand-held or lapel microphone? Are there any specific worship songs that would be effective in helping to prepare the hearts of the people for his ministry? Is he planning a ministry time after the preaching? If so, does he need prayer counselors, ushers to set up ministry lines, or other ministers to help assist in ministry? Let him know if you have trained counselors available. Communicate how you normally do ministry so that he knows what the people are accustomed to. What type of response is he anticipating? Does he want the worship team back for the ministry time or does he prefer it to be quiet? Or would he prefer just a keyboard? Is he anticipating moving prophetically? Will he minister prophetically over individuals? If so, is there a tape player available to record the personal prophesies?

As a pastor, I would want a tape running for the entire service, recording everything that is taking place. More than once, the Lord released a prophetic word and afterwards the sound man said that he did not capture it on tape because he had not yet started taping the service. That report is always met with disappointment.

Who does the fivefold minister turn the meeting back to when he is finished ministering? Does he end the service with ministry time, or does he turn it back to the pastor? If someone other than the pastor is moderating, does it go back to the moderator or the pastor?

Ask him if he would like a taped copy of the message. Some ministers find it helpful to listen to the message again to critique themselves or provide the message for someone else to listen to.

If you were planning on receiving a love offering after the message, how will it mesh with the ministry time? Some pastors ask the fivefold minister to give a five minute testimony about his ministry before he preaches. This way the pastor receives a love offering for him before he gives his message, opening the door for a time of prayer ministry at the end of the service. Are there other announcements that need to be given before the close of the service? All of this is helpful to the minister so that he can be sensitive about how the Holy Spirit is leading and what the pastor has planned to happen at the end of the service. If this is shared before the service begins, it helps provide a divine flow at the end.

## 6. Bringing clarity to the message

In light of the Word that was preached, we should be open to any corrections or adjustments that are necessary. Any seasoned qualified fivefold minister, who has the kingdom of God in his heart, is there to help you build what the Holy Spirit is building. If he says something that needs to be corrected or adjusted for your fellowship, do it right away at the end of the service, if possible. It will be contained at that moment and clarified, leaving no doubts. An elder should be aware that his people will always watch him to see how he is responding with "nonverbals" while another minister is ministering.

Before I minister, I always ask the elder to feel free to bring clarity if I say something that is contrary to what he is ministering in his church. For example, if I refer to women in governmental ministry, and the church believes that women cannot have a role in governmental ministry, the elder needs to bring clarity to what was communicated. He should feel free to say something like, "I appreciate what Ron had to share this morning, but I want to bring clarity to what he said about women in governmental ministry. We believe that the Lord has instructed us such and such in this matter." As a fivefold minister, I will not be offended with this adjustment.

In the case of a new concept or thought, the elder could say, "I am not sure about what Ron shared today. I am going to study the scriptures and encourage you to do likewise and I'll have a response for you at a later date." If, as an elder, you believe a fivefold minister shares something clearly wrong, bring adjustment immediately at the close of the service: "We do not agree with (the specific issue) spoken here and we will be in dialogue with Ron about it at lunch." This case scenario would rarely happen, but you need to be prepared if it does.

If you clearly trust the individual, let him know you trust him and tell him, "I give you complete freedom and liberty in the Spirit today to minister all that is on your heart." If you want to draw parameters, do so before the fivefold minister speaks. "Our policy here is that all prophetic words be run by one of the elders before it is spoken publicly." Any policies or methods of ministry are important to communicate *before* ministry happens to avoid awkwardness and embarrassment for everyone.

Remember, as an elder, you have spiritual responsibility and authority for the field or sphere that the Lord has given you. Don't be afraid to exercise that authority. A fivefold translocal minister has been invited in to your "field" and he needs to honor the leadership of that field.[1] As the God-ordained leader of the fellowship you should, along with your elders, exercise good, godly government and leadership.

## 7. Reimbursement

As was mentioned before, at the end of the speaking engagement, communicate again with the minister about payment for his services. Make sure you know who the check should be made out to, especially if you are able to give him a check immediately. If you're going to mail a check, let him know when he can expect to receive it. Many fivefold traveling ministers use the finances they receive today to pay for an upcoming trip. They may need to receive their funds as soon as possible. Also, if they know that it will take a week to receive the check, they can plan for it. Once they leave, it is easy to remember the wonderful ministry time but forget to mail the check. Clearly communicate, so that they know what to expect.

## 8. Debriefing

The area of debriefing is extremely important. As soon as possible, talk to the fivefold minister and find out what he was sensing while he was ministering. Sometimes people from the "outside" are able to sense a whole lot more than people from the "inside." That is why it is so important to get a sense of what he was feeling during his time of ministry. Did he find the people receptive? Did he sense a freedom to minister? Was there any thing he sensed about your leadership? How can you be a more effective leader?

Make sure that after you have received all that the fivefold minister has to give to you, *you* minister to *him*. Affirm him. He is a servant of the Lord, a fellow soldier, and under the attack of the enemy.

An outside fivefold minister may be able to pick up on something that you are unable to sense in-house. Sometimes the fivefold minister may have a prophetic sense about an individual because he stands out. By asking for input, you are getting an insight of what is emanating from the people of the congregation. The fivefold minister may sense a specific area of oppression that needs to be broken or something that you should be focusing on in the next few months. Take his insights very seriously, but also remember, we have all had services when things did not flow well. Consequently, always take the fivefold minister's input before the Lord for adjustment.

An exceptional service with a fivefold minister does not mean the church will flourish, just as a horrible experience will cause a church to fail. The truth is that sometimes everything flows extremely well during ministry and the next time, no matter how hard we try and stay sensitive to the Spirit's leading, it just doesn't seem to go right. Be aware that God's grace is there to cover.

Make sure that after you have received all that the fivefold minister has to give to you, *you* minister to *him*. Affirm him. He is a servant of the Lord, a fellow soldier, and under the attack of the enemy. If he really ministered to you and your congregation, tell him. Avoid flattering words like, "awesome message," "tremendous ministry," "That was really wild!" These words are not quantifiable and can easily be misunderstood. Use descriptive words like, "I really felt you ministered the heart of the Lord this morning. What you shared today is exactly what we need as a congregation to move forward in the next step that the Lord has for us." Or, "I could really sense the anointing this morning. The presence of God was tangible today. Thank you for investing in us today. We so appreciate your willingness to come and give of your time and expertise."

## Follow up

Lastly, if there is a need for you to give input to the fivefold minister, now is the time to do it. This is probably a little more difficult to do, but necessary. If you have constructive input, say something like:

"I think you would be more effective in your ministry if you would..."
"When you said..., it put up walls that hindered the true Word of the
Lord from being heard today."
"In the future you might want to consider..."

Remember that you are in ministry together. You want to learn from his experience and you want to share with him from yours. It is a "give and take"—one in which everybody can win! An elder can be blessed by how the Lord ministers through the fivefold minister and the fivefold minister will be blessed by the way the elder honors and takes care of him. The Lord promises to bless us as we take care of His ministers. That is truly a win-win situation!

[1] For more on "Fields of Ministry" see Chapter 6 of this book.

# Index

E

egalitarian spirit, 126

elders

able to teach, 23, 38-39

able to manage his house, 26

above reproach, 19

accountability, 155-157

affirmation of elder, 54

co-equal, 11-12

entry level ministry, 53

evaluations, 55, 195, 216-218

first among equals, 12-13

free from love of money, 26

full of Holy Spirit, 31

gentle, 25

give correction, 43-44

give direction, 40-43

give protection, 35-39

good reputation, 27

govern, 1-5, 7-10, 42-43, 57-58

guard the church, 36

has endurance, 33

heart of a servant, 30

Holy Spirit calls, 46

hospitable, 22

husband of one wife, 20

humble, 24

in love with Jesus, 32

installment of elder, 54

knows he is called, 32

lay down lives for sheep, 37

loves what is good, 27

New Testament model, 2-3

not a new convert, 28

not given to drunkenness, 23

not overbearing, 24

not quick-tempered, 25

oversee 1-5, 7-10, 35-42, 60-74

plurality, 11-12

pray for those in their care, 38

respectable, 21

responsibilities, 35-45

rule, 40-42

safeguard against false, 39-40

self-controlled, 21

senior elder, 2, 12, 52, 78-83, 88

servant-leaders, 5, 30-31

shepherds, 7-11, 38-39

spiritually mature, 9, 163

spiritual fathers and mothers, 5,
161-168

teach the flock, 38

temperate, 21

term of office, 54

qualifications, 15-34

upright, holy, 28

willing, 19

willing to be tested, 29

endurance, 33

entry level ministry, 53

episkopos, 8, 10

episcopal government, 79-82

equipping leadership, 153

evaluations, 55, 195, 216-218


F

failures and mistakes, 131

false accusations, 207

false teachers, 36, 39-40

fasting, 185-187

field of ministry, 60-74

fight of faith, 119

finances, 43, 107-110

first among equals, 12-13

fivefold leadership, 153, 242, 255-268

Floyd McClung, 40, 123

Francis Frangipane, 72

free from love of money, 26

fruit, 68

full of Holy Spirit, 31

function, 94-104


G

Gene Getz, 21

general elders, 57

gentle, 25

George Barna, 21, 204

George Verwer, 132

gifts, 65, 255-268

give correction, 43-44

gives direction, 40-43

gives protection, 35-39

Golden Rule, 122

good reputation, 27

govern, 1-5, 7-10, 42-43, 57-58, 153

governmental elders, 4-5, 7-10, 57-58,
153

guard the church, 36

## Elders Audio Set

Included in this series are the New Testament leadership principles to train elders to provide protection, direction and correction in the local church. *Six Tape Set includes twelve topics.* $35.00
ISBN: 1-886973-59-8

## Elders DVD Training

Twelve sessions taught by the four authors of the book! The complete set includes a copy of *The Biblical Role of Elders* book, a leader's guide, three DVDs and six student manuals: **$89**
ISBN:1-886973-69-5

## House to House

The church is waking up to the simple, successful house to house strategy practiced by the New Testament church. *House to House* documents how God called a small fellowship of believers to become a house to house movement. During the past years, DOVE Christian Fellowship Int'l has grown into a family of cell-based churches and house churches networking throughout the world. *by Larry Kreider, 206 pages.* $8.95   ISBN: 1-880828-81-2

## The Cry for Spiritual Fathers & Mothers

**The Book** Returning to the biblical truth of spiritual parenting so believers are not left fatherless and disconnected. How loving, seasoned spiritual fathers and mothers help spiritual children reach their full potential in Christ. *by Larry Kreider, 186 pages.* $11.95 ISBN: 1-886973-42-3

**Audio Set** of six topics. *Six Tape Set.* $29.00
ISBN: 1-886973-53-9

**Group Video Training** Complete set includes six or twelve sessions for all sizes of group training. Set of three video tapes in a protective binder, a *Leader's Guide,* six *Participant Manuals*, and a copy of the book *The Cry for Spiritual Fathers & Mothers*.  $99.00
ISBN: 1-886973-47-4

## Helping You Build Cell Churches

A complete biblical blueprint for small group ministry, this manual covers 54 topics! Gives full, integrated training to build cell churches from the ground up. *Compiled by Brian Sauder and Larry Kreider, 224 pages.* $19.95  ISBN  1-886973-38-5

# Biblical Foundation Series

This series by Larry Kreider covers basic Christian doctrine. Practical illustrations accompany the easy-to-understand format. Use for small group teachings (48 in all), a mentoring relationship or daily devotional. Each book has 64 pages: **$4.99** each, 12 Book Set: **$49** ISBN: 1-886973-18-0

# Biblical Foundations for Children

Creative learning experiences for ages 4-12, patterned after the Biblical Foundation Series. Takes kids on the first steps in their Christian walk. By Jane Nicholas, 176 pages: **$17.95** ISBN: 1-886973-35-0

# Evaluation Tools

This notebook of reproducible evaluation tools helps to get feedback to determine strengths, solidify vision and mission, open dialogue and discussion, and to provide goals. Evaluations for elders, ministry leaders and staff team. *by Steve Prokopchak, 50 pages.* $19.99 ISBN: 1-886973-61-X

# Healthy Leaders

How to develop a clear sense of identity and direction as a leader. This book covers the dynamics of godly leadership including insights to these questions: Do we know how to detach from the conflicts while at the same time fully identifying with other people? How do we respond when people react to our direction? *by Keith Yoder, 88 pages.* $8.95 ISBN: 1-886973-31-8

# Advanced Cell Group Ministry 201

**Video Training** Gain strategy to reach a new level in cell group ministry. There are seven sessions—each with a half hour teaching followed by questions for discussion. Training set includes: three DVDs, a copy of the book *House To House*, a group leader's guide and six participant manuals: **$89** ISBN:1-886973-70-9

### Advanced Cell Group Ministry 201 Audio Set

Hear Ron Myer share from his many years' experience. Gain strategy to reach a new level in cell group ministry. There are seven sessions. Four tape set: **$23.99** ISBN: 1-886973-71-1

# Cell Groups and House Churches: What History Teaches Us

A historical backdrop to much of what is happening in cell groups and house churches today. Explore the writings and practices of the Reformers such as Luther and Bucer, as well as the Pietists, Moravians, Methodists and others. These writings show clearly that when God moves in restoring His church, there is a renewal of small groups to aid discipleship and growth into holiness, often resulting in a greater concern for reaching the lost. *by Peter Bunton, 108 pages.* $8.99   ISBN: 1-886973-45-8

# Youth Cells And Youth Ministry

Learn the values behind youth cells and custom-design cells for your youth. Gives the specifics of implementing youth cell ministry, including a cell leader's job description, creative ideas for cells, and how churches can transition. *Compiled by Brian Sauder & Sarah Mohler, 120 pages.* $8.50   ISBN: 1-886973-33-4
**Youth Cells and Youth Ministry Audio Set** $45.00
ISBN: 1-886973-55-5

# Destination Cell Church

How do you move from a program-based to a cell-based church? This book is the story of how a church transitioned to make cell group ministry its central focus. Learn specific keys to help unlock the doors to walk in faith so your church can implement the needed changes in vision and values. *by Paul Gustitus, 80 pages.* $8.95   ISBN: 1-886973-43-1

# The Tithe: A Test in Trust

This book answers key questions about tithing based on the scriptures, explaining it as both an Old Testament and a New Testament teaching. Written with a variety of illustrations, this book has been used to help believers understand that the tithe is a test in trust—trust in God and trust in our spiritual leadership. By Larry Kreider. 32 pages: **$2.95** ISBN: 1-886973-17-2

# Prosperity With a Purpose

Unveils God's plan to finance the Great Commission. Is it God's will for Christians to live in the desert with only enough to get by or in the Promised Land of God's "more than enough"? If we only have enough to meet our needs, how can we meet the needs of others? In this book, Brian Sauder unapologetically provides solid, biblical teaching and sometimes comical testimony of his discovery of the God of more than enough. 96 Pages, by Brian Sauder **$9.99** ISBN: 1-886973-65-2

# House Church Networks

A new model of church is emerging. Discover how these new house church networks offer community and simplicity, especially as they fit the heart, call and passion of the younger generations. These house church networks will work together with the more traditional community churches and mega-churches to show the transforming power of Christ to our neighborhoods. *by Larry Kreider, 118 pages.* $9.99 ISBN: 1-886973-48-2

**House Church Networks Audio** With Larry Kreider and others involved with house churches from four nations. *Two Tape Set.* $9.99 ISBN: 1-886973-60-1

# Fivefold Ministry Audio

Designed to release healthy, effective fivefold ministry in the local church. Taught by experienced leaders. Topics: *Fivefold Ministry, Role and Function of Apostles and Prophets, Role and Function of Evangelists, Pastors, and Teachers, Qualifications of Fivefold Ministers, Ministry Motivation, Fivefold Fathering, Fields of Ministry, Fivefold and the Church Plant, Financing the Fivefold, Prayer and Fasting Audio Set of 10 Tapes.* $39.00 ISBN: 1-886973-52-0

# Counseling Basics

You can be an effective people helper! This manual is specifically geared to train small group leaders and potential leaders to counsel others. Packed with helpful scriptural references with eighteen essential areas covered. *by Steve Prokopchak, 88 pages.* $14.95 ISBN: 1-886973-39-3

**Counseling Basics Audio Set**The seminar on tape for your home, car or office. Taught by Steve Prokopchak. Includes a set of six tapes and a *Counseling Basics* book. $29.00 ISBN: 1-886973-54-7

# Called Together

*Pre and Postmarital Workbook*
This unique workbook, specifically designed for couple-to-couple mentoring use, prepares couples for a successful and God-honoring marriage. *Called Together* supplies down-to-earth Biblical wisdom to help couples get off to a positive start. *Called Together* also includes postmarital checkups at three and nine months. Special sections for remarriage, intercultural marriages and remarriages of senior adults. *by Steve and Mary Prokopchak, 250 pages.* $12.99 ISBN: 0-87509-991-2

# Spiritual Fathering & Mothering Seminar
Practical preparation for believers who want to have and become spiritual parents. Includes a manual and the book *The Cry For Spiritual Fathers & Mothers.*

# Elder's Training Seminar
Based on New Testament leadership principles, this seminar equips leaders to provide protection, direction and correction in the local church. Includes the book *The Biblical Role of Elders in Today's Church* and a manual.

# Small Groups 101 Seminar
Basics for healthy cell ministry. Session topics cover the essentials for growing cell group ministry. Each attendee receives a *Helping You Build Manual.*

# Small Groups 201 Seminar
Takes you beyond the basics and into an advanced strategy for cell ministry. Each attendee receives a *House To House* book and a seminar manual.

# Counseling Basics for Small Group Leaders
This seminar takes you through the basics of counseling, specifically in small group ministry. Includes a comprehensive manual.

# Marriage Mentoring Training Seminar
Trains church leaders and mature believers to help prepare engaged couples for a strong marriage foundation by using the mentoring format of *Called Together.* Includes a *Called Together Manual.*

# Youth Cell Ministry Seminar
Learn the values behind youth cells so cell ministry does not become just another program at your church. For adult and teen leaders!

# Church Planting Clinic
Designed to help you formulate a successful strategy for cell-based church planting. For those involved in church planting and those considering it. Includes a *Helping You Build Cell Churches Manual.*

# Fivefold Ministry Seminar
A seminar designed to release healthy, effective fivefold ministry in the local church. Includes a *Helping You Build Cell Churches Manual.*

For complete brochures and upcoming dates:
## Call 800.848.5892
www.dcfi.org        email: info@dcfi.org

**Steve Prokopchak** A Christian family and marriage counselor for more than twenty years, Steve ministers worldwide, training pastors and elders in biblical counseling and church leadership principles.

**Ron Myer** has served in areas of leadership in cell-based church ministry for more than twenty years. He travels regularly, teaching and imparting practical principles of leadership throughout the United States and the world.

**Larry Kreider** served as senior pastor of a church that grew from 25 to a church of 2,300. He currently is the Int'l Director of DOVE Christian Fellowship International. An author and featured speaker at conferences and churches, he travels extensively training leaders.

**Brian Sauder** is a 20 year veteran of cell ministry and directs the DCFI Church Planting and Leadership School, training others to fulfill the Great Commission. He also oversees DCFI churches and church planting in Canada.